The Practice of Network Security

ISBN 0-13-046223-3

94999

9 780130 462237

Prentice Hall PTR Series in
Computer Networking and Distributed Systems
Radia Perlman, Series Editor

The Practice of Network Security

Deployment Strategies for Production Environments

Allan Liska, CISSP

PRENTICE
HALL
PTR

Prentice Hall PTR
Upper Saddle River, NJ 07458
www.phptr.com

Library of Congress Cataloging-in-Publication Data

A CIP catalog record of this book can be obtained from the Library of Congress

Production Supervisor: Wil Mara
Executive Editor: Mary Franz
Cover Design: Anthony Gemmellaro
Cover Design Director: Jerry Votta
Editorial Assistant: Noreen Regina
Marketing Manager: Dan DePasquale
Buyer: Maura Zaldivar

© 2003 Pearson Education, Inc.
Publishing as Prentice Hall Professional Technical Refererence
Upper Saddle River, New Jersey 07458

Prentice Hall books are widely used by corporations and government agencies for training, marketing, and resale.

For information regarding corporate and government bulk discounts, please contact Corporate and Government Sales, at 1-(800)-382-3419, or corpsales@pearsontechgroup.com.

Other company and product names mentioned herein are the trademarks or registered trademarks of their respective owners.

Printed in the United States of America
10 9 8 7 6 5 4 3 2 1

ISBN 0-13-046223-3

Pearson Education LTD.
Pearson Education Australia PTY, Limited
Pearson Education Singapore, Pte. Ltd
Pearson Education North Asia Ltd
Pearson Education Canada, Ltd
Pearson Educación de Mexico, S.A. de C.V.
Pearson Education—Japan
Pearson Education Malaysia, Pte. Ltd

To Roseanne and Bruce—
Thank you for making my life complete

About Prentice Hall Professional Technical Reference

With origins reaching back to the industry's first computer science publishing program in the 1960s, Prentice Hall Professional Technical Reference (PH PTR) has developed into the leading provider of technical books in the world today. Formally launched as its own imprint in 1986, our editors now publish over 200 books annually, authored by leaders in the fields of computing, engineering, and business.

Our roots are firmly planted in the soil that gave rise to the technological revolution. Our bookshelf contains many of the industry's computing and engineering classics: Kernighan and Ritchie's *C Programming Language*, Nemeth's *UNIX System Administration Handbook*, Horstmann's *Core Java*, and Johnson's *High-Speed Digital Design*.

PH PTR acknowledges its auspicious beginnings while it looks to the future for inspiration. We continue to evolve and break new ground in publishing by providing today's professionals with tomorrow's solutions.

PRENTICE
HALL
PTR

Contents

Chapter 1

Chapter 2

Security Model   23

Chapter 3

Understanding Types of Attacks   41

Chapter 4

Routing   59

Chapter 5

Switching   97

Chapter 6

Authentication, Authorization, and Accounting   121

Chapter 11

The DMZ   217

Chapter 12

Server Security   231

Chapter   13

DNS Security   273

Chapter   14

Workstation Security   299

Chapter 15

Managing Network Security   313

Chapter 16

Monitoring   327

Chapter   17

Logging   345

Chapter   18

Responding to an Attack   369

Acknowledgements

Writing is an invigorating process; it can also be long and involved. A book like this means spending a lot of time working with a lot of really smart people, and learning from their experience.

There were so many people involved in the creation of this book that I am not sure where to start, so I will go chronologically.

I want to thank Li Glover, Tony Wynes, and Sean Murhpy for their guidance and support at UUNET, they helped me learn the network, and explore where it was vulnerable. They also covered for me when I went too far.

Shoeb Siraj and Steve Shippa were incredibly understanding while I was writing, providing me the necessary leeway to produce a great book.

Neil Salkind and Vicki Harding were great at unearthing this opportunity and smoothing things over with Prentice Hall when I fell behind.

Mary Franz, at Prentice Hall, has the patience of a cactus. Working with a first-time author, especially one with a newborn, a fulltime job, and no apparent concept of deadlines can be trying. Thank you for your understanding and helpfulness along the way.

Ed Skoudis provided very insightful input to the original proposal, and helped to tighten the focus of the book. Ben Liska also provided great assistance with the original proposal, and throughout the book.

Jorj Bauer and Todd O'Boyle, who reviewed this book, were amazing. Their guidance, suggestions, and challenges to my original text helped transform this work into a much better book.

Jeff Gunther at Intalgent Technologies, Mike Sweeney at Packetattack, George Simmons and Ken Durazzo from Cisco, and James VanBokkelen and the staff at Sandstorm Enterprises for their expertise and assistance with various parts of the book.

Tina Bird and Norm Laudermilch both served as great sounding boards for some of the ideas in this book and really helped me refine those ideas.

Elizabeth Martin and Wil Mara were incredibly helpful during the final stages of this book. Wil pushed to make sure that every little detail was taken care of, improving the final product significantly, and Elizabeth for reviewing the text and producing a much more polished work than what I originally submitted.

I would also like to thank the people whose tools or websites are mentioned throughout this book. Without access to some of these tools protecting a network would be significantly more expensive and time consuming. In addition to great tools, I want to thank the people sharing security information. Companies and web sites like CERT/CC, CIAC, Security Focus, MITRE, and Whitehats provide an invaluable service to the networking community.

Finally, I would like to thank my wife, Roseanne, and my son Bruce. I realize there were a lot of late nights and time away over the last six months. Your unwavering support and love during this period means the world to me, and reminds me how truly blessed I am to have such a wonderful family. I love you both.

Introduction

As I am writing this introduction an alert has just come in about a newly discovered vulnerability in Cisco's CatOS. The vulnerability, a buffer overflow in the CatOS HTTP daemon, is one that is commonly found on devices that have stripped down HTTP daemons used for management purposes.

A couple of years ago this vulnerability would not have raised too many eyebrows. After all, how often is a device within the network infrastructure attacked? Attacks are targeted toward servers, and insecure workstations not routers, switches, firewalls, or other network infrastructure, right? That's not the case any more. As networks have become more complex so have the attackers that try to infiltrate them. Network security is no longer simply about protecting servers and workstations. Network security now requires a holistic understanding of the network, and an awareness of vulnerabilities both at the edge and in the core.

As attackers have become more sophisticated, so have the tools they use to infiltrate networks. These tools, most freely available, have filtered down to chat rooms and "warez" web sites, making it easier for less knowledgeable users to launch an attack against a network, or multiple networks. Attacks against networks are now routinely launched by disgruntled teens, angry customers, ex-employees, or someone who just wants to see if it can be done.

All these changes have combined to make the job of security and network professionals much more difficult. The number of devices that must be protected has increased, while the security budget has remained the same or shrunk.[1] Security administrators must now spend time determining whether an attack is orchestrated by someone who knows what they are doing and is trying to gain access to confidential information, or some kid who wants to test out the last Denial of Service (DoS) tool.

In addition to these problems there is often a blending of the roles that security, network and server administrators play in protecting the network. Separating the responsibilities of different groups, while ensuring that communication between the groups still occurs is an important responsibility.

Purpose of This Book

Throughout this book there are real world examples of attacks used against networks, and suggestions for ways to protect networks against these attacks. However, it is important to keep in mind that a book is static; information within these pages is designed as a guideline, to help administrators develop a network security strategy.

Because each network is unique, it is impossible to deliver an all-encompassing strategy in a single book. Using the fundamentals provided in this book can help administrators find holes in current security strategies, or even start a discussion about security within the company.

I know that many people who pick up this book and thumb through it are going to think, at first glance, that much of what is listed here is a waste of time. Many network administrators are too busy plugging holes in the network to take the time to develop a security strategy, and the idea of trying to work with senior management to explain something as complicated as a DoS attack seems impossible. As difficult as these two task might seem, they are both important because, in the long run, they make the job of securing the network easier.

Putting a security process in place helps to refine the roles that different groups will play in the security process; it also serves to divide up the work that needs to be done when securing a network. A security process can also help create security baselines that make the job of administering a network much easier.

The purpose of this book is to make the job of securing the network easier. By offering suggestions, based on real world experience, of how to streamline the

---

1. Of course.

security process and some common mistakes to watch for, this book can be used to help create a unique security strategy for your organization.

This book should not be used alone. If your organization is serious about having a current and complete security strategy you should use as many tools as possible. In addition to this book, I would recommend the following books:

- *Network Security: Private Communication in a Public World,* by Charlie Kaufman, Radia Perlman, and Mike Speciner
- *Applied Cryptography: Protocols, Algorithms, and Source Code in C,* by Bruce Schneier

Of course, books should not be your only source of security information, the world of security changes too fast to rely solely on books for information. It is important to work with your server and network vendors to keep up to date on the latest vulnerabilities, and the recommended fixes. Vendors also have a lot of insight and advice about current best security practices for their products.

Finally, using the Internet as a tool to keep up to date with the latest security information can be important. As with any information on the Internet it is usually a good idea to get a second opinion. There is a lot of really good security information, but there is also a lot of bad information and some that is just wrong. Usually surveying the top security web sites, as well as vendor web sites can provide you with enough good information. Some of the security sites I recommend and personally use are (in no particular order):

- Security Focus (http://www.securityfocus.com/)
- The SANS Institute (http://www.sans.org/)
- Network Security Library (http://www.secinf.net/)
- CERT® Coordination Center (http://www.cert.org/)
- Insecure.Org (http://www.insecure.org/)
- Computer Incident Advisory Capability (http://www.ciac.org/)

The information on these web sites is usually reliable and can help you keep your network protected.

The Complaint Department

Knowing network and security engineers they way I do, I know there are going to be people who have complaints about things in this book. Some will feel I should have mentioned a tool that I did not, or that advice I gave was wrong.

If you are one of those people, I want you to tell me. You can e-mail me at allan@allan.org with any suggestions, flames, criticisms, or even if you want to compliment the work.

As I said before, the world of security is constantly changing, no doubt there will be a second and third edition of this book, and your comments can help make those next editions even better, so I welcome them.

1

Defining the Scope

Growing up you may have played the Milton Bradley game *Stratego*. The concept of the game is fairly simple: There are two players, each player has a flag, and the goal is to defend your flag while trying to capture the enemy's flag.

Stratego is a good analogy for network security. When designing a network security strategy your ultimate goal is to protect your corporate infrastructure, your flag, from attackers—both internal and external.

This book is designed to help you develop your network security strategy. Because each company has a different approach to network security, it does not attempt to define a specific strategy for you. Instead, the book concentrates on ways to help you reach your ultimate goal in network security: protecting your network infrastructure.

This chapter defines the scope of network security, as covered in this book, discusses various types of network security, and outlines some of the costs associated with lax security policies.

In addition to the theoretical aspects of network security, it covers common network security mistakes, and describes a typical corporate network.

Pay close attention to the diagrams in the last section of this chapter. They will be referred to throughout the book, as potential security holes are plugged. The final chapter will present a redesigned and more secure network.

1.1 What is Network Security?

The first step in any discussion about network security is defining network security. If you ask 10 different administrators for a definition of network security you will probably get 10 different answers.

For the purpose of this book the definition that originated from the United States National Security Agency will be sufficient: Network security is the protection of networks and their services from unauthorized modification, destruction, or disclosure. It assures that the network performs its critical functions correctly and there are no harmful side effects.

This is, admittedly, a very broad definition, but a general definition better prepares network administrators to deal with new types of attacks. If a network security plan is broad in scope, then the tools will be in place that help deal with new types of attacks. Some security incidents are obviously network problems. A distributed denial of service attack (DDoS) is an obvious network issue. A DDoS attack occurs when multiple systems flood a network, or network device, with traffic (such as Ping floods), rendering it unusable by legitimate users. DDoS attacks have to be stopped before they reach the server; in other words, at the network level.

On the other hand, e-mail worms are an example of an attack that is more of a gray area. An e-mail worm is a file that is sent as part of an e-mail. The file exploits security holes in popular e-mail programs to cause damage to a machine's file system, and then sends itself to other people via the address book, continuing to wreak havoc. At first glance an e-mail worm might be considered a problem for server administrators to deal with, but worms, in addition to flooding servers, also clog the network, and, in extreme cases, may force you to remove your network from the Internet, while the worm is being dealt with.

1.1.1 Network Security and Compromise

As with all security, network security is about compromise. As shown earlier, even defining the scope of network security involves compromise. A network security policy is not developed in a vacuum. Network administrators have to work with other departments, especially a company's legal department, and within the confines of a limited budget to determine the scope of an organization's network security policy.

Unfortunately, compromise often leaves a network administrator in the position of being damned if you do, and damned if you don't. Network administrators often find themselves in the hot seat for incidents that might have been prevented if the requested budget had been allocated.

Network security compromise is often a combination of education and risk management. Security personnel have to remain abreast of the latest security vulnerabilities, and communicate new information to others in their group, and often to the chief information officer (CIO), directly or through the normal chain of command. The CIO is then responsible for communicating the information to the rest of the organization.

NOTE

Throughout this chapter you will see references to the CIO. Depending on the size and structure of your company, the duties described may be handled by a chief technology officer (CTO) or an information technology (IT) manager.

When communicating security information to others in the company, it is often necessary to act like a salesperson. Security problems should be explained in terms of benefits not features—explain what can happen rather than the technical aspects of an attack. If a new security hole may allow DDoS attacks against a server, don't discuss the minutiae of the ISO OSI reference model or the Transmission Control Protocol (TCP). Instead focus on the fact that if this security hole is exploited it may cause your website to become unreachable by legitimate users.

Another tactic is to explain problems in terms of cost. If bandwidth is billed using a burst model (e.g., you have a 10-megabit connection, but can use up to 45 megabits) a DDoS attack can cause the organization to use its fully allotted bandwidth, thereby incurring a quantifiable additional expense.

In fact, the more often a security risk can be quantified, the easier it is to convince others to approve, or facilitate, the ability to act.

1.1.2 Risk Management

Quantification of network problems also allows network administrators to better handle risk management. Risk management is the process of assessing the potential threat from a security risk.

Risk management also means understanding when cost is not a factor. While this section largely focuses on determining the true cost of implementing security solutions, it is important to remember that there are some solutions that are so important they need to be implemented no matter what the cost.

Effective risk management requires an understanding of the full impact of every security threat. Full understanding of a risk gives network administrators the ability to weigh the true costs involved in not fixing a security hole. For instance, if mail servers are left unsecured, so anyone can send a message through them, there is a potential security hole that has a high risk of being exploited. Risk management involves looking at the costs of fixing the server versus not fixing it. The cost of fixing the mail server is relatively minor: Simply do not allow anyone outside the local network to relay through the server, or, if an organization has many remote users, implement a security system that requires people to authenticate before they can send mail. The cost of not fixing it is great. There is the obvious cost of someone using your server, and network connectivity to send mail to millions of people. But there are also administrative costs involved in a situation like this: angry e-mail from people who received the mail, losing the ability to send mail to some people because your mail server is blacklisted, and having to restrict access to the mail server anyway.

In April 2002, the FBI and the Computer Security Institute released the results of their "2002 Computer Crime and Security Survey." The survey, which collects data about security practices from randomly selected companies, provides information about the frequency of common network attacks. Table 1.1 lists the percentage of companies that reported successful attacks.

Computer worms are by far the most common type of network attack detected[1] and reported. The operative words are *detected* and *reported*. Obviously,

---

1. The second most common type of attack, not listed in the chart, is one originated internally by an employee, or group of employees.

Table 1.1   Reported Network Attacks

TYPE OF ATTACK	PERCENTAGE REPORTING SUCCESSFUL ATTACKS
Computer virus/worm	85
System penetration	40
Denial of Service attacks	40
Web server penetration	38

not all attacks are detected—and even some that are go unreported—so the percentages may not reflect the true number of network attacks experienced by these businesses.

Some companies feel that there is a stigma associated with network attacks and, despite the fact that network attacks are a common occurrence, the Computer Crime and Security Survey continually suffers from underreporting by companies.

Why is data like this important? It helps to give network administrators an idea of how an organization's resources should be distributed when developing a network security strategy. If it is known that a company is twice as likely to be the victim of a virus or worm than any other type of attack, server administrators can plan appropriately.

Many companies use a form of risk profiling to determine the cost of implementing a network security policy. Risk profiling involves evaluating a security risk from four perspectives and using the number gained to assign a priority to each threat.

As with the other aspects of risk management risk profiling has to be handled by a security group, and needs direct involvement from the CIO, senior management, and the legal department.

The risk profiling method developed by the National Institute of Standards and Technology involves creating a matrix that evaluates the threat, visibility, consequences, and sensitivity of a potential threat. This type of risk assessment fits well into most network security models, as discussed in the next chapter.

To create a risk profile, first create two charts (Table 1.2 and Table 1.3).

Table 1.2   Risk Profiling: Threats and Visibility

THREAT	RATING
No currently identified threats	1
Unknown, or multiple exposures	3
Active threats, multiple exposures	5
VISIBILITY	RATING
Very low profile, no publicity	1
Occasional publicity	3
Active publicity	5

Multiply threat value by the visibility value.

Table 1.3   Risk Profiling: Consequences and Sensitivity

CONSEQUENCES	RATING
Consequences have no cost, are within budget, or the risk can be transferred.	1
May impact internal functions, cause budget overruns, or there may be opportunity costs.	3
External functions may be impacted, and revenue loss will occur.	5
SENSITIVITY	RATING
Part of the cost of doing business, no organizational impact.	1
Unacceptable impact for a specific business unit and good-will costs.	3
Unacceptable management costs, and business relationships affected.	5

Multiply consequence value by the sensitivity value.

Apply all four measures to a risk; multiply the threat and visibility values. Multiply the consequences and sensitivity values. Add the two results, and you have a risk profile.

After the measures have been applied to a risk it can then be assigned to one of the three categories in Table 1.4.

Table 1.4   Risk Profile: Final Assessment

COMBINED VALUE	RISK PROFILE
2-10	Low
11-29	Medium
30-50	High

Also note that this type of risk profiling should be included as part of any new network project completed. Analyzing and understanding security risks inherent in a new project is important to minimize future security risks to your company.

1.2 What Types of Network Security Are Important?

When a company first sets out to create a network security plan, there are usually two questions asked: Where should we start, and what is the most important part of the network? The answers depend on many factors, and the answers are different for every network.

Generally speaking, one person, or department, will not be able to answer both of these questions and one department should not develop the network security policy. The network security policy, as all security policies, should be disseminated through the CIO, and should be approved by the legal department and signed off on by the heads of all other departments. Network and server administrators may be called on to develop the first draft of the policy, but it is up to senior management to finalize, implement, and enforce the network security policy.

There are some questions administrators can ask to begin the development of the corporate network security policy.

1.2.1 How Sensitive Is the Data?

Any business has confidential data. Whether it is the customer database, proprietary software, a product design, or some other sensitive data, there is undoubtedly something that has to be protected. Such data should always be your first priority when developing a security strategy. In some cases, especially for companies that deal with medical or financial records, there are legal ramifications for not properly securing this data.

Of course, core data is useless if no one can access it. Second to protecting the core data is protecting the means by which people within an organization, or customers, access that data. The lines of communication to data—the network—have to be kept available.

In addition, employee phone lists or human resource records, important data but not as critical, need to be protected. The protection for this information does not need to be as draconian as the measures you should take for your core data, but it absolutely must be in place.

The involvement of the CIO and other groups is necessary at all levels of network security. One group cannot be sure how to rank the various databases within an organization. Someone from senior management will need to assign ranks to all data sources, so it can be determined how limited resources should be deployed.

Of course the less sensitive the information is, the more difficulty there is in securing it. Employee phone lists generally need to be accessed by other people within the company, and an internal website is probably available to everyone.

In some ways, the more available the data, the harder it is to secure. It is easy to prevent anyone from accessing information. It is harder to allow only certain people to access information, and enforce those access restrictions.

1.2.2 Secure Your Servers

The first step in securing your corporate data is to secure the servers where the data is stored.

How you go about securing a server depends largely on what operating system you are running. There are some guidelines, however, you can follow that apply to any operating system and any server, no matter what its function. These steps are discussed in greater detail in Chapter 12, but this should give you a good overview.

There are two levels of server security: access to the server and environmental control. Access covers who can access the server and how they can do it. Environmental control covers the level of access that users can have—what they can do once they are on the server. These two types of server security are intertwined. If good access policies are enforced, but all users are allowed access to system files after they have logged onto the server, a security breach is waiting to happen. Should an attacker gain access he or she would have no limitations on what he or she could do to the server.

A server access policy should:

- Control who can log into your servers.
- Never send clear text passwords.[2]
- Force minimum password lengths.
- Impose character restrictions on passwords (mixed case, numbers, and punctuation).
- Force passwords to be changed at regular intervals.
- Set a maximum number of login tries before locking out an account.

Once a user has access to a server, there should be environmental limits that prevent users from gaining unauthorized access to system files or secured data. A good environmental control policy will include:

- Running virus scanners on all servers, especially e-mail servers. If a virus never makes it to an end-user's system it can't spread.
- Using, whenever possible, single-function servers (e.g., don't use the same server for mail and web services).
- Not storing proprietary information on public servers (e.g., do not put your customer database on your web server).
- Disabling all unused services, and if possible uninstalling those services.
- Closing all ports not being used.
- Changing all default passwords.
- Deleting unnecessary user accounts.

---

2. Expect to see this comment about 30 times throughout the book.

- Limiting users who have administrative access to the server.
- Deleting any sample files that ship with installed programs.
- Storing user files separate from administrative files (either on a separate partition or file system).
- Logging all movements by administrative users.
- Updating the system frequently with vendor security patches.

These steps are a good start toward securing your server, and protecting the data on those servers.

1.2.3 Secure the Network

Of course, the sooner you can stop a potential intruder, the better. This is especially true when dealing with server attacks. Ideally, you would like to prevent a potential intruder from ever reaching your server. Later parts of this book discuss strategies for securing your network in detail. Here are some useful guidelines that should be implemented on any network to help stop attacks:

- All machines in the network, except for the edge routers, should be behind a firewall.
- Authenticate all network protocols in use on the network (BGP, OSPF, VRRP, etc.).
- Restrict access to secure parts of the network by Media Access Control (MAC) address.
- Do not allow external traffic into the secure network areas.
- Use virtual local area networks (VLANs) for added levels of switch security.
- Change default passwords.[3]
- Use virtual private networks (VPNs) for employees who need to access sensitive information remotely.

These are general guidelines that should help administrators start forming a network security policy that works for an organization. As the book progresses, the policy can be refined.

---

3. This is another comment you can expect to see repeated.

1.2.4 Monitor it All

Never be complacent when it comes to network security. No matter how great the security measures taken, the fact is that a skilled and determined hacker will probably find a way into your network.

If that does happen, it is best to know about it quickly, and be prepared to stop it. To do that, monitor everything on the network. Anything that may be deemed as suspicious has to be brought to your attention. Monitoring is discussed in detail in Chapter 16.

In addition to monitoring, extensive logging of network activity should take place. It is unrealistic to expect the administrator's staff to have the time to scour hours of log files every day, but if an incident does occur, good, uncorrupted log files will be essential in tracking down how security measures were breached, and in trying to track down the attacker. At that point, you will be grateful for extensive logging.

A good monitoring strategy involves collecting a lot of data, and recognizing patterns within that data that may resemble attacks. These patterns generate an alarm, which will allow administrators to manually investigate the network or servers, and determine if there really is an intruder, or if it is simply a logging anomaly.

Some security experts advocate the use of honeypots as part of a monitoring strategy. A honeypot is a system that is intentionally left open to attract potential intruders. An attacker takes the bait and tries to break into the system. All interaction with the system is extensively monitored, and the honeypot becomes a tool to help network administrators learn more about security flaws in their system.

1.3 What Is the Cost of Lax Security Policies?

There are really two costs involved with lax network security: quantitative and qualitative. Quantitative costs, the ones most often discussed, are those that have the most immediate impact on the corporate bottom line, but qualitative costs can be just as important to a company in the long run.

According to The Yankee Group, network attacks accounted for $1.2 billion in lost revenue in 2000. That number doubled in 2001, and is expected to double again in 2002. Lost revenue is an example of a quantifiable cost of a security incident.

There is no universal formula to calculate the quantifiable costs of a network attack. There are, however, some commonalities that you can use to help develop your own, internal, formulas.

Some of the costs are easy. If you have an e-commerce site that is interrupted by a DDoS, or an attacker manages to gain entrance to one of the servers, forcing you to take your website offline for X number of hours, then one of your quantifiable costs will be the amount of revenue lost during that time. If your site normally generates $100,000 an hour, and it was offline for six hours, then one of your costs was $600,000.

Loss of revenue is not the only quantifiable cost. If it took you six hours to restore the website from backup and rebuild the database, then time becomes a quantifiable cost, as does the time spent researching the incident and reporting it to the proper authorities. There is also the cost involved in implementing a security fix, so a repeat attack cannot happen.

In addition to time, it is necessary to calculate the lost productivity of other groups within your company. If a design team made changes to the site after the last backup, then their changes will all have to be redone; their time is another quantifiable cost.

Qualitative losses are more difficult to measure, but can be just as important, and increase with the severity of an attack.

Using the example of an e-commerce site again, if someone were to force the website offline, in addition to the outlined quantitative costs, there are several qualitative costs. The most obvious is the loss of future customer revenue, and, depending on the severity and length of the attack, the loss of customer confidence.

If a customer cannot get to the site, he or she visits a competitor's site, has a good experience, and not only is the revenue lost, but future revenue may have been lost as that customer may continue to visit the competing site. If the attack is particularly successful, an attacker may gain access to your customer database, which is often enough for the attack to make the news. Now, on top of the potential loss of future revenue, other customers may not feel comfortable returning to the site, and potential customers may never shop at the site. There is also the added, quantifiable expense of hiring a public relations firm to deal with the problem.

A final qualitative cost is the loss, or delay, of future revenue from projects that were put aside because of the time spent dealing with an attack. If six hours is spent restoring a compromised system, that puts at least a six-hour delay on other projects. If the majority of time is spent dealing with security issues other projects may face an indefinite delay or cancellation. The revenue that would have been gained from those projects is now lost.

1.3.1 The More Severe the Attack, the Greater the Cost

It may seem like an obvious statement, but it is important to remember. The more severe an attack is—the further an attacker is able to penetrate into your network—the greater the cost, both in terms of qualitative and quantitative expenses.

A successful attack against one e-commerce website is relatively trivial, compared to more extensive attacks.

As mentioned earlier, an e-mail worm can paralyze an entire network, to the point of having to shut down e-mail servers and even force a company to disconnect from the Internet. Such an attack can cost a large company several million dollars in lost time and productivity.

Undoubtedly the most expensive attacks against a company are those that compromise data confidentiality and integrity. The compromise of confidential data, such as an e-mail system, corporate intranet, or a customer database can have long-term negative consequences. An attacker who gains access to these tools may not disrupt your network, but will have proprietary information that can be sold to competitors, or used to try to blackmail the company. If this attacker is discovered days, weeks, or even months after he or she has gained this level of access to your network, the cost to track down how the network was breached, and to find all of the security holes, can be extraordinary. Not only will you have to plug the initial security hole, but also each server and network device will need to be thoroughly audited to determine if the intruder left any trapdoors that would allow easy entry back into the network.

Data integrity attacks occur when an attacker gains access to—and modifies—confidential data. Sometimes the modifications are puerile and juvenile, such as defacing a website. Unfortunately, if an attack is targeted specifically to your company, data modifications can be more subtle, and their ramifications greater.

It is almost impossible to calculate the costs of a data integrity breach. Having to audit an entire customer database or verify the validity of confidential customer information can cost millions, not to mention the other costs normally associated with these attacks.

Data confidentiality and integrity attacks bring in the possibility of two new costs associated with security breaches: lawsuits and fines. If confidential information about the customer database or dealings with other companies is leaked, an organization may be open to a lawsuit. Even if it can be demonstrated that reasonable security measures were taken there are still legal costs associated with the lawsuit, as well as the aforementioned negative publicity and loss of customer confidence.

Depending on the type of data that is breached, a company may also be fined by the government. There are several bills before the United States Congress that would fine companies that do not meet minimum standards for network security. Some of these bills would allow companies to be fined up to $1 million if their networks are successfully breached.

1.3.2 Creating the Formula

Creating a company-specific formula that will help measure the cost of an attack is essential. If an organization is going to be able to implement a new security policy, you have to be able to show that the cost of not implementing it is greater than the cost of implementing it.

Again, it is important to keep in mind this formula should not be created by one person or group. The CIO, working in conjunction with senior managers from all departments, should develop the formula jointly.

The formula will vary depending on the type of attack for which the organization is trying to determine the cost. The best bet is to try to divide attacks into broad categories. In Chapter 2 common attacks will be covered in detail. For now, divide attacks into four categories:

1. Network attacks: Attacks not directed toward a server, such as DDoS attacks.
2. Worms: E-mail or web-based programs that travel from computer to computer on your network.

3. Attacks on peripheral servers: Attacks on servers that do not contain core business data.

4. Attacks on core servers: Attacks against servers that contain data that is essential to a business.

More categories can be added, or unnecessary categories can be deleted, depending on the needs of a business. (For instance, some organizations may want to add a category that specifically deals with an e-commerce site.) After categories have been created, the next step is to develop a basic cost structure for each category.

DoS attacks are a good example. If you have a firewall, or routing policy, that will block DoS attacks, then your costs would be limited to productivity losses from not being able to connect to the Internet while the attack was ongoing. If a routing policy that will lessen the impact of a DoS attack is not in place, productivity loss incurred while the network is unavailable may have to be factored. If a company generates revenue from the website, and it is located in a data center within the facility, then a DoS attack will cause loss of revenue from the website.

For each category created the goal is to develop as many fixed costs as possible. If it is known that it costs the company $100,000 an hour for every hour the website is down, that is a number that can be repeatedly factored into loss equations. If the company loses $90,000 an hour in productivity when the mail server is unavailable, that is also a fixed cost. Often, these numbers will be readily available from the appropriate departments.

1.4 Where Is the Network Vulnerable?

Before delving further into the book, it would be a good idea to assess network vulnerabilities. Being aware of some of the more common security problems found in a networking environment makes it easier to spot them on another network. A quick audit based on some common mistakes is a good start. As topics are covered in more detail, it should be easy to pick up other ideas to tighten security even further.

The most common mistake an administrator makes is using clear text passwords. Many administrators will disable telnet access to servers, but leave File

Transfer Protocol (FTP) access open, or they will use telnet to login into routers or switches, instead of creating a TACACS+[4] server. If possible, even e-mail login sessions should be done using encrypted usernames and passwords. Of course, encrypted logins have to be combined with a good password policy.

Domain Name System (DNS) servers are another commonly exploited vulnerability. The most popular program installed on DNS servers is the Berkeley Internet Name Domain (BIND). While recent versions of BIND have done a great job of increasing security controls, the vast majority of companies are still running older, less secure, versions of BIND.

Another common mistake network administrators make is to leave network passwords set to their default; this is especially true for the Simple Network Management Protocol (SNMP). The default passwords for reading data and writing to SNMP devices are generally public and private, respectively. Often administrators activate SNMP without thinking about the consequences of an attacker having full control of their routers.

Firewalls can also lead to poor security practices. Many administrators assume because they have a firewall in place their networks are secure. Firewalls do not solve all security problems. In fact, a firewall with poorly implemented rule sets offers little or no protection for a network. A firewall with good rule sets is important, but it is only a small part of a security policy.

Whenever possible, use managed switches instead of hubs. A managed switch offers security features such as VLAN control and MAC address control. These additional security features enable you to control what machines have access to your network, and can even allow you to control traffic within your network.

A wireless LAN (WLAN) is an incredible technology: It frees employees from their offices or cubicles and allows them to connect into the network from anywhere in your building. There is also a host of security concerns that need to be addressed before implementing a WLAN. Some of the security issues inherent in WLAN technology include the ability to easily port sniff other users connected to an access point, easy entry to your network for just about anyone, and of course, the use of an insecure default password.

---

4. TACACS is the Terminal Access Controller Access Control System, is documented in RFC 1492, and is an authentication and logging system.

1.5 The Network

The best way to learn is by example; to that end this section presents a typical corporate network for a 100-person company. This network is fairly insecure. Forging ahead, various chapters in the book will capitalize on the vulnerabilities in the network and demonstrate ways to correct them. Of course, there is no one correct security model. Security needs vary from company to company, but showing how to spot and correct weaknesses in corporate security helps administrators find holes in their own networks, and helps create better methods for dealing with security issues.

NOTE

In this example, the netblock 10.10.0.0 255.255.255.0 is used. This is one of the netblocks that has been reserved by RFC 1918 for private use. Think of it like using the 555 prefix for phone numbers in movies. The address block will function like a normal netblock, but the addresses are not routable across the wide area network (WAN).

1.5.1 The Network Infrastructure

Figure 1.1 shows the network infrastructure for this company. It is fairly simple: a router connected to a firewall that has three interfaces: public—to the router, and two private interfaces—one to the employee network and one to the server farm.

The firewall rule set is also fairly simple for this network. No traffic is allowed in to the employee network, all traffic is allowed in to the server network. The rules for the server network were tighter, but as new software was added to the servers in the server farm, it became difficult to keep track of which ports needed to be opened so all ports were opened.

The company uses a TCP/IP network infrastructure, but no auditing has been done to see what other network protocols are running on the machines. The netblock 10.10.10.0 255.255.255.0 (a Class C block of addresses) is assigned to the company. The IP addresses have been distributed throughout the network without subnetting them.

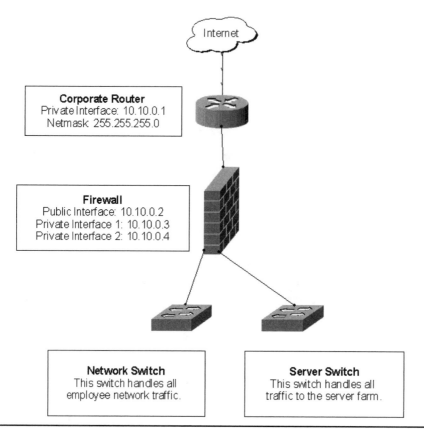

Figure 1.1   The network infrastructure

Finally, even though they are using managed switches, the network administrators have not assigned different VLANS to the ports on their switches; all machines connected to the switches are using the default VLAN.

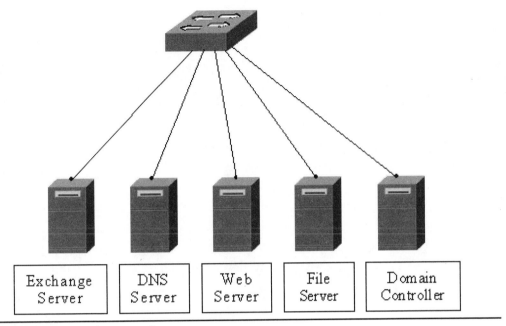

Figure 1.2   The server farm

1.5.2 The Server Farm

The server farm (Figure 1.2) consists of five servers; all but two perform unique functions. The File server also doubles as a Remote Access Service (RAS) server that allows employees to dial in to the network from home, while the domain controller doubles as a monitoring server.

The file and exchange servers and the domain controller are all running Windows NT, with service pack 4 installed. The web and DNS servers are both running Red Hat Linux 6.2.

New accounts are created on an as-needed basis, and there has been no auditing of account information to date.

1.5.3 The Employee Network

Various employee groups, such as human resources and accounting, are connected via hubs to the network switch (Figure 1.3). The employees use a mix of Windows 98, Windows NT Workstation, and Windows 2000 Professional workstations. Again, there has been no workstation auditing to date, and no one has set a policy to limit the type of workstations that can be added to the network. There is also no password auditing or policing system in place.

All workstations on the network are assigned IP addresses by the domain controller when they log onto the network.

The company is also experimenting with WLAN technology. The two conference rooms have been outfitted with access points that allow anyone with an 802.11b-enabled card or computer to connect into the network.

There are many gaping security flaws within this network. As each area is delved into more deeply, they should become more apparent.

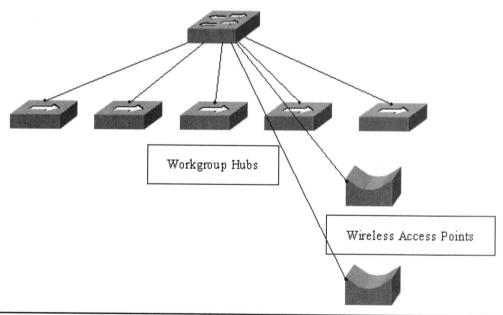

Figure 1.3   The employee network

1.6 Summary

Because networks are so commonplace within organizations, network security is important for all administrators. Maintaining good network security is a full-time task that has to involve the cooperation of all employees within an organization.

Because network security is so important, and involves all aspects of day-to-day operations, it is important that security policies be communicated from the top down, and that all managers are involved in the planning of network security policies.

Many organizations, especially small ones, don't feel that they need to worry about network security. The truth is, any organization that is publicly connected to the Internet has to make an effort to secure its border.

2

Security Model

Before a security policy can be put into place, the first step is to choose a security model. The security model is the framework within which you develop a security policy that is unique to your company. At its most basic level a security model acts as a checklist, ensuring that there are not gaping holes in your security policy.

But a security model is much more than that. It is a philosophy that guides the way your company approaches security. While most security models cover the same topics, the approaches can vary, as shown in the next section, so it is important to choose one that meshes well with your corporate philosophy.

Before proceeding, it is a good idea to define terms that will be used in this chapter, and throughout the book. These are words you may have heard used without being clear on their definition. It is important to understand these terms, because they will have to be communicated to your senior management—and all employees—if you are responsible for developing a network security policy.

For our definitions, we'll focus on:
- Security model
- Security policy
- Standards
- Guidelines

The security model is simply, as already mentioned, a framework. It is within this framework that security policies are developed. Different security models will lead to slightly different security policies.

Which brings up security policy. The security policy is a published, and communicated, set of "rules" that all employees, customers, or vendors are required to adhere to and observe. The security policy, or policies, are not optional. For example, if you determine that only laptops and workstations running Windows 2000 are allowed to plug into the network, that is a policy. If someone plugs a laptop with Windows 98 into the network, he or she is in violation of that policy.

Of course, for a network policy to be effective it has to be communicated and enforced. If no one knows about a policy, it is not going to be followed. Conversely, if the policy has been published, but no one enforces it, it is equally ineffective.

The security model you choose should allow you flexibility in developing and evaluating policies. If you are very concerned about password sniffing on the network, you may create a policy that requires all passwords be at least 10 characters, have at least two capital letters, two numbers, and two nonstandard characters ($, @, #, etc.), and be changed on a weekly basis. At first blush this seems very secure until you walk around and see little Post-It® notes, on which passwords are written, attached to everyone's monitor. In your effort to create a secure password policy, you have actually made it less secure.

Two other definitions that are integral to this chapter are standards and guidelines. Standards are system- or purpose-specific requirements. Standards provide guidance when choosing new equipment, or installing a new piece of hardware or software. An example of standards would be a set of requirements developed for switches. You may require that switches have to allow MAC addresses to be mapped to a specific port, or that all switches have to allow SNMP polling. A standard is not necessarily system specific, although it can be. Instead the goal is to set requirements that all equipment deployed on a network must meet; each type of network device will have different standards. More specifically you can also develop standards for specific devices or operating systems. If you deploy Cisco routers, you may outline specific services that have to be disabled, complete with step-by-step documentation.

Guidelines are similar to standards, but they are not required. Instead, they are strongly encouraged. A guideline might be that all switches allow remote access through SSH, and Telnet has to be disabled. While this is an excellent security precaution it may not be practical, as many switches simply do not support this capability. Of course, as more switches begin to allow SSH access, you may decide to make SSH-only access a standard.

Your network security policy will use policies, standards, and guidelines. Being as thorough as possible will prevent confusion in the implementation of the policy, and make it easier to follow.

The focus of this book is network security. Therefore when discussing security models, the focus will be on implementing a security model for your corporate network. Obviously, a network has to be integrated into a larger corporate security policy. In fact your company undoubtedly has a preferred security model, in which case, it may make more sense to use the company-wide security model as your network security model.[1]

Even if your company does not have a well-defined security model, you will still need to work with counterparts in other departments when developing a network security model, just as senior management will have to work with other members of senior management before determining which model will be used.

2.1 Choosing a Security Model

The first step is to understand what types of models are available. The more aware of different models you are, the easier it will be to choose the model that best matches the needs of your company.

The focus of this chapter will be on the OCTAVE (Operationally Critical Threat, Asset, and Vulnerability Evaluation) model. OCTAVE was, and continues to be, developed by the Computer Emergency Response Team at Carnegie Mellon University, better known as CERT®/CC (CERT Coordination Center).

The CERT®/CC was created in 1988 by the Defense Advanced Research Projects Agency (DARPA) to deal with computer-related security emergencies. The CERT®/CC grew quickly, and today it disseminates information about potential security problems throughout the Internet.

OCTAVE was chosen as an example model because it was designed to integrate with any existing security model. Because network security has to be a subset of a larger security model, you will need a model that makes this type of integration seamless, and painless.

OCTAVE is not the only security model that integrates well with other models; in fact, there are many others. However, the fact that it is maintained by

---

1. Of course if your company has a security model, steps to secure your network should have been taken when that model was first implemented.

CERT®/CC lends a lot of weight to its completeness and the quality of its design.

Before reviewing the benefits of OCTAVE, it is a good idea to review some of the other options available.

2.1.1 RFC 2196: The Site Security Handbook

The Internet Engineering Task Force (IETF) has developed a handbook for creating site security policies. This handbook called, conveniently enough, the *Site Security Handbook*, also known as RFC 2196, details the process by which administrators[2] can develop security policies and procedures.

One of the major appeals of the *Site Security Handbook* is that it is designed with flexibility in mind. This model can be applied to large and small companies, with many different types of network infrastructures.

The *Site Security Handbook* approaches the process of developing a security policy through a five-step process:

1. Identify what you are trying to protect.

2. Determine what you are trying to protect it from.

3. Determine how likely the threats are.

4. Implement measures which will protect your assets in a cost-effective manner.

5. Review the process continuously and make improvements each time a weakness is found.

This five-step model is fairly commonplace, and was originally documented in *Control and Security of Computer Information Systems* (Fites, Kratz, and Brebner, 1989).

The *Site Security Handbook* is nice because it provides readers with concrete examples of security policies that are commonly implemented. These examples provide guidance when first developing a plan by giving you a base of information to work from. The downside is that the *Site Security Handbook* was written

---

2. The authors of this RFC use the term administrators to refer to network and system administrators, as well as middle management, or decision makers.

in 1997. There are several holes in the advice provided, such as no discussion of VLANs or other methods of switch security, and no discussion of Border Gateway Protocol (BGP) security.

As with any good security model, the *Site Security Handbook* allows for these omissions by encouraging readers to keep policies flexible. While Step 4 is arguably the most time consuming, Step 5 is undoubtedly the most important. If administrators do not stay abreast of current security problems, then the security policy will eventually become useless.

The *Site Security Handbook* does not recommend developing policies for specific hardware; instead, policies should be developed for device classes: web servers, routers, workstations, and protocols: RIP (Router Information Protocol) Version 2.0, Open Shortest Path First (OSPF), DNS, and so on.

Finally, the *Site Security Handbook* helps users document the process for identifying, handling, and reporting a security incident. It also helps you develop a policy for the aftermath of a security incident.

NOTE

Find out more about IETF 2196 on the IETF website: *www.ietf.org/rfc/rfc2196.txt*

2.1.2 Cisco SAFE

Cisco has developed a security model specifically designed for networks. SAFE is not a stand-alone security model. In fact, the designers assume that users have their own security model in place; SAFE acts as an addendum specifically for network security.

The SAFE model has six security goals, listed in order of importance:

1. Security and attack mitigation based on policy
2. Security implementation throughout the infrastructure
3. Secure management and reporting
4. Authentication and authorization of users and administrators to critical network resources

5. Intrusion detection for critical resources and subnets

6. Support for emerging networked applications

At the core of the SAFE model is a layered approach to security. This is true with most network security models, but that layered approach is not often explicitly stated. In this case, layered security is the second listed goal of SAFE.

Another advantage of the SAFE model is that it uses a modular design. SAFE actually uses a two-tiered modular approach to security. The first group of modules contains broad network divisions, while the second group contains divisions within the larger modules.

There are two different SAFE models, the first covering the needs of enterprise organizations, the second covering the needs of small businesses. The module design for both models is the same (see Figure 2.1).

Within each module there are smaller ones that cover important network design areas. For instance, the Network Edge module has smaller modules for the gateway routers, VPN access, and public services (e.g., web, FTP, or DNS servers).

This type of modularity allows the SAFE model to be slowly integrated into a business. By implementing one or two of the second-tier modules at a time, rather than trying to convert an entire network, network administrators can easily keep track of what has been done, and what has yet to be completed.

The downside is that the modules may not reflect your network design. SAFE allows for this by not forcing you to use all available modules to develop your security policy. However, you may run into problems when even the equipment within a module does not match the the your network infrastructure.

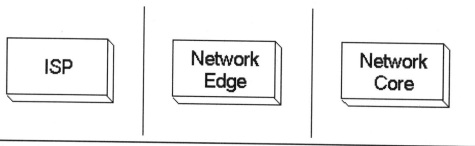

Figure 2.1   SAFE modules

SAFE excels at describing detailed ways to secure routers and switches. The network security aspect of this model is exceptional; it provides a lot of practical advice that is not platform specific. The advice SAFE offers for server security is not as detailed. This is undoubtedly because servers are not viewed as a network device—unfortunately, the reality is that attempting to separate public servers from the network is next to impossible, and oftentimes a network security team is very active in developing security policies for public servers.

NOTE

Cisco has detailed documentation for SAFE on its website: *www.cisco.com/go/safe/*

2.1.3 Common Criteria/ISO 15048

The Common Criteria for Information Technology Security Evaluation was released in May of 1998. The International Organization for Standardization (ISO), used Common Criteria as the basis for its security model, ISO 15048, released in June 1999. The most current version of Common Criteria is 2.1, which is ISO 15048 compliant.

Common Criteria is unique in that it evaluates systems and specific products. If an organization adopts Common Criteria as a security model, there are already products that are ISO 15048 certified which should integrate seamlessly into the organization.

Common Criteria refers to the system that is being evaluated as a target of evaluation (TOE). The TOE is evaluated for three types of failures: unauthorized disclosure, unauthorized modification, and availability.

Common Criteria focuses on IT security threats that involve human interaction, regardless of whether or not these threats are intentional or accidental. While this is adequate, it exposes two limitations with this model: It does not address other types of security issues, and it does not take into account non-IT security issues.

While Common Criteria can certainly integrate with other security models, it is easier to follow a single model throughout the entire security process. Having a separate security model for IT issues can only cause confusion.

Common Criteria breaks its audience down into three different groups:

1. Consumers—The group or person setting the requirements for the security level of a product or system. Consumers dictate what level of security is important, using a protection profile developed using Common Criteria.

2. Developers—Developers can use the Common Criteria method to certify their product before releasing it to the public. By following a standardized, or well-accepted, methodology in designing the security for a product or system, developers can indicate they are ISO 15048 certified.

3. Evaluators—Common Criteria provides evaluators with guidelines that can be used when a new product or system is being tested. Using these standard guidelines for evaluation can simplify the evaluation process.

The Common Criteria method is divided into three different parts. Each of the previously mentioned groups has different responsibilities within the different parts. The three parts of the Common Criteria model are:

1. Introduction and overview—This part presents the Common Criteria model and defines the process involved in evaluating the security of IT products. It also reviews the process and language involved in writing security requirements for IT products.

2. Security functional requirements—This part is used to build the catalog of security requirements for a specific TOE. Evaluators use this catalog to test a TOE.

3. Security assurance requirements—This part of the evaluation process uses predefined Common Criteria assurance levels to rate a TOE.

Common Criteria certification requires that each group complete all three steps in this process.

NOTE

More information about Common Criteria/ISO 15048 is available on the Common Criteria website: *www.commoncriteria.nl/*

2.2 OCTAVE

The CERT/CC has developed a security model, OCTAVE, based, in part, on best practices from ISO 15048 and RFC 2196.

OCTAVE uses a three-part approach to help guide an organization through the process of identifying and addressing security issues:

1. Build asset-based threat profiles.
2. Identify infrastructure vulnerabilities.
3. Develop security strategy and plans.

OCTAVE has been designed from the ground-up to be managed internally. CERT found that many organizations outsource their security assessments to third-party vendors. The problem with this method is that third-party vendors cannot adequately assess the security risks for a company. Every organization has different security needs, depending on what are viewed as core assets. A vendor hired to perform risk analysis may not be able to properly identify these core assets, which could lead to failure to protect them.

Before you fire your security consultant, understand that using OCTAVE does not negate the need for security consultants, but the approach has to be different. In fact, the OCTAVE method can work well with security vendors, because these vendors can provide areas of expertise that your staff may be lacking.

Security vendors can also help guide the conversations that are an integral part of the OCTAVE method. This is especially true in the beginning of the OCTAVE process. If your organization has never attempted to develop a security plan, you may be at a loss as to who to include in the meetings, and how to identify core assets.

More importantly, a security vendor can be especially useful in the second phase of OCTAVE. Your staff may not have adequate knowledge of the potential vulnerabilities in your infrastructure, and a security consultant can help point those out to you, and recommend fixes for those vulnerabilities.

2.2.1 The Core Team

The basis of the OCTAVE method is a core team consisting of three to five people, depending on the size of your organization. This team will make security assessments and guide the company through the three steps of the OCTAVE process.

This team should consist of people from the core business group as well as people from the various IT-based departments. The core team will not be expected to have all the answers—but they should have access to the resources needed to find that information.

This is the most important part of OCTAVE, or any other security method: senior management support. Without the support of senior management any security model will fail. Security permeates all aspects of an organization, which means that assistance from every department is required. If information requests do not originate from senior management, they may be given a low priority or ignored. The core team does not need to be comprised of senior management, but the first group that is briefed should be members of senior management to make sure the team has full support—this will be discussed in more detail shortly.

The core team must go through several steps during the process of the OCTAVE evaluation. These steps generally correspond with the three-part approach to the OCTAVE method and are used to create catalogs of practices and vulnerabilities. Again, these steps will often involve people outside of the core team, who can provide information or expertise in certain areas.

2.2.2 Getting Started

The first step, as mentioned earlier, is to get sponsorship from senior management. Ideally, the idea of using the OCTAVE model will originate at that level, but if it does not, it is important to approach senior management first, explain the process, and why the steps are necessary to ensure corporate security. The initial deployment of a security model can take a considerable amount of time. Senior management needs to understand this, and be prepared to have some of their employees take time away from their regular duties to support this.

After you have secured the support of senior management, the next step is to select the core group. As with senior management, the core group needs to understand the process, and the time that it will need to be devoted to this process. Obviously, senior managers should be involved in the selection of this group, but they do not necessarily have to be members of the panel. As mentioned previously, the core group should be comprised of three to five representatives from the business and technical side of the company.

The core group will need to be trained on the OCTAVE method. Either the member of the core group who initiated the process or a third-party security vendor can handle this. Each member will oversee aspects of the cataloging process. During the training members should be made aware of their role in this OCTAVE process.

After the core team has been trained, planning can begin. Areas of the organization that are considered vital to its security should be identified. When these areas have been selected senior management should communicate the relevant parts of the OCTAVE process to employees within those areas. As with the core group, senior managers should work with managers in the identified areas to select employees who will contribute to the OCTAVE process, on an as-needed basis.

The selected employees should be briefed on the full OCTAVE process and what will be expected from them.

When these initial steps have been completed, the core group can begin addressing the three parts of the OCTAVE process.

2.3 Build Asset-Based Threat Profiles

The first phase of OCTAVE is to build asset-based threat profiles. This is a fact-finding mission of sorts. The core group arranges meetings with different levels of staffing to identify assets that are critical to the company, and the negative impacts on the company should these assets be compromised.

By design there are separate meetings for each organizational level: senior management, middle management, staff, and the IT department. By separating the organizations in this manner, each group will be more inclined to speak freely, and not hold back anything for fear of reprisal. The nature of the topic dictates that the meetings have to be somewhat formal, but the gatherings should be as relaxed as possible so attendees are willing to share information.[3]

---

3. Food always helps.

Make sure that attendees are there because of their knowledge or skills, and not just because they are available at a certain time. It is important that everyone who attends is able to contribute to the discussion.

In each meeting, the attendees should determine what they perceive to be the most valuable assets in the organization. Assets can be data, people, equipment, software, or anything else that has a tangible value to the company. The next step is to rank the assets in order of importance. The importance of the asset, in this case, is relative to the impact on the organization if the asset is compromised. For example, if your customer database were lost the impact on your organization would be severe. On the other hand, if the employee phone book were compromised, the impact would be less severe.

Once the assets have been identified and ranked, the next step is to identify the threats to these assets. A threat, in this case, is defined as any undesirable event that could result in a compromise of an asset. Threats can be based on human error (an engineer configures the netmask on a switch incorrectly), or on nature (a tornado destroys your data center). Each asset should have a list of potential threats, as well as the possible results if that threat is executed. Make sure that the threats are kept somewhat realistic. While an asteroid crashing into your data center would undoubtedly be devastating, the likelihood of it happening, combined with the exorbitant costs involved in preventing it, make it unreasonable to list it as a threat.[4]

You have gathered the assets and the associated threats, as well as the impact of those threats. The next step is to define the security requirements for each asset. There are three guidelines that need to be used when creating the requirements for each asset: confidentiality, integrity, and availability. These are similar to the guidelines used to develop security requirements for data in the Common Criteria model.

Confidentiality is the process of keeping information that is private and sensitive away from anyone who should not have access to it. Integrity involves assuring that an asset has not been impaired, or modified in any way by someone or some process that is not authorized. Availability is how often authorized personnel are able to reach an asset.

Table 2.1 lists the matrix that is being developed for each asset.

---

4. Not to mention that it is not possible for an asteroid to hit a data center. When it enters into the Earth's atmosphere it becomes a meteorite.

Table 2.1   Security Evaluations

ASSET	THREATS	THREAT RESULTS	SECURITY REQUIREMENTS
Ranked list of assets	Threats to each asset	Worst-case scenario	Minimal security standards

At this point important assets have been identified, threats associated with those assets have been listed, and the security requirements have been created. The security requirements that have been listed for each asset are added to a catalog of security practices that the organization should strive to follow. This catalog of security practices should be the goal that the three parts of the OCTAVE process are striving to help your organization meet.

The next step is to identify the current security practices for each asset. These practices should be obtained using anonymous surveys at each of the group meetings. It is essential that an accurate picture of current security practices for each asset be obtained, even if it reflects badly on a department or individual. When gathering the current security practices, it is important to reassure people that there will not be negative repercussions for failures in the current security model. Employees have to be able to provide honest communication.

Listing the current practices will often make some of the security vulnerabilities become more apparent. Those that are not automatically apparent should still be identified within the survey. Nonapparent vulnerabilities can include things like running older software code on routers and switches, not updating operating systems with the latest service packs, and bad password policies. Vulnerabilities are different from threats in the way they approach a security problem. A threat would be an attacker launching a DoS attack against your web server; vulnerability would be running an older version of your web server software that is susceptible to the DoS attacks.

The security evaluation chart now looks like Table 2.2.

Keep in mind that each group will have its own chart, and the charts represent the opinions of each individual group. Expect the charts from each group to be very different, especially when comparing the results from the senior management and the staff meetings.

The differences are why the core group is so important to this process. The core group has to evaluate the lists from each of the meetings and combine the

Table 2.2   Security Evaluations

Asset	Threats	Threat Results	Security Requirements	Current Security Practices	Known Security Vulnerabilities
Ranked list of assets	Threats to each asset	Worst-case scenario	Minimal security standards	Current security procedures	Areas where security could be improved

information to produce a master chart identifying the core assets of the organization and the perceived threats as well as the requirements necessary to secure against these threats. Now, the group can move on to Part 2: Identifying infrastructure vulnerabilities.

2.4 Identify Infrastructure Vulnerabilities

Part 2 of the OCTAVE method involves a comprehensive evaluation of your organization's technology infrastructure to determine what additional security measures need to be taken in order satisfy the security requirements laid out in Part 1 of the evaluation process.

Some of the changes in the infrastructure will be easy. The changes recommended by employees in Part 1 of the evaluation might be implemented quickly. What will probably be more difficult is correcting security vulnerabilities of which members within your organization are unaware. Determining and fixing additional vulnerabilities not gathered during the first phase may involve using a third-party vendor who specializes in this type of work.

Of course, if the skill set to perform these tests exists within your organization, feel free to use it, but you must understand the steps involved in testing a system, and how to properly interpret the results; otherwise, this crucial part of your security evaluation will be useless.

OCTAVE groups security vulnerabilities into three categories:

1. Design—A vulnerability that is a flaw based in hardware, software, or a protocol. This could be a security hole in an operating system or a prob-

lem with the version of a specification, such as the security flaws found in SSL 1.0.

2. Implementation—A vulnerability that lies in the way a system is being used, not in how it is deployed or designed.

3. Configuration—The most common vulnerabilities. Configuration vulnerabilities stem from administrative errors: a bad password, insecure system access, or other errors.

Each system within your IT infrastructure will most likely have multiple vulnerabilities that span all three categories. In order to maintain best practices while testing the system, OCTAVE requires that an organization use an established catalog of vulnerabilities.

2.4.1 CVE

The most popular catalog of vulnerabilities is the Common Vulnerabilities and Exposures (CVE) dictionary, sponsored by the Mitre Corporation (*cve.mitre. org*). CVE is used by many organizations as a way to standardize vulnerabilities across multiple platforms. Rather than act as a database or a repository (similar to BugTraq) of information, CVE provides a standard naming convention for vulnerabilities. Other organizations that support CVE use the names defined within CVE in their products. From an end-user perspective, this means that all devices that are CVE-compliant will list CVE-2001-0494 as a buffer overflow problem with the IPSwitch SMTP Server.

Dictionary systems, such as CVE, provide a valuable tool to network administrators because they make it easier to determine what vulnerabilities an intrusion detection system (IDS) tool will detect. The downside to tools like CVE is that, because it tries to be vendor neutral, incidents that are added to the CVE database are determined by a group of industry experts. This can mean that the official CVE database can lag several months behind the report of a security incident.

Fortunately, CVE also supplies a list of candidates for inclusion into the database. Candidates have not been officially added, but many CVE vendors will include them in their tools in an effort to be as complete as possible. Candidates are distinguished from actual dictionary entries by their titles. A dictionary entry includes the letters CVE, followed by the year, and the incident number. In the example given earlier, the IPSwitch vulnerability is incident number 494 of 2001. Candidates have the letters CAN, followed by the year and the incident number. The incident CAN-2002-0085 describes a potential Apache exploit involving PHP, which was reported in February 2002. Before it can be listed in the dictionary it has to receive enough accept votes from members of the CVE board. Voting, and detailed information about the incident, are available with each listing.

A wide range of IDS tools uses the CVE system. The tools that use CVE include VLAD the Scanner, an open source scanner available from BindView, and Cisco IDS (formerly known as NetRanger). The CVE website lists more than 1,600 systems that use the CVE dictionary.

2.4.2 Assess the Results

Using whatever dictionary and IDS system your organization's staff feels comfortable with, analyze your critical IT systems.

When the analysis is complete, another meeting needs to be held with the core group and the IT staff. The results of the testing should be analyzed and placed into three separate groups:

1. Vulnerabilities outside the organization
2. Vulnerabilities within the organization
3. Vulnerabilities in each system

Every vulnerability should be reviewed, within the context of its group, by the organization's IT staff before moving on to Part 3 of the OCTAVE evaluation.

2.5 Evaluate Security Strategy and Plans

In Parts 1 and 2 of the OCTAVE evaluation the core team, with assistance from select other groups within the organization, has built a database of critical assets, threats to those assets, and vulnerabilities of the assets. The goal of Part 3 of the OCTAVE evaluation is to determine how to reduce risk to the critical assets.

A risk, in this situation, is defined as a threat combined with the impact on an organization if that threat is carried out against a critical asset. Risk can be defined as either a qualitative or quantitative value; OCTAVE focuses on the qualitative aspect of risk evaluation.

Before deciding how to respond to the risks that emerged from Parts 1 and 2 of the OCTAVE evaluation, an organization must conduct a risk analysis. There are three steps involved in the OCTAVE risk analysis process.

1. Examine the threats to assets deemed critical. Each threat should be evaluated in terms of the impact of vulnerabilities that affect the asset's confidentiality, integrity, and availability. This creates a risk profile for each threat.

2. Create a benchmark against which each risk profile can be examined. The benchmark should consist of simple qualitative values, such as high, medium, and low, that can be assigned to each profile.

3. Assign the values created in the benchmark phase to each profile. This is done by the core team.

After every risk profile has been assigned a value, there are three possible resolutions to the vulnerabilities:

1. Develop new security practices.

2. Continue to maintain current security practices.

3. Fix identified vulnerabilities, without changing existing security practices.

The core group, working in conjunction with the affected departments and IT, develops a list of steps to be taken to address the threats, or change existing policy. As with the other steps in the OCTAVE evaluation, this requires the involvement of senior management to ensure that all departments are cooperative in this process.

An OCTAVE evaluation is not a one-time phenomenon. Instead, it should be carried out continuously throughout the year. The initial OCTAVE evaluation may cause some confusion as employees may not be used to this type of security methodology. However, as employees get used to it, it will begin to make sense, and subsequent evaluations will become faster and easier. It will also provide your organization with a way to become more proactive with regard to security issues.

Employee involvement is a critical aspect of OCTAVE evaluations. Code upgrades, and protocol security are not enough to create an effective security policy. Employees must participate willingly and fully. This is why the meetings are such an important part of the OCTAVE method. Meetings allow employees to give their input into the security policy of your organization as well as giving the core group a chance to explain why security steps are being taken and what the end result of the process will be.

By providing employees with as much information about the process as possible, you will build a stronger and more effective security policy.

2.6 Summary

This chapter has covered a variety of security models that can be used to develop a security policy for your organization. Security models are not a very exciting aspect of the security process, but a good security model is essential to developing a security policy that will be effective in the long term.

This chapter was not intended to be a comprehensive analysis of security models, but it should give you an idea of the issues involved in selecting a security model and using it to develop a security policy for your organization.

3

Understanding
Types of Attacks

MacGyver was a television series on ABC in the 1980s and early 1990s. On the show MacGyver, the main character, would come up with innovative ways to stop his foes. These methods usually involved using everyday household items to create bombs, and other things that exploded. The creators of *MacGyver*, wisely opting not to be sued, always left out at least one critical step in the bomb-making process.

The same rules cannot apply to a network security book. It is important to have all of the information possible, so administrators can understand the tools being used. The better attack tools are understood, the easier it will be to defend against the incursions.

The goal of this chapter is to provide network and security administrators an overview of the types of attacks that can be launched against a network. This chapter does not discuss, in any detail, ways to stop these attacks, or prevent them from occurring in the first place. That is what the rest of the book is for; this chapter is designed to educate administrators about the nature of the different types of attacks, and what they are designed to do. Whenever possible, existing attack tools are profiled, along with links to those tools. Attackers have access to this information; network administrators should have the same access.

One type that is not covered in this chapter, but is mentioned often in the press, is the DoS attack. Originally, a DoS attack referred to one launched against a network. An attacker would flood a network with malformed packets, causing all servers on that network to become unreachable, and, possibly, crashing gateway routers or firewalls.

The meaning of a DoS attack has morphed to the point that it no longer carries the same connotation. Instead, DoS refers to any attack that renders a network, part of a network, or a single server unreachable. Most network attacks fall into that category, so by broadening the definition of DoS attacks it has become a less useful as a description.[1]

The tools used throughout this chapter are relatively easy to download and install, most having precompiled binaries that run on either Microsoft Windows or Linux. The ease with which these tools can be downloaded and installed should be disconcerting, to say the least. Some very powerful tools are readily available for download. An ex-employee, an angered customer, a competitor, or someone who simply does not like an organization has an arsenal that can be used against that organization.

The pervasiveness of these tools has given rise to the pejorative term *script kiddie*. Script kiddie refers to someone who does not necessarily understand the tools being used, or the logic behind them—instead the script kiddie simply wants to cause as much damage as possible. Think of a script kiddie as someone who likes to graffiti buildings; the primary goal is defacement, not theft or information gathering. Of course the tools available to script kiddies are akin to making a do-it-yourself safe-cracking kit. Just because someone does not understand the logic behind the tool does not make him or her any less dangerous.

NOTE

Script kiddies can cause serious damage. In February 2000, a script kiddie managed to knock eight of the world's largest websites offline for several hours using a DDoS attack. While there is still limited protection against DDoS attacks, the good news is that most other types of attacks can be prevented using good security practices.

Script kiddies rely on known weaknesses and systems that have not been properly patched, or upgraded, to launch successful attacks. A well locked-down

---

1. On the positive side, it has made it a lot easier for technology journalists to report security incidents.

system will almost always stop a script kiddie cold. A good understanding of the tools being used can help keep script kiddies out.

3.1 Sniffing and Port Scanning

The first step in any successful attack is sniffing, used to see what type of traffic is being passed on a network, and look for things like passwords, credit card numbers, and so forth. *Sniffing* is the term generally used for traffic monitoring within a network, while port scanning is used to find out information about a remote network.

Both sniffing and port scanning have the same objective—to find system vulnerabilities—but they take different approaches. Sniffing is used by an attacker already on the network who wants to gather more information about the network. Port scanning is used by someone who is interested in finding vulnerabilities on a system that is unknown.

There are many tools available for network sniffing. Two of the most common tools are Ethereal (*www.ethereal.com/*) and Snort (*www.snort.org/*). Both tools are relatively simple to use, and are designed to help troubleshoot problems, but can also be used to watch traffic.

NOTE

Always run programs like this on an isolated part of the network. While some of these programs are well known and have legitimate uses, others are specifically designed for launching attacks on other systems. It is possible there are Trojans within these programs that may wreak havoc on a network.

Figure 3.1 is an example of what a packet captured by Ethereal looks like. As you can see information about the transaction is included in the top window, while the bottom contains the contents of the actual packet. If the packet is not encrypted it is possible to read the information within it. It is also possible to string packets together to monitor an entire transaction.

A packet sniffer works by putting the network card into promiscuous mode so the network card listens for and processes all Address Resolution Protocol

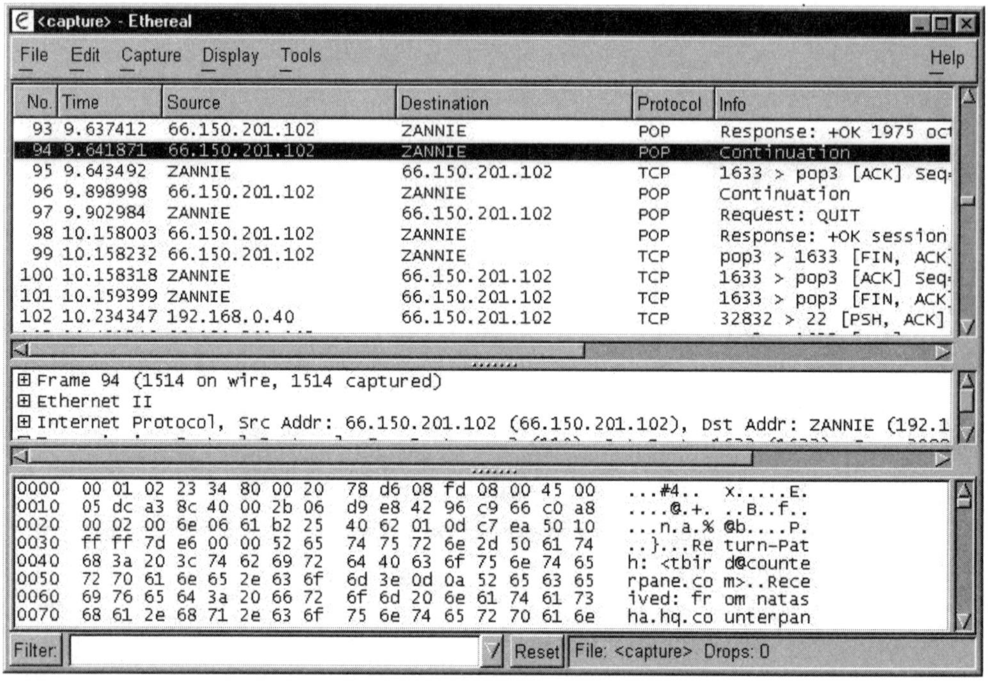

```
┌────────────────────────────────────────────────────────────────────────────────────┐
│ @ <capture> - Ethereal                                                    _ □ ×     │
├────────────────────────────────────────────────────────────────────────────────────┤
│ File   Edit   Capture   Display   Tools                                      Help    │
├────────────────────────────────────────────────────────────────────────────────────┤
│ No. Time       Source           Destination        Protocol Info                     │
│  93 9.637412   66.150.201.102   ZANNIE              POP      Response: +OK 1975 oct   │
│  94 9.641871   66.150.201.102   ZANNIE              POP      Continuation            │
│  95 9.643492   ZANNIE           66.150.201.102      TCP      1633 > pop3 [ACK] Seq    │
│  96 9.898998   66.150.201.102   ZANNIE              POP      Continuation            │
│  97 9.902984   ZANNIE           66.150.201.102      POP      Request: QUIT           │
│  98 10.158003  66.150.201.102   ZANNIE              POP      Response: +OK session   │
│  99 10.158232  66.150.201.102   ZANNIE              TCP      pop3 > 1633 [FIN, ACK]  │
│ 100 10.158318  ZANNIE           66.150.201.102      TCP      1633 > pop3 [ACK] Seq    │
│ 101 10.159399  ZANNIE           66.150.201.102      TCP      1633 > pop3 [FIN, ACK]  │
│ 102 10.234347  192.168.0.40     66.150.201.102      TCP      32832 > 22 [PSH, ACK]   │
├────────────────────────────────────────────────────────────────────────────────────┤
│ ⊞ Frame 94 (1514 on wire, 1514 captured)                                             │
│ ⊞ Ethernet II                                                                        │
│ ⊞ Internet Protocol, Src Addr: 66.150.201.102 (66.150.201.102), Dst Addr: ZANNIE (192.1 │
├────────────────────────────────────────────────────────────────────────────────────┤
│ 0000  00 01 02 23 34 80 00 20   78 d6 08 fd 08 00 45 00   ...#4..  x.....E.          │
│ 0010  05 dc a3 8c 40 00 2b 06   d9 e8 42 96 c9 66 c0 a8   ....@.+.  ..B..f..         │
│ 0020  00 02 00 6e 06 61 b2 25   40 62 01 0d c7 ea 50 10   ...n.a.%  @b....P.         │
│ 0030  ff ff 7d e6 00 00 52 65   74 75 72 6e 2d 50 61 74   ..}...Re  turn-Pat        │
│ 0040  68 3a 20 3c 74 62 69 72   64 40 63 6f 75 6e 74 65   h: <tbir  d@counte        │
│ 0050  72 70 61 6e 65 2e 63 6f   6d 3e 0d 0a 52 65 63 65   rpane.co  m>..Rece        │
│ 0060  69 76 65 64 3a 20 66 72   6f 6d 20 6e 61 74 61 73   ived: fr  om natas        │
│ 0070  68 61 2e 68 71 2e 63 6f   75 6e 74 65 72 70 61 6e   ha.hq.co  unterpan        │
├────────────────────────────────────────────────────────────────────────────────────┤
│ Filter:                                             √ Reset  File: <capture> Drops: 0 │
└────────────────────────────────────────────────────────────────────────────────────┘
```

Figure 3.1   A captured packet displayed in Ethereal

(ARP) requests on the network segment, not just ARP requests destined for that machine.

Obviously, for a packet sniffer to be effective it has to be attached to the network. A packet sniffer is used either by someone who has compromised a machine on a network, or by an internal attacker.

A packet sniffer is hard to detect because it operates passively. It simply collects information, rather than actively searching for data. Many network intrusion detection systems (NIDS) attempt to detect promiscuous mode by watching for certain behaviors, but these methods are not always effective.

3.1.1 Port Scanning

Prior to sniffing a network an attacker has to gain access. Attackers gain access by scanning devices on the network for vulnerabilities, then exploiting them. Port scanning can either be targeted or random. An attacker interested in a particular network will attempt to track down information about that network and scan for vulnerabilities. Alternatively, attackers will put large netblocks into a port scanner and let it run for days, trying to find any machine that is available and able to be exploited. This highlights the difference between an attacker and a script kiddie.

NOTE

A knowledgeable attacker is looking for specific information; a script kiddie simply wants to destroy things.

A tool commonly used for port scanning is nmap (www.insecure.org/nmap/). It allows users to enter a range of IP addresses, choose the type of scan desired, and let the program run in the background. When it has completed its sweep it will produce a report showing the ports which responded, on each network device:

```
[root@test root]# nmap -sT www.datacenterwire.com

Starting nmap V. 2.99RC2 ( www.insecure.org/nmap/ )
Interesting ports on (66.150.201.102):
(The 1589 ports scanned but not shown below are in state: closed)
Port State Service
21/tcp open ftp
22/tcp open ssh
25/tcp open smtp
53/tcp open domain
80/tcp open http
81/tcp open hosts2-ns
110/tcp open pop-3
443/tcp open https
587/tcp open submission
3306/tcp open mysql
5432/tcp open postgres
10000/tcp open snet-sensor-mgmt

Nmap run completed -- 1 IP address (1 host up) scanned in 48 seconds
```

Nmap can be configured to scan all TCP and User Datagram Protocol (UDP) ports, or just the ports that generally have services running on them. Using the information collected in the example, notice there were 12 out of 1,589 scanned ports responding on the server.

Once the list of ports and host names has been compiled, the next step is to try to exploit weaknesses in the various server configurations. This involves knowing what the weaknesses of the different servers are and exploiting those weaknesses.

3.2 Exploits

An exploit allows an attacker to take advantage of known weaknesses in operating systems or applications to gain access to a server. Exploits can be performed in many ways; however, it is becoming increasingly common for an exploit to be written into a software application that can be easily pointed at any server.

NOTE

Exploits as programs make it very easy for script kiddies to wreak havoc, but they also separate true attackers from the script kiddies. One developer, having set up a honeypot on a FreeBSD system, went into a well-known script kiddie chat room and told them about a "vulnerable" Microsoft Windows IIS server he had discovered. Seconds after his announcements the honeypot server began getting attacks designed to exploit vulnerabilities in the Microsoft Windows server. Not one person bothered to verify whether it was really a Microsoft Windows server.

Before an exploit can be run, it is important to know what operating system is running on the network device. Some exploits work on some systems, but not others. There are many tools to do this, but since nmap has built-in operating system fingerprinting capabilities, it is often easiest to use:

```
[root@test root]# nmap -O www.datacenterwire.com

Starting nmap V. 2.99RC2 ( www.insecure.org/nmap/ )
Interesting ports on (66.150.201.102):
(The 1587 ports scanned but not shown below are in state: closed)
Port State Service
21/tcp open ftp
22/tcp open ssh
25/tcp open smtp
53/tcp open domain
80/tcp open http
81/tcp open hosts2-ns
110/tcp open pop-3
443/tcp open https
587/tcp open submission
```

```
886/tcp  filtered unknown
3306/tcp open mysql
5432/tcp open postgres
10000/tcp open snet-sensor-mgmt
32787/tcp filtered sometimes-rpc27
Remote operating system guess: FreeBSD 4.5-RELEASE (or -STABLE) (X86)
Uptime 72.083 days (since Fri May 17 17:15:58 2002)

Nmap run completed -- 1 IP address (1 host up) scanned in 685 seconds
```

The attacker now knows that the site is running FreeBSD, Version 4.5, on an Intel processor. With that knowledge the attacker can:

- Attempt to exploit known vulnerabilities in the operating system.
- Try to access the server through security holes in the applications running on the server.

FreeBSD is a fairly secure operating system. Rather than try to crack the operating system directly it is usually easier to exploit security holes in applications running on the server.

In June 2002 a serious security flaw was found in the Apache web server, used by more than 18 million websites around the world. This security hole caught many people off guard, and given the large install base, it will be a while before the majority of Apache web servers will be upgraded. A good attacker knows this, and will check to see if the server is vulnerable.

Fortunately there are numerous tools that can be used to test for application weaknesses. Network administrators use scanning tools to find security holes within their own network. Unfortunately, there is nothing preventing an attacker from putting these tools to the same use.

A common application used for tasks like this is Nessus (*www.nessus.org*). Nessus is designed specifically for remote security scanning; that is, it is built to emulate the actions of an attacker attempting to break into a network. The developers of Nessus maintain a database of known vulnerabilities. Administrators—or attackers—can use this database to find known security holes in various servers on the network. Administrators can patch the holes; attackers can exploit them.

In this case, the attacker already knows that he or she wants to try an Apache exploit, so there is no need to use Nessus, because there are programs that will simply check for Apache vulnerabilities. A fairly common tool is the Retina Apache Chunked Scanner, developed by eEye Digital Security (www.eeye.com).

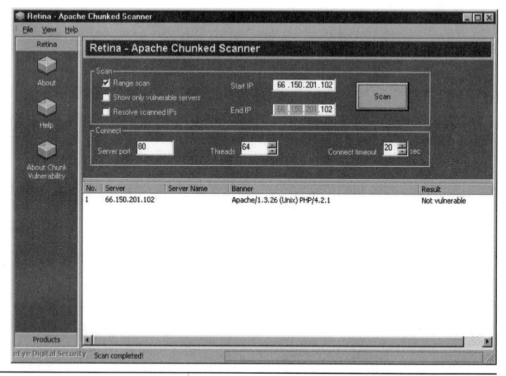

Figure 3.2   The Retina Apache Chunked Scanner checks for a specific Apache vulnerability. Other tools will check for a wider range of vulnerabilities.

Simply enter the IP address, or range of IP addresses to be scanned, and it will check for the vulnerabilities. Figure 3.2 shows that the server is not vulnerable to this particular attack.

This server is not vulnerable to the Apache exploit, so what is the next step? That depends on the attacker. If the attacker is specifically targeting this server, he or she will attempt to find another way in. If the attacker is simply looking for a server to attack, and does not have many tools with which to launch the attack, then he or she will probably move on to another server that is vulnerable, as in Figure 3.3.

It is not uncommon for an attacker, especially a script kiddie, to have a limited arsenal of weapons with which to launch an attack. This is especially true if the attacker does not understand how the attack works, and is relying on tools developed by someone who does. This type of attacker is not going to try a sys-

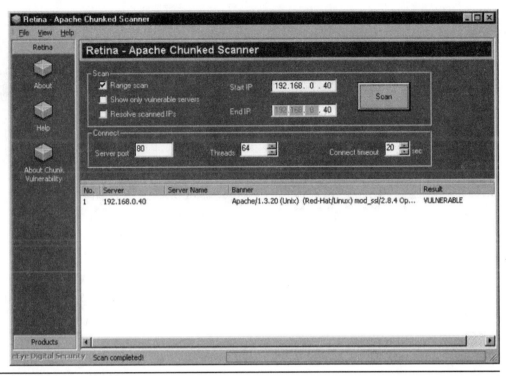

Figure 3.3   This server is most likely vulnerable to the Apache Chunk exploit. The next step would be to attempt to exploit the server.

tematic approach to a server attack; instead, the attacker will move on to a less secure server.

Figure 3.3 shows a server vulnerable to the Apache Chunk exploit. Once the attacker finds a server that is vulnerable, the next step is to exploit it. Again, this can be done by understanding the weakness and developing a program to take advantage of it. Alternatively, if a script exists to do this for the attacker, that script can be used.

NOTE

The Apache Chunk exploit is a bug in the way Apache deals with files being uploaded when the server is unable to determine the file size.

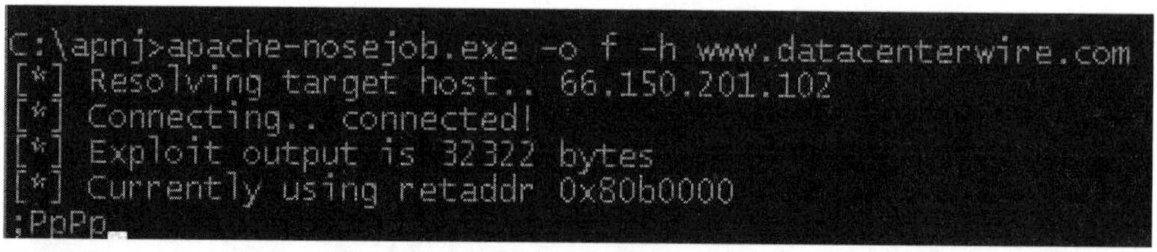

```
C:\apnj>apache-nosejob.exe -o f -h www.datacenterwire.com
[*]  Resolving target host.. 66.150.201.102
[*]  Connecting.. connected!
[*]  Exploit output is 32322 bytes
[*]  Currently using retaddr 0x80b0000
;PpPp
```

Figure 3.4   Using the program to launch an attack against a website and exploit a security hole in the Apache web server

In this case, the code to take advantage of the Apache Chunk exploit is available in a compiled format from the Packet Storm security website (packetstorm.decepticons.org/filedesc/apache-nosejob.zip.html). Download the code, target the server (as in Figure 3.4), and an attacker can gain root access to the remote web server.

Often it takes very little skill to break into a server, especially a web server. It is simply a matter of knowing the tools needed for the job and implementing them.

3.2.1 Rootkits

When an attacker gains access to a server, the first goal is to cover his or her tracks. Installing a rootkit often does this. A rootkit has two purposes: to cover the tracks of the attacker and to gather information about the server and its users.

Rootkits usually kill logging services and monitor the keystrokes of system users looking for passwords and other useful information. A rootkit will contain several programs that hide the activity of the attacker.

A good example of a rootkit is Tuxkit, developed by Tuxtendo (www.tuxtendo.nl). Tuxkit has all of the classic features that make a rootkit useful for an attacker: easy to install, leaves a backdoor on the system, covers the tracks of the user, and replaces system files with compromised binaries that are used to gather server intelligence. Tuxkit consists of several files and an installation script:

```
-rw------- 1 1209 1209 502884 Dec 4 2001 bin.tgz
-rw------- 1 1209 1209 406 Dec 4 2001 cfg.tgz
-rw------- 1 1209 1209 16213 Dec 4 2001 lib.tgz
-rw------- 1 1209 1209 3684 Dec 4 2001 README
-rw------- 1 1209 1209 461892 Jan 5 2002 sshd.tgz
```

```
-rw------- 1 1209 1209 1644819 Dec 4 2001 tools.tgz
-rwx------ 1 1209 1209 9489 May 15 14:59 tuxkit
```

For ease of use the installation script, Tuxkit, requires that only a single variable be changed:

```
#!/bin/sh
# Tuxtendo Linux Rootkit v1.0 By Argv[]

# Your e-mail address
EMAIL="allan@allan.org"

# You don't need to edit anything below this
```

All an attacker has to do is execute the install script. The attacker's tracks are covered and Tuxkit begins to gather information. It also sends a nice e-mail to the attacker with the IP address and backdoor information to the server:

```
ssh 192.168.0.40 -l root -p 4000 # test.allan.org password: R0s3ann3
psyBNC: 4001
```

This allows Tuxkit to be used in an automated fashion: Load a large netblock into a security scanner, looking for exploitable servers; when a server is successfully compromised, install Tuxkit. The e-mail is sent to the attacker, who may be able to take control of several dozen servers in a few hours.

On a well-secured network, a rootkit should not go unnoticed very long. If unusual traffic is generated from a server, or an administrator notices that syslog is disabled, this should set off alarms. In addition many administrators run chkrootkit (*www.chkrootkit.org/*) to check for rootkit installations. Not only does chkrootkit look for specific rootkits, it also looks for modified files and alerts administrators that they have been modified. On a system infected with Tuxkit:

```
[root@test chkrootkit-pre-0.36]# ./chkrootkit
ROOTDIR is `/'
Checking `amd'... not found
Checking `basename'... not infected
Checking `biff'... not found
Checking `chfn'... not infected
Checking `chsh'... not infected
Checking `cron'... not infected
Checking `date'... not infected
Checking `du'... INFECTED
Checking `dirname'... not infected
Checking `echo'... not infected
Checking `egrep'... not infected
Checking `env'... not infected
```

```
Checking `find'... INFECTED
Checking `fingerd'... not infected
Checking `gpm'... not infected
Checking `grep'... not infected
Checking `hdparm'... not infected
```

While relatively easy to spot, rootkits are popular because, like some of their companion exploits, they can be quickly installed and manage many tasks that some attackers do not have the skills to perform.

3.3 Spoofing

An IP spoofing attack is one in which the source IP address of a packet is forged. There are generally two types of spoofing attacks: IP spoofing used in DoS attacks, and man in the middle attacks.

IP spoofing-based DoS attacks are relatively straightforward. An attacker sends a packet to the target host with a forged IP address (SYN)—often an IP address in the RFC 1918 address space, though it does not have to be—the targeted host sends an acknowledgement (ACK) and waits for a response. The response never comes, and these unanswered queries remain in the buffer of the targeted device. If enough spoofed queries are sent the buffer will overflow and the network device will become unstable and crash.

Man in the middle attacks are much more onerous. Here, the attacker intercepts traffic heading between two devices on the network. The attacker can either monitor information or alter the data as it passes through the network. This is illustrated in Figure 3.5.

Typically a man in the middle attack works like this: An attacker sits on the network and watches traffic. When another user on the network sends an ARP request to a network device, the attacker sends a response saying the compromised machine is the requested device. Even if the actual device responds, the second response will override the first. The user now sends all data destined for the original device to the compromised machine.

It is possible for an attacker to use this method to intercept enough data to effectively monitor and log all network traffic and gain important information such as usernames and passwords. Users may never know that the traffic is being intercepted, because each packet will eventually be forwarded onto its intended destination.

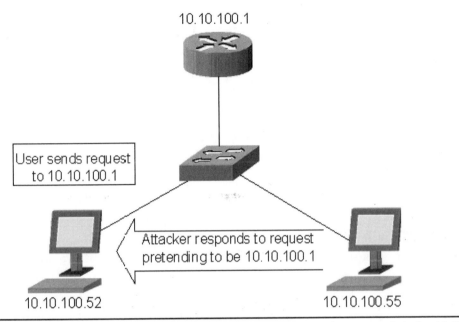

10.10.100.1

User sends request
to 10.10.100.1

Attacker responds to request
pretending to be 10.10.100.1

10.10.100.52   10.10.100.55

Figure 3.5   User sends a request to 10.10.100.1. The attacker pretends to be 10.10.100.1 and sends a response to that effect. The user then forwards all packets destined for 10.10.100.1 to the attacker.

NOTE

As with the other attacks described in this chapter, there are pre-compiled tools that help attackers carry out man in the middle attacks. One of the most popular tools used for man in the middle attacks is Ettercap (*ettercap.sourceforge.net/*). Ettercap binaries are available for Windows, Solaris, BSD, and Linux.

3.4 Distributed Denial of Service Attacks

DDoS attacks use a combination of the techniques described in this chapter to launch a large-scale attack against a network or network device. DDoS attacks are very effective in knocking their targets offline, because they are focused attacks that generally exploit a small number of weaknesses.

A DDoS attack is relatively simple: An attacker scans a series of network blocks looking for specific vulnerabilities. When a vulnerable host is found it is exploited and used to scan for other hosts with the same vulnerability or group of vulnerabilities. This creates a chain of computers that are under control of the attacker.

The tools used to launch DDoS attacks are automated: when the DDoS tool locates a vulnerable host, it is automatically compromised and a rootkit is installed. The first set of vulnerable hosts are called *handlers*. The handlers are then used to locate a second set of vulnerable hosts, known as *agents* (this process is outlined in Figure 3.6). By creating a two-tier system the attacker is able to keep his or her source IP address from being discovered. Instead the attacker launches the attack from the handlers.

DDoS attacks serve only one purpose: to make a network or host unavailable. This is accomplished by using compromised hosts to issue a large stream of TCP requests against the target. The large number of TCP requests use up system resources on the target host or network, making it unavailable for legitimate traffic.

There are several tools used to launch DDoS attacks. The most well-known, and the first DDoS ever detected is Trin00 (also spelled Trinoo) and its cousin for Microsoft Windows, Wintrinoo. Trin00 works by sending a large number of UDP packets with four bytes of data. These packets are sent from the same source port on the attacking machine, but sent to various source ports on the target host or network. The target host or network responds with ICMP port unreachable messages, until all available resources are used up and the system shuts down.

The Tribal Flood Network (TFN) behaves in much the same manner as Trin00 except in the way the attacker communicates with the handlers. Trin00 uses UDP packets to send information among attacker, handler, and agent. UDP packets are easily detected by an IDS so TFN relies on ICMP packets for communication between the levels.

The attack structure is basically the same between TFN and Trin00, but the use of ICMP packets for communication makes TFN much more difficult to detect than Trin00 attacks.

A third tool is Stacheldraht. Once again Stacheldraht's attack model is the same as TFN and Trin00, but the communication between devices is different.

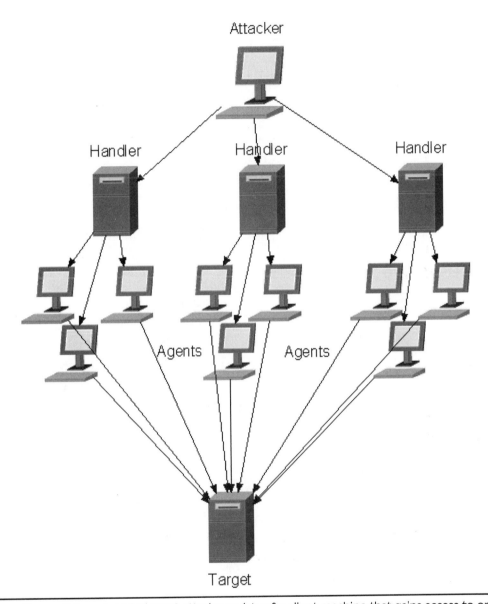

Figure 3.6   A typical DDoS attack consists of a client machine that gains access to one or more intermediary machines, known as handlers. The handlers use the DDoS tool to gain access to even more machines, known as agents. The agents are the machines that launch the actual attack.

Stacheldraht uses a combination of ICMP and TCP to communicate between the attacking hosts. In addition, Stacheldraht encrypts all information sent between the attacking hosts using symmetric key encryption.

As administrators have started taking network security more seriously, large-scale DDoS attacks, like those that affected eBay and Amazon in February 2000, have become less common. However, smaller DDoS attacks still occur with amazing frequency. Because it is hard to stop DDoS attacks once they have been launched, the most effective method of prevention is to not let them start in the first place. This requires keeping systems properly patched to prevent hosts from being used as either handlers or agents. If a script kiddie is unable to find any hosts from which to launch the attack, the attack will not occur.

3.5 Viruses and Worms

The most common types of network attacks are the virus and the worm. A virus is a program used to infect a computer. It is usually buried inside another program—known as a Trojan—or distributed as a stand-alone executable.

Not all viruses are malicious; in fact, very few cause extensive damage to systems. Most viruses are simply practical jokes, designed to make it appear, or scare recipients into thinking, that something is wrong with Windows. Unfortunately, the viruses that are destructive are often extremely destructive. A well-designed virus can disable an entire network in a matter of minutes.

NOTE

Viruses and worms can be expensive. Information technology research group Computer Economics (*www.computereconomics.com/*) estimated the cost of clean up and lost productivity for the Love Bug worm at $2.62 billion worldwide.

Worms are often confused with viruses, but they are very different types of code. A worm is self-replicating code that spreads itself from system to system. A traditional virus requires manual intervention to propagate itself, by copying it unknowingly to a floppy, unwittingly embedding it in an attachment, or some other method. Worms do not require assistance to spread; instead, a worm can automatically e-mail itself to other users, copy itself through the network, or even scan other hosts for vulnerabilities—and then attack those hosts.

A worm resides in active memory; the program is executed, does what it is going to do, and propagates itself. A virus typically overwrites, or attaches itself to, system files.

The distinction is often difficult to follow: It is not uncommon for a virus to be paired with a worm prior to launch. The virus does its job, and the worm transports the virus to the next group of victims.

Worms have become much more dangerous with the advent of application integration. Many worms take advantage of code that allows that programs to automatically execute code to automate common office tasks. E-mail applications are often especially vulnerable to worms. Sometimes worms are sent as attachments that execute when a user attempts to open them, but more often the malicious code can be executed simply by previewing the message, without even reading the message.

3.6 Summary

A lot of attacks can be launched against networks. The tools to accomplish these attacks are becoming more widespread and easier to use every day. It is important to stay ahead of the attackers. It is next to impossible to keep out a determined attacker, especially a skilled attacker.

Fortunately, attacks launched by skilled attackers are less common than attacks launched by unskilled attackers, the so-called script kiddies. Administrators should concentrate on protecting their networks from basic attacks, and remain vigilant against skilled attacks.

Vigilance is best maintained by tracking security issues closely. Monitor vendor security information and independent security websites and mailing lists. Probably the best independent research point is the BugTraq mailing list, which is part of the Security Focus website (*www.securityfocus.com*) and publishes information quickly. Another excellent source for information is the Common Vulnerabilities and Exposures list, maintained by the MITRE Corporation (*cve.mitre.org*). Finally, both CERT (*www.cert.org/*) and CIAC (*www.ciac.org/ciac/*) publish alerts which are not as timely as those on the BugTraq mailing list, but there are also fewer false positives.

4

Routing

Router security has traditionally been of little concern to network administrators. Routers, for the most part, simply run. They forward packets across the WAN and do not usually cause, or exacerbate, security problems.

That thinking has changed a lot over the last few years. As attackers become more network savvy, they realize that routers often make excellent targets. This is especially true for small companies that do not have dedicated network support staff. Often default router access passwords are left in place, or default SNMP passwords are unchanged. Even if a password is changed, many administrators will continue to telnet to the router, leaving their login and password information available to anyone with a sniffer.

In addition to the lack of system security, attackers find that routers are good targets because they generally sit outside the firewall and oftentimes access and configuration data are not logged.

Routers are also fast. An attacker who gains access to a router can often use it to launch DoS attacks against other servers. A more nefarious attacker may decide to route all traffic from the router to a network controlled by the attacker, allowing him or her to sniff all data coming from the compromised network.

If nothing else, an attacker who gains access to a router will have detailed information about a network, and, if TFTP is used to back up router configuration, will know of a server with at least one vulnerable service.

The goal of router security should be to make the router the first line of defense against an attacker. This entails not only securing the router, but also using it as a tool to help prevent the attacker from ever reaching the network. If an attacker is prevented from gaining access to the network at the edge it places less of a burden on the firewalls or the servers.

4.1 The Router on the Network

Older network designs sometimes made extensive use of routers. To keep broadcast traffic under control routers were sometimes used to create network segments—although bridges were more commonly used for this purpose—and to help distribute traffic load. Newer network designs replace the routers with multilayer switches.[1] A network built around multilayer switching technology allows you to keep your network design more streamlined, and means that you only have a single router, or pair of routers, to worry about.

Figure 4.1 shows a typical edge network design.

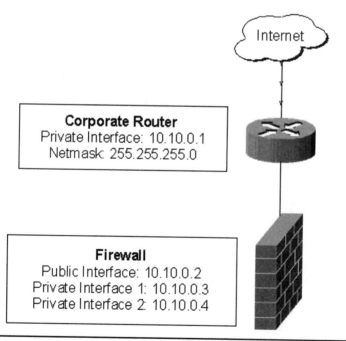

Figure 4.1   Typical edge network design

---

1. Multilayer switches are discussed in detail in Chapter 5. They are switches that combine the speed of Layer 2 switching with the intelligence of Layer 3 routing.

There are several problems with this design, the most glaring of which is that it provides an attacker with a single target. Whenever possible, a network should have multiple connections to the Internet. In addition to improving WAN response to and from the network, a dual-homed connection is a lot less susceptible to a DoS attack.

Of course a dual-homed design does involve some additional risk, as it requires the enabling of an Exterior Gateway Protocol (EGP), such as BGP. You will also have to enable the Virtual Router Redundancy Protocol (VRRP)[2] so the routers can share a connection internally. A new, more robust design will look more the one in Figure 4.2.

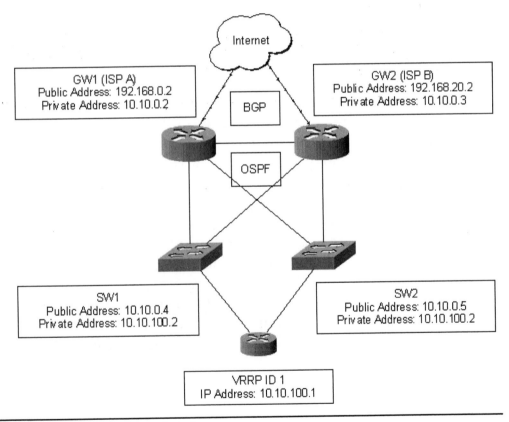

Figure 4.2   A new network design

---

2. Or one of its proprietary cousins, such as Extreme's Extreme Standby Router Protocol, or Cisco's Hot Standby Router Protocol.

In addition to running BGP on the external network, the new design uses OSPF on the internal network. Depending on what type of switches used behind the routers, the VRRP address may be configured on a second pair of routers, instead of multilayer switches.

Notice the two routers are connected to different ISPs. It is not enough to have two connections to the same ISP; a network should be as diverse as possible—given the limitations of ythe budget.

Enabling these enhanced services will be discussed in detail later in this chapter.

4.2 The Basics

There are some basic steps that need to be taken with any router to help increase network security. Not all of these steps will be possible in every environment, but as you develop a security strategy for your network, you can incorporate the options that are appropriate for your security needs.

Keep in mind that edge routers have at least two interfaces on them. Many times a network administrator will tighten down the external interface, leaving the internal interface wide open. If someone does manage to invade the network, he or she can use internal servers to launch attacks against other networks. If the internal interface is locked down to the same degree as the external interface on the router, it increases the chances of stopping an attack that originates from within the network.

In Chapter 3 we discussed smurf attacks, which are launched by pinging the broadcast address of a netblock and allowing the responses from the hosts within that network to flood another host.

A very simple way to defeat smurf attacks is to not allow packets to broadcast an address through the router. If the attacks are stopped at the router level, they cannot cause any damage. In Version 12.0 and higher of IOS, Cisco disables access to broadcast addresses by default. If you are running an earlier version of IOS, you should disable it manually for all interfaces:

```
gw1(config-if)#no ip directed broadcast
```

Some vendors, such as Juniper and Extreme, automatically disable directed broadcast access.

In Chapter 3, several spoofing attacks were also described, including one involving source routing. The router can be used to stop all source routing requests:

```
gw1(config-if)#no ip source-route
```

Remember, both of these commands should be applied to all interfaces on your router.

4.2.1 Physical Security

Have you ever forgotten the password to a router, or worse walked into a new job where no one knew the passwords for the routers? You are not alone. Because routers often function with little, or no, manual intervention, they can be left untouched for months, or even years, perhaps even buried under a stack of papers by someone who assumes that it is important, but has no idea what it is.

NOTE

It may sound unbelievable that a router would be buried under a stack of papers, but if you talk to anyone who has worked in the support department of a large ISP, they will tell you it happens more often than you think.

Router companies realize this, which is why most have developed password recovery procedures for most of their products. Cisco even has a nice page that lists all of its networking equipment along with the associated password recovery procedures (*www.cisco.com/warp/public/474/*).

The downside is that anyone with a little bit of knowledge can access this information and use it to log into your routers. Keeping routers physically secured can help prevent this type of physical attack.

The ideal location for core network equipment is in a clean data center, with redundant power sources and multiple cooling sources. A setting like this will help increase the lifetime (availability) of routers as there will be less dust, less temperature fluctuation, and no power surges, all of which have detrimental effects on routing and server equipment.

Realizing that not everyone has the budget for a carrier class data center, there are still precautions that should be taken to keep core networking equipment secure. Start by locking the equipment in a closet or in a room used only by networking personnel, rather than a room with a lot of traffic. Networking equipment should be racked, rather than stacked on a table or a shelf. Racking the equipment helps keep it cooler, and makes it more difficult for someone to walk away with it. Specifically, if the networking equipment is in a room, consider buying an enclosed rack with a lock—and make sure you use the lock.

A small cooling/filtering unit is also a good idea; at the very least make sure that the area where the equipment is stored has good ventilation. Finally, a high-end uninterruptible power supply (UPS) is important. A UPS serves two purposes: It massages the power, making sure there are no spikes that may damage the equipment. It keeps the equipment running in the event of a power failure. This is important not because you want to keep your network up (though I am sure you do), but more because a hard shut down can damage the router, forcing it to be replaced—and causing additional downtime.

Once you are confident that your networking equipment has been properly secured, the next to step is to secure the router operating system.

4.2.2 Banners

It has become a common practice to create login banners outlining the security practices of an organization. In part this practice is to let people who may be just snooping know that they should not be. Generally you want to make your welcome message as succinct as possible, and do not use the word *welcome*. Some people have contended that the word *welcome* indicates they are being invited to investigate; since that is not the case, it is a good idea to make your point clear. Text like this is usually effective:

```
**************************************************
        Organization Name
        RESTRICTED ACCESS

        No Unauthorized Access.
Contact(s):
Joe Smith:jsmith@example.com
Jane Doe:jdoe@example.com
**************************************************
```

This will probably not deter an attacker who has successfully gained access to the system, but it may assist in the event you are able to track down and prosecute the attacker.

4.2.3 Access Lists

Access control lists (ACL) are commonly used to filter unwanted packets at the router. An ACL is a rule, or a group of rules, used to manipulate packets as they pass through the router. Some organizations will attempt to use a router ACL to replace a firewall. This is not a good idea for two reasons:

1. An ACL does not have the same level of functionality as a firewall.
2. ACLs can often place a heavy CPU burden on routers. The heavy CPU burden can cause serious performance degradation, and, if the router is not powerful enough to process the incoming information, make your internal network unreachable.

If a company is going to rely on ACLs to help filter unwanted traffic it is a good idea to "super size" the router. Whatever router is recommended by your vendor for your level of connectivity, select a more powerful model. In addition, if you are going to have multiple connections to the Internet, which is good—where practical—maintain separate routers for each connection, and allow your internal network to determine the best route.

Each router manufacturer handles ACLs in a slightly different manner, but they all basically follow the same pattern:

```
Number | Traffic | Destination IP | Source IP | Action
```

A typical Cisco access list will look something like this:

```
access-list 110 deny ip 192.168.0.0 0.0.255.255 any \
log-input
```

NOTE

A line of code that ends with a \ indicates that everything should be on one line, but would not fit because of the book margins.

On a Juniper router, this same type of entry is referred to as a route list, and would look something like this:

```
policy-options {
    policy-statement from-hall2 {
        term 1 {
            from {
                route-filter 192.168.0.0/16 reject;
            }
        }
        then accept;
    }
}
```

This is a very common ACL rule. It tells the router that all IP traffic destined to any address on the network from the 192.168.0.0 netblock should be denied, and the information should be logged. As mentioned in Chapter 1, the 192.168.0.0 netblock is reserved for private networks only. Packets from the 192.168.0.0 netblock should not be traveling across the WAN,[3] so any traffic originating from addresses within that netblock can be denied.

There are other ACL rules that can be effective, but they are more controversial. While they do have their merits, they might meet with resistance inside your organization. One such rule is:

```
access-list 110 deny icmp any any redirect log-input
```

This rule will block all Internet Control Message Protocol (ICMP) traffic into, and out of, your network. ICMP requests are usually sent using Ping. Ping is a very common tool that is used to test system availability:

---

3. Barring very badly configured routers—and you don't want their traffic anyway.

```
[root@test root]# ping -c 5 192.168.0.1
PING 192.168.0.1 (192.168.0.1) from 192.168.0.40 : 56(84) bytes of
data.
64 bytes from 192.168.0.1: icmp_seq=0 ttl=150 time=864 usec
64 bytes from 192.168.0.1: icmp_seq=1 ttl=150 time=749 usec
64 bytes from 192.168.0.1: icmp_seq=2 ttl=150 time=769 usec
64 bytes from 192.168.0.1: icmp_seq=3 ttl=150 time=741 usec
64 bytes from 192.168.0.1: icmp_seq=4 ttl=150 time=745 usec

--- 192.168.0.1 ping statistics ---
5 packets transmitted, 5 packets received, 0% packet loss
round-trip min/avg/max/mdev = 0.741/0.773/0.864/0.055 ms
```

Ping can also be used to launch attacks against a network. Attacks like the Ping of Death exploit weaknesses in the ICMP architecture on certain systems, in order to crash those systems. Ping can also be used as an exploratory tool; attackers use it to determine what systems within a netblock are available. The ICMP architecture itself makes it easily exploitable. ICMP requests do not rely on a specific port, so ICMP requests are not logged, which makes them hard to track if they are used as a weapon to attack your network.

NOTE

The Ping of Death is an exploit introduced in 1996. It was determined that sending Ping packets that exceeded the legal size limit for such a packet (65,535 octets) would lock up certain operating systems, and cause them to be non-responsive.

The downside to disabling Ping packets in this manner is that it can make legitimate network troubleshooting more difficult. You will still be able to Ping hosts within your network, so local troubleshooting will not change, but remote troubleshooting may become more difficult. On balance, the added security gained from disabling ICMP packets through your routers offsets any loss in productivity.

ACL rules are generally processed until a match is found. Similar to firewall rules, which have an explicit deny as the last rule, ACLs usually end with an explicit deny statement (though not always, check with your router manufacturer to make sure). This means that you have to tell the router to allow traffic you are not denying through:

```
access-list 110 permit ip any any
```

Try to arrange ACLs so the most commonly used rules are processed first (which is one reason to log all rule matches to a syslog server). This will speed up connectivity for users, and lessen the load on the router. Also include rules that help speed the process of rule matching. Many network administrators will include a rule similar to this as their first rule:

```
access-list 110 permit tcp any any established
```

This rule says that connections that have already completed the three-way handshake should be allowed to pass through. By making this the first rule you are, in essence, giving users with established connections a priority pass through your router. This allows you to improve performance, while still putting in restrictive access lists.

In addition to the rules used in this section, some of the more common ACL rules used to increase security include:

```
access-list 110 deny ip 10.0.0.0 0.255.255.255 any \
log-input
access-list 110 deny ip 172.16.0.0 0.15.255.255 any \
log-input
```

One word of warning before you begin applying ACLs to your router: Whenever possible, it is best to connect to the router using a console cable when making ACL changes. Countless network administrators have locked themselves out of a router and blocked all traffic by not properly anticipating the results of their access lists. It is always better to test the effect of an access list in a lab before going live, but even lab testing cannot account for bad typing.[4]

NOTE

Most network administrators find it is easier to either "cut and paste" ACL rules into the router, or to manually edit the configuration remotely, then install it on the router.

---

4. Not that the author has ANY first-hand experience with being locked out of a router in this manner. No, definitely not.

4.2.4 NTP

The Network Time Protocol (NTP), defined in RFC 1305, synchronizes time settings, ensuring that the time on a device is always accurate, or, at the very least, in synch with the rest of the network.

If you intend to do remote logging of your router, you will undoubtedly want to have NTP enabled. When done properly, NTP can help assure that the logs collected by the remote server are valid, and contain good data.

NTP references the Universal Time Coordinate (UTC) system used by satellites and atomic clocks. NTP can be coordinated using a GPS receiver, phone line, or, of course, TCP/IP. NTP servers are arranged in different stratums, depending on the proximity of the server to a UTC source (e.g., an atomic clock). An atomic clock, or other primary UTC source, is considered to be a Stratum 0 source, a server that connects directly with a UTC primary source is considered a Stratum 1 source, a server that connects with a server that is connected directly with a Stratum 0 source is considered a Stratum 2 source, and so on. The further you drift from Stratum 0 sources the more time disparity devices on your network will have with regard to UTC.

For example, a Stratum 2 device will usually have a 30-millisecond drift from UTC, devices on the local network that are using that source will have a 35–40 millisecond drift from UTC and devices on the WAN will have 130–140 millisecond drift from UTC. For most organizations this level of drift is acceptable. If it is not for your organization, consider using a Stratum 1 device, which will cut the level of drift in half, or, if it is practical use an internal Stratum 0 source. A Stratum 0 source within your LAN will decrease network drift to approximately 5–7 milliseconds.

Before setting NTP up on the router, you will first need to create an NTP server on your network. There are many public NTP servers available, but NTP data is not encrypted by default, so you may leave your network vulnerable by sending NTP packets over the WAN. If you can justify the cost, using your own internal atomic clock is your best solution for an NTP server. If you must use a public server, pick one that allows you to do signed updates. Designate a single server on your LAN to be the NTP server. All other machines will get their updates from that machine. Setting up NTP on a server will be discussed in greater detail in Chapter 11.

On your routers, an NTP server should only be set on one internal interface. In fact, unless you are using your router as an NTP server, NTP should be disabled on all public interfaces, and all but one of the internal interfaces. Some vendors will enable NTP on their routers as a convenience to their customers. This practice is generally not recommended, as it can add unnecessary load to the router, and it may be used as an exploit to crash the router.

Traditionally, NTP has been run as a clear text service. The problem is it makes NTP susceptible to spoofing attacks that can be used to alter the time on a network device and render logged data useless.

NTP, Version 3.0, supports several levels of encryption that have to be enabled on both the client and the server. If NTP traffic will be restricted to the LAN then combining access lists on the server with public-key authentication between the client and the NTP server will provide sufficient levels of authentication, so you can be more assured that your logged data has maintained its integrity. As network attacks have become more common, and the integrity of log files from these attacks has become critical, the current level of security in NTP has been deemed inadequate. NTP, Version 4.0, currently in development, will address these issues and provide for even more robust security.

4.3 Disabling Unused Services

A router can run many services that are neither needed nor desired. It is a good idea to disable those services. It is often not advertised that these services are running, so it is a good idea to check your router vendor's website, and read through your documentation to determine if there are unnecessary services running.

Cisco, for example, up until version 12.0 of IOS,[5] enabled a group of diagnostic services: echo, chargen, and discard for both UDP and TCP connections. An attacker can use these services to launch a DoS attack against the router.

These services can be remotely accessed. Each time the service is accessed a little bit of CPU time is used. If enough requests are made, the router will become overwhelmed and no longer be able to respond to requests, or crash entirely.

---

5. IOS is Internet Operating System. It is the operating system that runs on all Cisco routers and many of the Cisco switches.

These services are generally not used in enterprise networks; if you do not use them it is wise to disable them:

```
gw1(config)#no service tcp-small-servers
gw1(config)#no service udp-small-servers
```

Other services to watch out for, such as Finger, DHCP, and router-specific protocols that you may not be using should be disabled:

```
gw1(config)#no service finger
gw1(config)#no service dhcp
gw1(config)#no cdp run
```

CDP is the Cisco Discovery Protocol, a Cisco proprietary service that allows Cisco devices to find and communicate with each other. CDP works on Layer 2; routers and switches use the protocol to share configuration information, and Cisco CallManager can use the information to update management programs, such as Cisco Works, with the latest data from the network devices.

CDP has been the target of attacks in the past. Because it operates strictly at the Layer 2 level, it does not have the error-checking capabilities of some of the higher level protocols, making it more vulnerable to attack.

One exploit common with older versions of IOS is to spoof CDP packets from another device on the network. The spoofed packets need to have random device identifiers, have the maximum expiration time set (255 seconds), and have the maximum CDP packet size (1,480 bytes). The router will attempt to write these large packets to memory, eventually filling up the buffer, which will cause the router to crash and reboot, or simply stop routing.

Fortunately, because you cannot ARP Layer 2 packets over the WAN, in order for someone to run an exploit like this they have to be on your network.

Every router vendor has services similar to CDP that ease the configuration process but can also leave large, possibly exploitable, security holes within a network. It is a good idea to review each vendor's website periodically to find out what current best practices in router security they recommend.

4.4 Redundancy

Even the best networking equipment can fail. This is an unfortunate fact of life, and something of which most network administrators are probably painfully aware. Having a router at the edge of the network fail can create endless headaches for administrators, and employees within your organization.

Recall from Chapter 2 one of the key tenets of a good security policy is availability. It is important that the core and the edge of the network be available as close to 100 percent of the time as possible. One way to help ensure a high level of network availability is by having redundant connections to the Internet. Of course it is not enough to have redundant connections; the connections should be to different providers, and terminate in different locations.

Termination is a factor often overlooked when setting up redundant connections. A traditional access line, such as a T1, T3, or OCX connection, runs over either fiber or a twisted pair connection—called a local loop—that is run by a telephone company to your location and terminated at a central office. From the central office, the connection is routed to your provider's point of presence (POP) and out to the WAN. If there are connections from two separate providers, there is a good chance they will both terminate at the same central office. If the phone company has a problem with the central office, then both connections fail. To avoid this, make sure that each connection is terminated at a different central office.

This same type of termination problem does not exist with other types of connections, such as wireless or satellite (of course they have their own problems). This type of problem also does not exist with the newer metro area service providers. These providers use optical Ethernet connectivity to bypass the traditional local loop, and do not require the involvement of a local telephone company. The downside is that these services are still new, and have not been used extensively by enterprise clients, so there may be reliability and security issues that have not surfaced.

If an organization has two connections to the Internet, running to two central offices, then they should also have two routers. After all, an organization does not want the single point of failure to be the only edge router.

Each connection to the Internet should be terminated to a different router. The routers should be configured with a BGP connection to the two different ISPs. This will provide multiple connections to the Internet. The BGP paths from the ISPs should be used to propagate an OSPF area that is shared between the private interfaces on the routers and either the switches, another set of core routers, or firewalls (if the firewalls support OSPF).

The primary function of the edge routers is to provide the greatest level of availability to the Internet. This means that there always has to be multiple paths from the core of the network to the edge. Because of this specialized need, the redundancy protocols, discussed in Chapter 5 (VRRP, HSRP, etc.) should not be used here. If you do not use multilayer switches, then the core of the network should include another pair of routers that have a public interface that is part of the same OSPF area as the edge routers. The private interfaces should be configured with a redundancy protocol.

4.5 Securing Routing Protocols

Within a network there are probably multiple routing methods. Most large networks use a combination of static routing. It is important when selecting a routing method to fully understand the potential security holes, and to take steps to address them. This section will address static routing, as well as three very common dynamic routing protocols: RIP, BGP, and OSPF.

An in-depth explanation of the configuration process for the routing options discussed in this section is beyond the scope of this book. So, while there are some configuration examples in this chapter, they are by no means intended to be complete. Most vendor websites offer configuration examples for the different protocols listed here.

4.5.1 Static vs. Dynamic Routing

If you go back and take a look at the network design presented in Figure 4.1, you will notice that the diagram presented a single link to the Internet, and a very flat network architecture. While this design may work well for smaller companies, as the complexity of a network increases it can lead to problems.

Many companies prefer to segment different departments within the company to make the management of network resources easier. Deploying this type of network design can involve the use of multiple routers, which are used to create the segments. While this is one way to provide the desired network segmentation, many networking experts recommend the use of multilayer switching rather than increasing the number of routers deployed. Multilayer switching, which is discussed in Chapter 5, has the same benefits as increasing the number of routers, while still keeping the network flat, and it generally has a lower cost.

Static routing is the simplest form of routing. It simply means that the path along which the router should direct traffic is manually configured. There are two ways of handling static routes. The first is to build a routing table defining what netblocks should be routed through an interface. For example, a router connected to ISP A, B, and C, can be configured to direct traffic destined for 10.10.0.0 through the ISP A interface, while traffic destined for the 10.100.0.0 netblock can be instructed to route through the ISP B interface.

The second way of creating a static route is to create a gateway for the router.[6] The gateway can either be configured so that all traffic is routed through it, or it can be used in conjunction with other static routes, so that it is only used if there is no static route for a destination IP address.

Static route interfaces and gateways both need to be directly connected to a router. If the router cannot reach the interface it will drop the packet.

Dynamic routing, on the other hand, does not involve manual interference with the routing tables. Instead, the chosen protocol is configured on a router interface and routing tables are generated and updated automatically. In addition to involving less manual intervention, dynamic routing protocols provide better performance, because data always traverses the optimal path.

Which of the two is more secure? The answer depends on what type of attack you are protecting against. Dynamic routing protocols rely on information from other routers. Any time you are going to allow another device, even one that is controlled by you, to update equipment the risk exists of falling prey to an attack. An attacker who gains access to the network can interject bad routing statements that will be picked up by all other routers in the network.

Star Trek fans are familiar with the alien race known as the Borg. The Borg were interconnected, and they all had simultaneous access to the same information. They were defeated because the crew of the *Enterprise* was able to interject the command "sleep" into their collective consciousness and put them all to sleep.

Dynamic routing works in much the same way. If you do not limit the devices that have access to update routing information, then an attacker can shut down the network, or possibly route all network data through a device he or she controls, giving an attacker with a sniffer access to all information that traverses the network.

---

6. In Cisco-speak, this is the Gateway of Last Resort.

Using static routes prevents an attacker from poisoning routing tables with bad information, but presents another problem. With a single default route, a network is more susceptible to a DoS attack. If you are connected to diverse backbones and using a dynamic protocol to route traffic using the best path, it is more difficult for an attacker to launch large attacks, because there are multiple paths into and out of the network. Of course, if an attacker has access to enough bandwidth to flood a network, multiple connections are going to do little good.

All things being equal, a dynamic routing protocol used with proper security precautions will be more secure than a static routing protocol.

4.5.2 Interior and Exterior Dynamic Routing

Before discussing dynamic routing in more detail, it is important to distinguish between interior and exterior protocols, because the security approaches taken for the two types of protocols are vastly different.

Interior and *exterior* refer to whether a packet will be routed within or outside an autonomous system. Interior Gateway Protocols (IGP) direct traffic within an autonomous system; conversely, EGPs direct traffic between autonomous systems.

An autonomous system is a network, or series of networks, that is controlled by a single organization. Most organizations are assigned groups of IP addresses—netblocks—by their ISP. The organization has complete control of routing within those assigned netblocks, and only uses the ISP to hand-off traffic to the WAN.

As an organization grows, additional netblocks are added, and netblocks from other ISPs may be used. This makes it extremely difficult to use contiguous netblocks, making routing more difficult.

Fortunately, the Internet Assigned Numbers Authority (IANA) developed a system for distributing Autonomous System Numbers (ASN) in RFC 1930. An ASN is a unique identifier distributed by the three regional registries:

1.   American Registry for Internet Numbers (ARIN): *www.arin.net*

2.   Reseaux IP Européens (RIPE): *www.ripe.net*

3.   Asia Pacific Network Information Centre (APNIC): *www.apnic.net*

Each registry is assigned a block of numbers that it is responsible for maintaining. Organizations that require an ASN, and can justify the allocation of one, receive it from the appropriate registry (each registry is responsible for certain geographic areas).

An ASN is used by IGPs to route traffic within the system and can also be used with EGPs to route traffic between systems. Using an ASN versus manually editing routing tables can save network administrators enormous amounts of time.

NOTE

It is a common practice to use the acronyms AS and ASN interchangeably. However, throughout the book, if you see AS it will refer to a network controlled by a single organization. If you see the term ASN, it refers specifically to an IANA-assigned number to identify a network.

4.5.3 RIP

RIP is one of the oldest and most widely accepted protocols in use on the Internet. Xerox originally developed RIP in the 1970s; in the 1980s, it was ported to the LAN, and then the WAN.

RIP is an IGP protocol based on the Bellman-Ford algorithm. The Bellman-Ford algorithm is a method for returning the shortest path between two points; this type of algorithm is also referred to as a distance-vector algorithm. Most routing protocols use some sort of distance-vectoring algorithm to determine the distance from Point A to Point B on a network. When RIP is enabled on a router, the router is constantly examining the paths available to it, and using that information to build a routing database. All RIP-enabled routers on an autonomous system update each other with the information in their databases, using the UDP. In some instances routers can update each other as often as every 30 seconds. The standard update interval, except for core routers, is 180 seconds.

To better understand how RIP works, take a look at Figure 4.3. Let's say that Router A needs to deliver a packet to Router B, and all these routers are part of the same autonomous system. The first thing Router A will do is determine

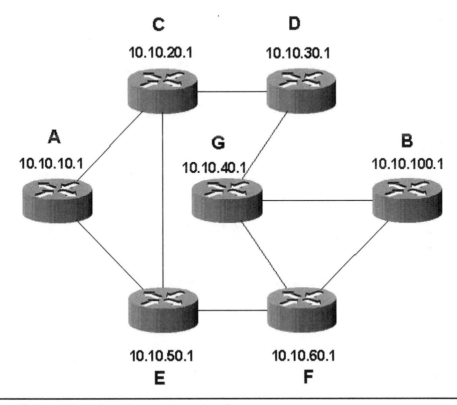

Figure 4.3   An autonomous network

whether or not it has a direct connection to Router B. Because it does not have a direct connection, Router A will examine its routing tables to determine if it has a path for this address. If it does not, it will simply forward the packet to its default gateway.

If you look at the diagram you will notice that there are multiple paths a packet can take to get from Router A to Router B. RIP determines the shortest path from Router A to Router B. In this case, Router A is three hops away from Router B: D to E to B, as shown in Figure 4.4.

An RIP-enabled router automatically learns new routes from the other routers in the autonomous system. The RIP routing tables will tell the router the

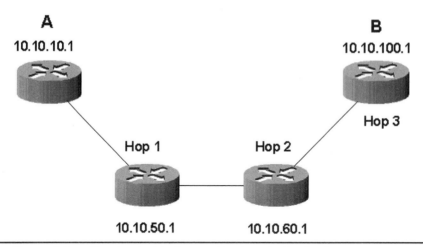

Figure 4.4   The shortest path from Router A to Router B

path a packet takes to get to a destination. Take a look at this sample from the routing table of Router *A:*

```
gw1#show ip route

R 10.10.60.0/24 [120/1] via 10.10.50.1, 00:00:6, Serial0
R 10.10.70.0/24 [120/1] via 10.10.50.1, 00:00:4, Serial0
C 10.10.10.0/24 is directly connected, Serial0
R 10.10.50.0/24 [120/1] via 10.10.10.1, 00:00:8, Serial0
```

Automating the routing table updates in this manner allows the network to automatically failover in the event of a failure. The downside is that RIP does not automatically update when there is a failure—the routers directly connected to the failed router will not notify the rest of the network until it sends out its next RIP update. If the update interval is set to 180 seconds, then the rest of the routers will continue to send traffic along the wrong path for up to three minutes after a failure.

Using the network in Figures 4.3 and 4.4, we can examine the failure process. In the next scenario Router *F* will fail, as shown in Figure 4.5.

After Router *F* fails, the network has to renegotiate the routes. The first step is that Router *E* has to realize that it has lost connectivity to *F.* After it has realized that it no longer has a connection to *F,* Router *E* will update its routing

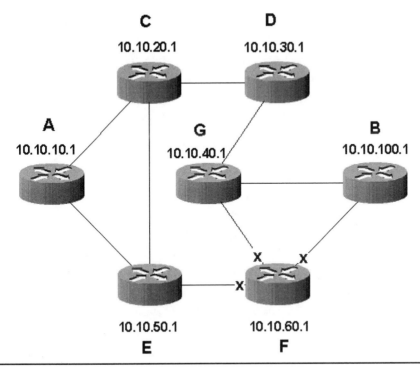

Figure 4.5   A failure occurs in Router F

tables to reflect the change in the network topology. The new routing tables are updated throughout the network the next time *D* sends out its routing table.

When Router *A* has received the new information it will renegotiate the shortest route to *B*. Router *A* will negotiate a four-hop path to Router *B* (*C* to *D* to *G* to *B*). This new path will remain in effect until a shorter path is introduced into the topology, and communicated to Router *A*.

RIP is the first example of an SPF protocol. Different SPF protocols have methods other than Bellman-Ford algorithm to determine the shortest path. Modern SPF protocols, like OSPF, also use distance and latency as well as hop number to determine the shortest path.

4.5.3.1 RIP Security

The original RIP protocol was deployed, as is the case with many of the original Internet protocols, with no thought to security. In fact RIP and RIP Version 1.0 have so many security holes that it is recommended that they not be run in production environments.

There are two areas where RIP security falls dangerously short:

1. RIP does not verify the information sent to it.
2. RIP does not include any form of authentication.

Both areas revolve around the fact that RIP has no way of verifying the authenticity of the information it has received.

The first compromise stems from the fact that RIP does not verify that the information sent to it. An attacker with a spoofed IP address and an understanding of your network and the RIP protocol would be able to inject bad routes domain. An attacker who just wanted to be spiteful could inject large routing lists that could cause the routers to crash if they are unable to process all of the information within the list. Even if the new lists did not cause the network to crash, they would continuously flood the network with traffic every time they were exchanged; this could bring the network to a crawl.

Having the network crash is actually the less costly of the two scenarios. If that same attacker were attempting to gather information about the network, he or she could simply reroute traffic to a different location and sniff through the packets looking for the desired information.

These scenarios are exacerbated by the fact that RIP and RIP Version 1.0 do not offer any way for routers to authenticate information. There is no password or public key verification capability specified within the original RIP protocol. Some vendors have attempted to add this functionality into their implementation of the protocol—unfortunately, that raises vendor incompatibility issues.

4.5.3.2 RIP Version 2.0

RIP Version 2.0 was introduced in 1993 to address some of the security concerns inherent in the initial RIP and RIP Version 1.0 specifications. Version 2.0 is identical to previous versions in the way it handles routing failover issues, but it adds a security layer to the protocol.

RIP Version 2.0 was introduced in RFC 1388 and was updated by RFC 2453 in 1998.

Version 2.0 was introduced with password-based authentication. In order to maintain backward compatibility with older versions of RIP, the password is sent in a separate packet; if a router is only running RIP, it will ignore the password. RIP Version 2.0 devices can be configured to accept updates from older versions of RIP with no password authentication, or they can be configured to drop the packets. The problem with this, of course, is that clear text passwords are not much of a challenge to a determined attacker.

In 1997 Fred Baker and Randall Atkinson proposed, in RFC 2082, that Version 2.0 be enhanced to support keyed MD5 (message digest) encrypted passwords. The keyed MD5 algorithm is the standard method of authentication for IP headers. The keyed MD5 algorithm allows RIP Version 2.0 packets to use an encrypted key to handle authentication. While keyed MD5 encryption is not the best manner of key exchange, it is very suitable for short message segments that expire quickly—which is why it is a good match for Version 2.0.

4.5.4 OSPF

OSPF is a routing IGP protocol developed, in part, to address many of the limitations of RIP. OSPF Version 2.0, the current version, is specified in RFC 2328.

OSPF is, by design, much more secure than RIP and provides increased functionality and performance on larger networks. Some of the advantages of OSPF include:

- No limit to the number of hops a router will support (RIP has a limit of 15).
- OSPF sends out updates using a multicast address, so that only routers listening for OSPF updates will receive the packets, helping to conserve bandwidth.
- OSPF has faster convergence than RIP; changes in network topology are communicated instantly; and only the changes are communicated, not the entire routing table.
- OSPF is very useful for load balancing traffic between routers.
- When selecting a route, OSPF calculates a cost based on available bandwidth as well as hop count.

OSPF determines the path to take through the network using the Dijkstra algorithm. As with RIP, OSPF uses the algorithm to determine a cost for each link. Each router builds a unique network topology based on its location within the autonomous system, while maintaining the same link-state information as the rest of the network.

Figure 4.6 shows a network similar to the one used to illustrate RIP. However, link speeds have been added between the different routers. Again, we want to see how Router *A* will get to Router *B*.

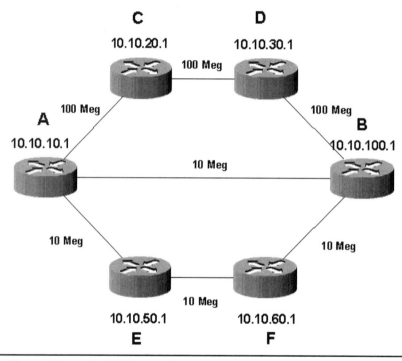

Figure 4.6   An OSPF network

The first step in determining the route is to examine links costs, also called metrics. OSPF uses a very simple formula to determine the cost of a link:

```
Cost = 100000000/Bandwidth (expressed in bits per second)
```

Take a look at the top of the diagram. Each of those routers are connected via a 100-megabit link. 100 megabits is the same as 100 million bits, so the cost for a 100-megabit link would be calculated like this:

```
Cost = 100000000/100000000=1
```

Each cost in the path has to be added together. The cost from A to C is 1, the cost from C to D is 1, and the cost of D to B is 1, so the total cost of traversing from A to B using the top group of routers is 3. You'll notice, using this calculation, that even though A is directly connected to B, the cost for that link is actually higher, with a value of 10. Of course it seems pointless to have a direct link that is not used, so OSPF assigns a cost of 0 to networks that are directly connected. In this case, even though the top route has a lower cost, traffic will still traverse the direct A to B link.

In Figure 4.7 the direct A–B link has been removed, and all bandwidth has been set to 100 megabits.

In this newly redesigned network the cost of getting from Router A to Router B is equal for both paths. OSPF can handle this situation in one of two ways:

1. If left on its own, it will automatically load balance traffic between the two paths. Some traffic will use the C–D path, while other traffic will use the E–F path.

2. If load balancing is not desired, OSPF allows you to manually set the cost for each connection. You can increase the cost of the A–E connection, so it raises the cost of the E–F path and traffic will be routed along the C–D path, unless there is a failure.

OSPF also allows you to create areas. Rather than receive updates from all routers on the network, you may want to group the routers in smaller units. The routers will only share OSPF information with other routers in their area.

The primary area for an OSPF network is Area 0. This area should be at the logical center of your network, with other areas touching it. Areas are defined on the interface of the router, and routers that belong to two areas are considered border routers (see Figure 4.8).

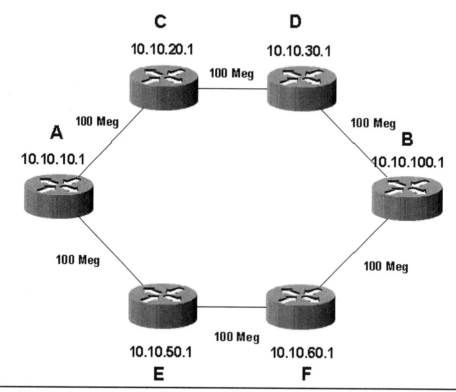

Figure 4.7   Revised OSPF network

Figure 4.8 shows an OSPF network with areas enabled. By limiting the number of routers in each area, you can limit the number of broadcasts that each router has to process, and make routing across the network easier.

4.5.4.1 OSPF Security

You have already seen one of the best security features that OSPF offers: areas. When an OSPF-enabled interface on a router receives an update from another device that has a different area, it ignores it. Of course, because OSPF packets are sent as clear text, it would be trivial for a determined attacker to find the area number and inject bad routes into a network, so other measures of security are needed.

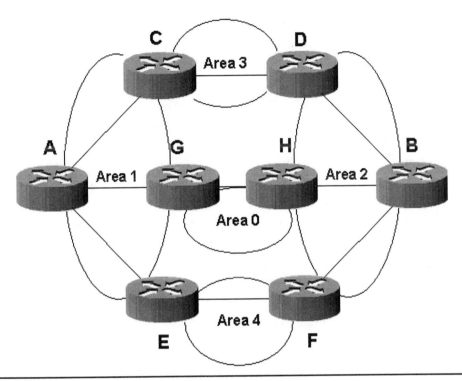

Figure 4.8   OSPF areas

In addition to defining OSPF areas, network administrators can also explicitly state who the OSPF neighbors in a network are. OSPF is a broadcast protocol by default. More specifically, it is a multicast protocol, so an OSPF-enabled interface will send out routing updates to all interested parties whenever there is a change. You can lessen this problem by forcing OSPF to send directed updates. This is a two-part process: (1) disable broadcast and (2) manually configure the OSPF neighbors. This will limit the number of network devices that the router will send to and receive OSPF information from.

OSPF has password authentication enabled. Unfortunately, the default is usually set to no password. There are two types of password authentication supported natively in OSPF: plain text and MD5.

While plain text authentication does have some serious limitations, if authentication also requires a specific area, and is from one of the trusted neighbors, it may provide enough security for your organization. This is actually one of the really nice features about OSPF security: If the authentication header does not meet all of the predefined security parameters, it will be rejected by the router. This allows network administrators to layer the security measures used in the network, making things more difficult for an attacker.

MD5 authentication provides a greater level of security. To enable MD5 authentication, the same password must be defined on all router interfaces participating in an OSPF area. When a network device sends routing updates to other devices in the same area, it includes a message based on the key, the key-ID, and the OSPF packet. The receiving device translates the message, and matches it against the password it has stored; if the two passwords match, the router accepts the update. At no point is the password sent; instead, the message in the header is deciphered by the receiving device to see if it matches the password.

Because OSPF areas reside within controlled networks, security is sometimes not strictly enforced on OSPF devices. This is a bad strategy; a good security policy has to work at many levels to be effective. Protecting the internal network is a good first line of defense in the battle to keep servers and your data protected.

The next protocol—BGP—is an exterior gateway protocol, and it has a whole new set of security concerns.

4.5.5 BGP

BGP, like OSPF and RIP, is used to exchange routing information, but BGP is unique because it can be used as both an IGP (IBGP) and an EGP (EBGP), though it is most often used as EBGP. Figure 4.9 shows a simplified BGP configuration.

The original specification for BGP was published in 1991 under RFC 1267. The current version of BGP, BGP Version 4.0, is outlined in RFC 1771 and 1772.

In Figure 4.9, AS1 represents a typical ISP backbone, while AS2 and AS3 are either smaller ISPs or enterprise customers of that ISP. AS2 and AS3 will run EBGP with AS1, and AS1 runs an IGP on its internal network.

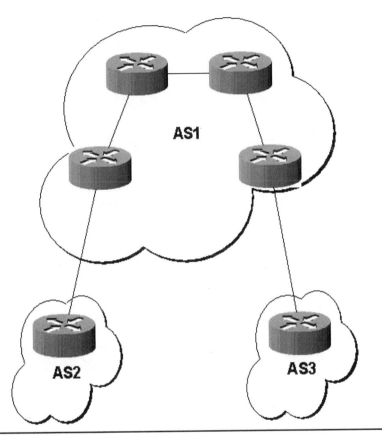

Figure 4.9   A BGP network

As you would expect, the routing process is automated; AS2 and AS3 will automatically update AS1 with any changes in the network, and AS2 and AS3 will receive any changes in network topology that occur within AS1.

A BGP-enabled network device will only communicate changes in its routing tables to other devices, and a BGP device only defines a single path—the best one—to a destination on its network.

BGP is very robust; the number of advertised routes on the Internet has gone from fewer than 20,000 in 1994 to more than 100,000 today. This means that the routing table for a core Internet router can contain more than 100,000 entries.

Attempting to share more than 100,000 routes between every router on the Internet would be a waste of bandwidth, and completely unnecessary, so BGP allows users to restrict the amount of information that is propagated to other routers. These restrictions are called *attributes* and are defined as part of the protocol.

BGP transmits information over TCP, using port 179 rather than using the direct connection model supported by OSPF and RIP. Because BGP runs over a reliable transport protocol, rather than UDP as OSPF does, error control and retransmission are automatically done and do not need to be addressed within the protocol.

When two BGP-enabled routers establish communication, the first thing they do is exchange full routing information about their respective networks. Each router uses this information to build a network map of the remote AS. The remote network is built using the path to each destination along with attributes about that path. The path attributes for each destination are stored in a table, like Table 4.1, that contains required and optional information.

Table 4.1   AS Path Attributes

PATH ATTRIBUTE	FUNCTION	OPTIONAL OR MANDATORY
ORIGIN	AS from where the path originated.	Mandatory
AS_PATH	List of AS segments the packet has to traverse.	Mandatory
NEXT_HOP	The next border router in the path.	Mandatory

Table 4.1   AS Path Attributes *(Continued)*

PATH ATTRIBUTE	FUNCTION	OPTIONAL OR MANDATORY
MULTI_EXEC_DISC	In cases where there are multiple exit points to an AS, this allows you to weight them.	Optional
LOCAL_PREF	Used within an AS to define a router's preference for a route.	Optional
ATOMIC_AGGREGATE	Used within an AS to share that a less-specific route will be advertised.	Optional
AGGREGATOR	Contains the last AS of an aggregate route and the IP address of the router that formed the route.	Optional

The path attributes serve two purposes aside from determining the route to a destination: to help prevent routing loops and to detect changes in the network topology of the remote AS.

After the initial connection between two BGP-enabled devices has been made, there are four different types of messages that can be sent:

1. Open: Used to establish the BGP parameters between the two devices. The devices exchange BGP version, AS numbers, hold time values, and identifier (usually the device's IP address).

2. Update: Contain information about reachability within the AS, as well as connectivity with other AS.

3. Keepalive: Sent out periodically to ensure that both devices are responding properly. The message contains the BGP header, with no additional information.

4. Notification: Sent when an error occurs between the two devices. After a notification message is issued, no further BGP information will be

exchanged between the two devices until the error is resolved and connectivity is re-initiated between the two devices.

Unless otherwise specified, an AS with multiple connections will always choose the optimal path. If there is a tie between two paths, the path with the lower IP address will be chosen. This is not always an optimal solution, as it creates the problem of an unused BGP device[7], while the other BGP device is probably overburdened. You can resolve this by load balancing your BGP connections.

4.5.5.1 BGP Security

BGP has some built-in security measures that prevent it from accepting multiple routes to the same AS, and are used to control what other devices a BGP-enabled device will share information with. Overall, BGP provides very poor security.

There are several areas in which BGP is lacking in security:

- There is no authentication of BGP packets.
- All data is sent clear text across the WAN.
- There is no verification of the route information that is exchanged.
- A misconfiguration by one of the BGP peers can cause traffic to be black holed, or lead to replay attacks, where routes are continuously fed into a router, causing a routing loop that can crash the router.

As with RIP and OSPF, an extension has been added to BGP to support authentication of BGP headers using MD5 encryption. This is outlined in RFC 2385. While this increases the level of security between BGP neighbors, it does not address the problems associated with bad routes being interjected across AS, nor does it address misconfiguration errors.

With security performance this poor, you may wonder why BGP is used so widely. The truth is that there is not another protocol that is robust enough to handle the number of routes that BGP is able to support. In addition, because BGP is so widely deployed, it would take a complete reengineering of the Internet backbone to implement another protocol.

Rather than throwing out BGP, several engineers from BBN have developed an enhanced version of the BGP protocol, Secure BGP (S-BGP). S-BGP builds on the fundamentals of the BGP protocol, but adds several security enhancements.

---

7. Most likely, an expensive one.

The creators of the S-BGP protocol advocate taking several steps to relieve the security problems inherent in BGP. The underlying methodology for securing BGP would be a series of Public Key Infrastructure (PKI) certificates that could be used to verify the authenticity of a BGP neighbor, the advertised IP blocks, the AS, and that the router is authorized to share information about the AS.

S-BGP has a lot of potential to resolve many of the issues currently associated with BGP, and to vastly improve the security of the core Internet backbone. At this time, none of the major router vendors have implemented support for S-BGP, so its widespread deployment is at least several years out.

4.6 Limit Access to Routers

Protecting routers from being corrupted by remote attacks is important, but a more basic control overlooked by many network administrators is restricting who can access their routers. Many networks have fewer than five routers in place. In smaller networks a full-blown authentication system, like TACACS and RADIUS (covered in Chapter 6), is probably overblown. However, even in smaller networks, access to the router should be limited, both in terms of securing it against external unauthorized access and restricting personnel within your organization who have access.

An attacker who gains access to the network and is able to sniff, or guess, the router password can easily take the network offline, and may be able to damage an ISP's backbone. The same is true of an unknowledgeable or malicious employee who is given access to the networking equipment, or uses another employee's password. Because the potential for damage is greatest at the network level, this is where the most precautions should be taken.

4.6.1 Telnet, SSH, and HTML

Telnet should be disabled on routers, and SSH should be used to access them remotely. On Cisco routers SSH was introduced into IOS with Version 12.0.5. Other manufacturers, such as Juniper, have had SSH enabled from the start. Remember that enabling SSH on an interface is not enough; you also have to make sure you explicitly disable telnet. This will prevent anyone from accidentally logging in using telnet.

There are several steps involved in enabling SSH on a Cisco router.

```
gw1(config)#ip domain-name example.com
gw1#crypto key generate rsa
gw1#config t
Enter configuration commands, one per line. End with CNTL/Z.
gw1(config)#ip ssh
gw1(config)#ip ssh timeout 60
gw1(config)#ip ssh authentication-retries 3
```

Similarly on a Juniper router:

```
services {
     ssh {
          root-login (allow | deny | deny-password);
          protocol-version [v1 v2];
          <connection-limit limit> ;
               <rate-limit limit>;
                    }
     }
```

The first step is to set a domain name for the router. Only set the top-level domain, as the host name is already set (gw1 in the example). The next step is to generate an Rivest-Shamir-Adelman (RSA) encrypted key in the exec mode. Finally, enter back into the configuration mode and enable SSH. Set the authentication time-out and the number of failed attempts.

Now that SSH has been enabled on the router, it is a good idea to disable telnet. Of course, make sure to test that SSH has been properly enabled before disabling telnet.

```
gw1(config)#transport input ssh
```

Secure remote login is now enabled for the router, and telnet is disabled. It is also a good idea to check with the router vendor to find out what version of the SSH protocol is enabled on its routers. SSH Version 1.0 has several security holes, including a root exploit. These will be discussed in detail in Chapter 11, but it is a serious enough problem to note that you should check with your vendor.

Many network devices include an HTML interface. The HTML interface is convenient because it gives users a graphical tool which can be used to manage the network device. This can be nice for users not familiar with the command line, but the truth is, because of limited processing power on the router, HTML interfaces tend to be slow and cumbersome, and cannot perform all of the tasks that can be done through the command line.

HTML interfaces also present a serious security risk. Like telnet, information transmitted during an HTML session is sent unencrypted. Again, anyone with a sniffer on the network will be able to gather username, password, and configuration information for the router. To further exacerbate this problem, many router vendors have separate default usernames and passwords for the HTML interface, which means that unless you specifically disable the HTML interface it can be a security hole, even if it is not used. On a Cisco router, the command is:

```
gw1(config)#no ip http server
```

If, for some reason, a web interface is required for configuration, consider asking your vendor for an SSL option, or try using a remote configuration tool that sends encrypted information between your workstation and the router.

Now that we have restricted the protocols people can use to access your router, the next step is to restrict the interfaces they can use to access it.

4.6.2 Restricting Interfaces

Whenever possible, remote access should be disabled for all public interfaces. If remote access to a router is needed, you should do it using the internal interface, or an out-of-band interface designated for remote administration. If you are using the out-of-band method, make sure the IP address is not advertised anywhere, and disable ICMP access to it, so it is not discovered by someone using a scanner.

If an out-of-band interface is out of the question, and you need to allow access to the public interface to make troubleshooting easier, it is a good idea to apply a strict access list to the virtual terminal on the public interface.

Different router vendors have different ways of restricting remote access to virtual terminals. Many vendors allow administrators to apply a standard ACL, as described earlier in the chapter, like you would to an interface, while others have special ACLS designated for virtual terminals only.

Cisco refers to an ACL for a virtual terminal as an access-class. Access-classes can be defined for incoming or outgoing traffic. This allows administrators to limit not only who can telnet into the system, but also where they can go once they have gained access.

An ACL for a virtual terminal is configured in the same manner as a standard access list, except administrators have to define which of the virtual terminal(s) it should be applied to (in Cisco-speak, which line(s) it should be applied to):

```
access-list 50 permit 192.168.105.0 0.0.0.255 line 1
access-class 50 in
```

This will only allow IP addresses in the 192.168.105.0–255 netblock to open a virtual terminal on the router. As with interface-based ACLS, there is an implicit deny at the end of this ACL.

Of course, there can be problems with creating this type of ACL. If your home ISP assigns a dynamic IP address every time a connection is made, you may not be able to create a single rule like the one in the example. If you begin adding every netblock you may get assigned into your virtual terminal ACL, you will effectively render it useless.

One way to avoid this is to use dynamic access lists. Dynamic access lists, also called lock and key security, allow a user to make a connection to the router, and authenticate. If the authentication is successful, then a temporary access list is created allowing the user to access the router and the network beyond the router. When the user has finished the connection, the dynamic access list is automatically deleted, after a time-out period.

A dynamic ACL allows administrators to keep router configuration cleaner by not having to add additional ACL entries that may become security holes. Of course, you are opening the public interface on your router to anyone from your remote IP address with a password, so it is still important to send encrypted data to your router. Also, using a dynamic ACL means that good password security is even more important. Anyone who can successfully authenticate will now be able to access the router. Enable them only if absolutely necessary.

NOTE

Another way to increase router security is to limit router access to a single machine located in the firewall demilitarized zone (DMZ). The machine can be secured using whatever server firewall software necessary, and access to the routers can be restricted to SSH. This provides a very secure solution.

4.7 Change Default Passwords!

Table 4.2 lists the default username/password combinations for commonly deployed devices. While these combinations are not necessarily the default on all devices manufactured by these vendors, they are used on enough devices that administrators should be concerned. If an attacker comes across one of these devices, the default combination is going to be the first tried. That's why it is important to create an account, and then remove the default account.

Table 4.2   Default Usernames and Passwords

VENDOR	USERNAME	PASSWORD
Bay Networks	Manager	Manager
Cisco	cisco	cisco
Extreme	admin	
Juniper	root	
Nortel	admin	setup

Often, an administrator will create one, or several, accounts, without deleting the default account, leaving a gaping security hole. It is important to delete all default accounts and replace them with more secure account name and passwords. Unfortunately, it is easy to overlook the different accounts on a network device, so make sure you use this checklist to cover your bases:

- Virtual terminal user
- Console user
- Superuser (enable user on Cisco routers)
- HTTP user (unless you are disabling remote access)
- SNMP read password (unless you are going to disable SNMP)
- SNMP write password
- Default passwords for any vendor-specific protocols (unless you are disabling these services)

Removing default users and changing default passwords make it more difficult for remote users to access network devices. Coupling these steps with only using encrypted access from internal network devices significantly reduces the chances that an outside attacker will be able to gain access to the network through its routers.

That being said, after these precautions are taken, it is important that the passwords are not shared with anyone who does not need them. If more than a handful of users access the network equipment, it is a good idea to use a TACACS or RADIUS server. If there are fewer than five users, each user should be assigned a unique username and password combination, and his or her access level should be appropriately distributed.

There is a temptation when only one or two users access the system to use a single login and password. If you are logging connections to your networking devices, you should not do this. If there is no distinction between the users, then there can be no accountability should a mistake or a malicious act occurs.

4.8 Summary

A lot of thought and planning has to go into securing your routers, especially at the edge of the network. It can't be said enough that the best type of security approach is one that is layered. Stopping an attack at the edge puts less strain on your internal infrastructure and keeps attackers that much further from your data.

From the edge of the network, the next step is to protect the core of the network. The core of the network is another line of defense. As with the edge, it does take some planning to ensure that you have the greatest level of protection and availability.

5

Switching

Like routers, security precautions for switches are often overlooked. This is obviously a mistake. Switches serve as entry points to the network. Not only are they the handoff point from routers, they are also the way users connect into the core of your network.

Continuing the layered security model started in Chapter 4 with routers, switches are a second line of defense in network protection. As with routers, switch security needs to focus on stopping unwanted incoming and outgoing traffic. This means securing who has access to your switches, routing on multi-layer switches, and restricting machine access to the switches.

In addition to access restriction, switches are used to help build a redundant, scalable, and highly available network. Because availability is a core component of a secure solution, it will be discussed extensively in this chapter.

Most people don't think about switches because a switch sits on the network and forwards traffic to the edge, with very few failures. As enterprise networks have become more complex, the switch has taken a more central role in the deployment of those networks. To that end, switch selection has become more important than ever to an enterprise network. It is important to choose switches that will make it easier to manage the network, and that are able to scale as traffic on the network grows.

Before beginning a discussion on switch security, it is important to understand what to look for when purchasing a switch. Undoubtedly, you already have a network infrastructure is already in place, so this advice may not be of immediate assistance to you, but it may be useful for future purchases.

For an enterprise network, a switch is always preferred over a hub. Hubs work in broadcast mode: A packet sent from one machine is broadcast to all other machines plugged into the hub. This generates a lot of excess traffic and is a security risk, because it means that all of the machines plugged into that hub can view the traffic destined for all of the other machines on the network.

Switches behave in a different manner. A switch maps a physical address (the MAC address) to a logical address (an IP or IPX address), and terminates all broadcasts at the originating port. This means that if a packet leaves a machine headed for the gateway address, it is forwarded directly to the port to which the gateway is attached, making it very difficult for other users to sniff traffic from the machine.

Even better than a switch is a managed switch. Managed switches provide a network administrator with a lot more control over the network. Managed switches allow you to:

- Set port speed
- Control access by MAC address
- Gather statistics about bandwidth usage on a per-port basis

This type of detailed statistics collection makes network troubleshooting and planning a lot easier because you can quickly determine the location of problem areas on your network and decide if you need to upgrade equipment or talk with a specific user who may be using excessive resources.

The downside to switches, especially managed switches, is that they are significantly more expensive than hubs. A 24-port 10/100 hub will run you about $200, a 24-port 10/100 unmanaged switch will cost you around $700, and a 24-port 10/100 managed switch will cost you more than $1000.[1]

5.1 The Switch on the Network

Switches make up the core of an enterprise network. Depending on the type of switch it can be used to route traffic between internal networks, and out to the Internet.

---

1. Often a lot more.

There are two types of switches that should be used in your network: (1) managed Layer 2 switches and (2) multilayer switches—which will be discussed in greater detail in the next section. Traditional Layer 2 switches, also called workgroup switches, are fairly static and reliable. They are the networking devices closest to workstations and servers, and they simply act as forwarders to send TCP or UDP requests to their ultimate destinations. Depending on how employees are spread throughout the building, a typical 100-user network will have four or five workgroup switches plugged into two core switches, which will make routing decisions.

Figure 5.1 shows a typical network layout using a combination of workgroup and core switches. The workstations are all assigned a gateway of 10.10.10.1; they connect to the workgroup switch, which has two connections, one to each of the core switches. The core switches have configured a VRRP address of 10.10.10.1. Traffic flows to the core switch that is active for the address 10.10.10.1 and on to its destination.

Should something happen to the primary core switch, the second one would take over and start answering queries for the address 10.10.10.1.

5.1.1 Redundancy Protocols

Before continuing the discussion of the core network, it is a good idea to discuss redundancy protocols. VRRP, defined in RFC 2338, is a way to increase availability by allowing two devices to share an IP address. VRRP is based on the Cisco proprietary protocol Hot Spare Router Protocol (HSRP) and the Digital Equipment Corporation proprietary protocol IP Standby Protocol (IPSTP), although many other networking companies also have their own proprietary redundancy protocols.

VRRP is an excellent way to increase availability within a network while still maintaining security. Prior to VRRP, the only way to provide redundancy within a network was to use dynamic routing protocols, such as OSPF or RIP. Obviously, trying to manage a large network with every node belonging to an OSPF or RIP area would be a logistical and security nightmare. VRRP allows a network administrator to configure static routes on workstations and servers, only relying on dynamic routing to move traffic through the network core.

Configuration of VRRP is surprisingly simple. A virtual router is configured between two or more interfaces that are part of the same subnet. Each virtual

VRRP Address 10.10.10.1

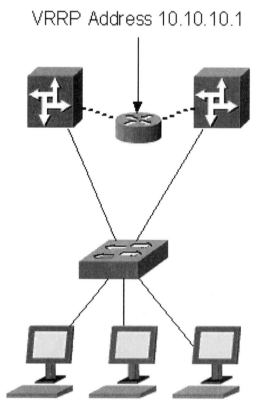

Workstation's Gateway Address: 10.10.10.1

Figure 5.1   A typical network design using Workgroup 2 switches in conjunction with multilayer switches

router is assigned a virtual router ID (VRID), so an interface can be part of multiple virtual routers. One of the interfaces participating in a virtual router is declared the master; the rest are backups.

Figure 5.2 outlines a typical VRRP network design. Router *A* and Router *B* are both part of 10.10.10.0/24 netblock. They are also both participating in VRRP for 10.10.10.1. The master, in this case Router *A*, can be automatically determined, or an administrator can assign a priority between 1 and 255 to each interface during the configuration process. The virtual router responds to

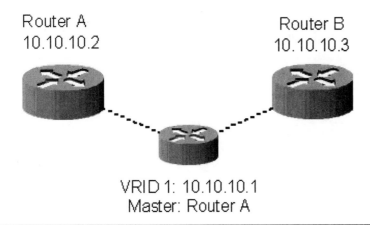

Router A
10.10.10.2

Router B
10.10.10.3

VRID 1: 10.10.10.1
Master: Router A

Figure 5.2   A typical VRRP configuration

all ARP requests with a special MAC address designated for VRRP. The address is 00-00-5E-00-01-[VRID]. Using a special MAC address means that the routers will not have to wait for the ARP cache of the switches to expire before the new device takes over. When the backup device begins responding to requests, it responds using the same MAC address, so the flow of data does not need to be interrupted.

The master router sends multicast packets every second announcing that it is alive. If the backup devices do not receive this multicast packet, they will begin the negotiation process to determine which device should become the new master. The new master will remain the master until the older master returns to service (assuming it is configured with a higher priority).

Where VRRP falls short is that it is not a load-balancing protocol. While the master router is responding to queries, the backup router is not doing anything. From a cost perspective it is hard to justify a $10,000, $20,000, or more expensive device that sits on the network and does not pass any traffic unless there is a problem.

Many administrators have overcome this limitation by creating multiple VRIDs that are shared by the same interfaces. Some workstations will use the first VRID as their gateway, while others will use the second VRID as theirs.

Figure 5.3 demonstrates configuring two virtual routers. Each router has a different VRID, even though both are served by the same set of routers. Assuming

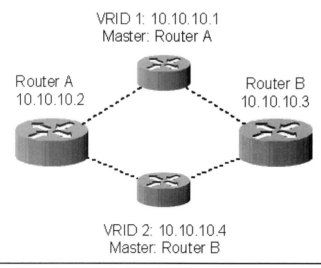

VRID 1: 10.10.10.1
Master: Router A

Router A
10.10.10.2

Router B
10.10.10.3

VRID 2: 10.10.10.4
Master: Router B

Figure 5.3   A VRRP configuration with two virtual routers

the DHCP server on the network is configured to return the two gateways, traffic will be load balanced between the two devices, so resources are not wasted.

VRRP is a great protocol when creating a redundant gateway within a network that is not homogenous. On the other hand, if you are using the same devices throughout your network, you probably want to consult your vendor's documentation about the enhancements they have made to VRRP.

NOTE

These enhancements are sometimes called *SRP. You already know Cisco has the HSRP, but Extreme Networks has the Extreme Standby Router Protocol (ESRP), and Foundry Networks has the Foundry Standby Router Protocol (FSRP).

5.1.1.1 Redundancy Security

VRRP provides for several levels of security within the protocol. At its most basic level, there is no authentication of VRRP packets. Of course, this is unacceptable, so the developers of the VRRP standard have included several levels of packet authentication. In addition to packet authentication, interfaces will ignore VRRP packets that originate from other networks. This means that VRRP should not be susceptible to remote attacks. Unfortunately, VRRP is still susceptible to local attacks.

Similar to the dynamic protocols discussed in Chapter 4, VRRP allows administrators to force either clear text password or MD5 header authentication. If you choose to use clear text authentication on your network, understand that the password will be broadcast from the master router every second. Since the password is clear text, anyone who has gained entry to your network may be able to sniff it. While passwords may make life more difficult for an attacker, it will be only marginally more difficult.

MD5 header authentication provides significantly more security. Unfortunately, network devices are not required to support MD5 header authentication to be considered VRRP compliant. Check with your vendor to ensure that they will support this type of authentication.

5.2 Multilayer Switching

Multilayer switching is a relatively new technology that combines a router and a switch into one device, giving an administrator the best of both worlds. More and more enterprise networks are switching from routers in their core to multilayer switches. Multilayer switches offer a lower per-port cost than a typical router, while providing enhanced services, such as dynamic routing protocols and ACL support.

A multilayer switch can work in one of two ways:

1. It can be a chassis that has both switch and route processor cards.
2. It can be workgroup-style switch that has a CPU, or multiple CPUs, dedicated to routing, as well as an Application Specific Integrated Circuit (ASIC) for the switching fabric.

Multilayer switching provides many benefits over a traditional routed network. The primary advantage is that a multilayer switch allows administrators to collapse their network, creating fewer layers, while still maintaining the same level of redundancy. In Figure 5.1, the network consisted of two layers: access and core. If that network were to be redone using a traditional network configuration, another layer would need to be added into the mix, as in Figure 5.4.

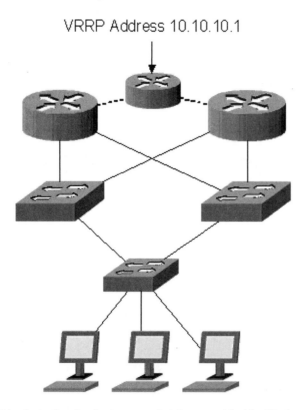

Figure 5.4   A traditional network with redundancy

The more layers a network contains, the greater the security risks. Not only are you forced to keep track of more devices, but there are more points of entry for an attacker. This type of network design is also difficult to expand. If the network grows at a fast pace, it will eventually outgrow the two core switches, and will be forced to add two additional switches, which means you will have to add more to your routers. Router expansion is generally limited, and new cards for routers are significantly more expensive than new ports for a switch.

A complex network is also difficult to troubleshoot; the more layers administrators have to sift through to find a problem, the longer it takes, and more downtime is experienced. The other problem with a complex network infrastructure is that it is easier to make a mistake that disables the entire network. When troubleshooting one problem, it is very easy to "correct" a configuration error that causes a much bigger problem. With proper documentation, this should never happen, but in reality even the most conscientious network administrator can make mistakes.

Aside from the security advantages to a multilayer-switched topology, there is a performance advantage. Multilayer switches are generally faster than traditional routers. When traffic is sent through a router, each packet is inspected and forwarded using the router's processor. Multilayer switches do not work in the same way; they perform an operation often referred to as "route once, switch many." A packet enters the switch, and is fed to the route processor (the router portion of the switch). The route processor learns the new route and sends the information back down to the switch. The switch then forwards all packets with the same header information to the same destination. The routing decision needs to be made only once; from then on the packets stay only within the ASIC. Packets are almost all forwarded at wire speed, which is why there is such a performance increase.

The route processor of a multilayer switch has the full capabilities of a router. Multilayer switches are capable of performing OSPF, BGP, and other advanced routing protocols, as well as often being able to support more ACLs than a traditional router.

This type of switching has become so popular that some networking companies, Extreme Networks and Foundry Networks in particular, no longer make distinctions between routers and switches, because the same underlying technology is used in both devices.

5.3 VLANs

VLANs are a common way to increase security on switches. A VLAN is a way to segment ports on a switch so that each port appears to be part of a different network. While the benefits of VLANs are readily apparent, many administrators do not like them, and in fact actively despise them. The arguments against VLANs tend to focus more on the platform than the actual VLAN concept.

The arguments against VLANs basically boil down to this: Given the lax security policies most administrators apply to switches, using VLANs is like putting a steel lock on a paper chain. Administrators who rely on VLANs, or any other single security measure for that matter, to protect their network, are leaving themselves open to attacks. On the other hand, VLANs used in conjunction with the other security measures outlined in this chapter will provide a network with an added layer of security.

VLANs help control traffic by breaking up a large broadcast domain into smaller, more manageable domains. This decreases the amount of broadcast traffic, and helps to keep data segmented. In practical terms, this turns a switch into two, three, or 24 switches. This keeps traffic levels down, and allows administrators to extend the life of switches, in terms of bandwidth, and in large switch deployments it can even collapse your switching infrastructure into three or four large switches, instead of 10 smaller switches. Most switching vendors support 4,084 VLANs per switch but check to make sure that your switch does support that many.

Refer again to Figure 5.1. The entire network uses one large netblock: 10.10.10.0/24. A lot of broadcast traffic can be generated across a large, flat network when all nodes are part of the same netblock. One way to reduce the amount of traffic is to subnet the IP block into more manageable chunks. Then administrators can assign the different chunks to each workgroup, or business unit. This method of segmentation can be hard to manage. VLANs are essentially the same as subnetted netblocks, a packet must travel through a router or other Layer 3 device to move from one VLAN to another.

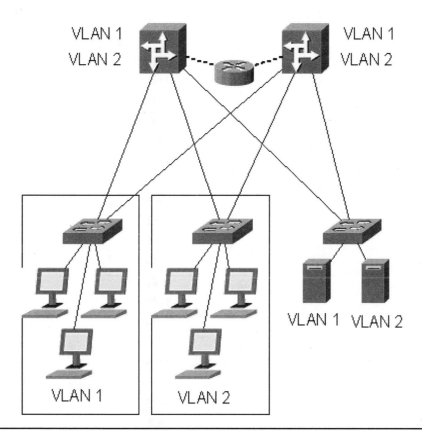

Figure 5.5 A flat network that uses VLANS to limit broadcast domains

In Figure 5.5 the network presented in Figure 5.1 is fleshed out a little more, and VLANs have been added. There are three switches. All of the active ports on Switch 1 have been assigned to VLAN 1, while all of the active ports on Switch 2 have been assigned to VLAN 2. The two core switches are both part of VLANs 1 and 2.

Generally VLANs are most useful when you share the information between multiple switches. When VLAN information is passed from one switch to the next it is referred to as tagging. The Institute of Electrical and Electronics

Engineers (IEEE) has established the standard for VLAN tagging as 802.1Q. Using 802.1Q to share VLAN information is recommended, though many switch vendors have developed their own ways to share information. For example Cisco has a proprietary protocol called Inter-Switch Link (ISL) that behaves similarly to 802.1Q. Check with your vendor to see what type of VLAN tagging is supported.

At this point, we have managed to significantly contain broadcast traffic. Instead of Switch 1 and Switch 2 seeing all traffic destined for the other switch, they now only see broadcast requests for machines on their own switch.

To contain broadcast traffic even more, the next step is to configure VLANs on the third switch. The third switch only has file servers attached to it. Each group has its own file server, and obviously the users are continuously accessing these file servers. Because the file servers do not move often, each port can be assigned to the VLAN that corresponds to the VLAN of the group that uses that file server. If there are ten different groups within an organization—therefore 10 file servers—broadcast traffic can be reduced by an additional 50 percent by assigning each port on the file server to a different VLAN.

If members of an organization are heavy laptop users who move from location to location within the network, you can also create dynamic VLANs. A dynamic VLAN is configured based on the MAC address of the device connecting to the switch. The MAC address is added to a database on the switch. Because VLAN information is shared among all switches, whenever that MAC address plugs into any switch on the network it is automatically added to that VLAN and is able to talk to the rest of the machines in that VLAN.

VLANs are a great way to help ensure availability on the network, and they can isolate traffic, but do they have any other security value?

5.3.1 VLAN Security

As discussed in the previous section, VLANs help to increase availability, and they can keep traffic isolated, preventing others from sniffing data they should not. However, VLANs can also help restrict access to your network—if they are deployed properly.

Switches are generally viewed as "plug and go" equipment. A network administrator purchases a switch, plugs it into the network, plugs workstations/servers into the switch, and it starts working. This ease of deployment is one of the reasons that switches have such a poor security reputation. For switches that support VLANs, all ports on the switch are initially configured to be part of the default VLAN (usually VLAN 1). While this makes switch installation very simple, it also makes it very easy for someone to gain access to the network using the switch.

To improve security on switches, remove the default VLAN. Each port on the switch should have to be added to the appropriate VLAN. Even if all machines on a switch are part of the same VLAN, any empty ports should be configured with no VLAN. Or, if the switch does not support removal of the default VLAN, the active ports on the switch should be switched to a different VLAN.

Removing the workstations/server from the default VLAN is important, but it is imperative that the port connected to the upstream switch or router be removed from the default VLAN as well. Because the upstream port is tagged with all of the VLANs, an attacker who is able to determine the default VLAN for the tagged port may be able to sniff all traffic on the network. Not only should the trunked port not be in the default VLAN, but it should have a native VLAN number that is unique.

NOTE

The SANS Institute performed a test, using an intrusion detection system, on VLAN security. It found that with a little bit of testing an attacker could successfully sniff traffic on a LAN that used default VLAN configuration settings. SANS engineers recommend not using VLANs as the sole method of enforcing switch security policy. They also recommend not putting the trunking ports in the native VLAN. Read more about the study online on the SANS Institute website (*www.sans.org/*).

5.4 Spanning Tree

There is a flaw in the design of the access to the core network we are building: the access switches all have two connections to the core switches. If the network devices were talking Layer 3, this would be no problem, but of course, the switches are speaking Layer 2. This means that they cannot use dynamic routing protocols to determine the best path. Why is this a problem?

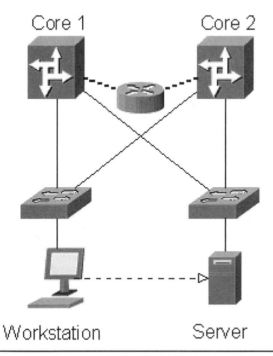

Figure 5.6   A redundant switched network can cause problems if not properly configured

Figure 5.6 shows a typical network scenario in which the user at his workstation needs to get to a server connected to a different switch. Because redundancy has been implemented in the core of the network, the access switch has two paths to get to the core switches. The person at the workstation wants to get to the departmental server, connected to a different switch. The packet has two paths to travel to get to the second switch; it can go through Core 1 or Core 2, either of which can forward it to the destination switch. When the workstation sends a packet out to the server, both Core 1 and Core 2 receive the packet and forward it on to the server's switch. Core 1 and Core 2 see that a packet has been transmitted from the other core switch and now think that the workstation is directly attached to the other core. When the response comes from the server switch, Core 1 and Core 2 will attempt to forward it to the other core switch, creating a routing loop. Some packets will manage to travel from workstation to server, but most will not.

In a large network, this type of routing loop can cause a broadcast storm, which is capable of making the network unavailable.

The Spanning Tree Protocol (STP) helps remove these types of routing loops on redundant Layer 2 networks. STP, a standard defined by the IEEE as 802.1D, creates a series of active and inactive ports on the switches. Traffic is forwarded only through the active ports, while the inactive ports listen for a failure so they can take over.

STP determines which ports will be active and which will be inactive by using the spanning tree algorithm (STA). The STA selects a base of operations, called the *root bridge*, and calculates all of the paths on the network based on that root bridge. The STP is able to determine the best way for data to travel throughout the network.

When a switch is first added to the network, it assumes it is the root bridge, and it sets its identification, called the bridge ID, equal to the root bridge. The bridge ID is a combination of the two numbers, the 16-bit priority, which is configured by default to be 32768 on most switches (Cisco, Foundry, Nortel, Bay Networks, Extreme, etc.) and the 48-bit MAC address. The switch sends the information to the rest of the switches in the network using a message format called bridge protocol data units (BPDU). The switch with the lowest bridge ID and MAC address becomes the root bridge in the network.

Once a root bridge has been selected, all switches participating in STP listen on all ports for BPDU messages. If the switch receives BPDU messages on multiple ports, it will choose the port with the lowest cost to the root bridge to be the active port; the other ports will go into standby mode. If multiple ports have the same cost to the root bridge, then the port with the lowest port ID will be chosen as the active port.

5.4.1 Spanning Tree Security

One problem is that there is no inherent security in STP. An attacker who is able to gain physical access to a network could plug a switch into the network, configure it to join an STP group, and force it to be the root bridge, thus controlling the flow of traffic on the network, and being able to sniff all traffic that comes into the interloping switch.

STP is also an all or nothing protocol. It has to be enabled for all ports or none. This only serves to make it easier for the attacker described in the previous example to take over a switched network. The attacker does not even have to guess which ports are activated for STP (unlike VLANs, which are configured on a per-port basis), because they all are.

The lack of any security precautions inherent in STP has forced vendors to develop their own security enhancements to STP. While it is good that vendors are taking a proactive response, it also means that one vendor's version of STP may not be implemented the same as other vendors.

For example, Cisco Root Guard prevents other switches in the network from becoming the root bridge, unless the designated root bridge fails. Root Guard allows a network administrator to keep the network intact, while still providing failover. Root Guard is built into all Cisco switches that support STP. Root Guard configuration is relatively simple: Decide which port should be the bridge root, and declare it to be guarded. You can even select a port that is not currently the root bridge. To make this configuration on a Cisco switch running CatOS use the following command:

```
core1> (enable) set spantree guard root 1/24

Rootguard on port 1/24 is enabled.
Warning!! Enabling rootguard may result in a topology change.
core1> (enable)
```

If the switch is running Cisco IOS, the commands are:

```
Core1(config)#interface fastEthernet 0/12
Core1(config-if)#spanning-tree rootguard
Core1(config-if)#^Z
*Mar 15 20:15:16: %SPANTREE-2-ROOTGUARD_CONFIG_CHANGE: Rootguard
enabled on port FastEthernet0/12 VLAN 1.
Core1#
```

There are a number of vendor-specific enhancements that will make STP safer to run on switched networks. As long as a network is homogenous it is a good idea to refer to vendor documentation to determine what type of STP security you can apply to the access and core layers.

5.5 MAC Addressing

To this point we have primarily discussed availability within the switched portion of the network. While availability is an important part of network security, protection against unauthorized intrusion is equally important. A properly configured switch can assist in this type of protection as well. If an administrator can prevent an attacker from plugging directly into network, it will be that much more secure.

Most networks have several unused ports on their switches. These ports are potential security holes, as anyone can plug into an unused network jack and have access to your network. One solution is to disable all unused ports, and then enable/disable them as needed. This solution is problematic for two reasons:

1. It takes time away from network administrators who have to constantly enable/disable ports on switches. This is especially true if you have several conference rooms at your location. Every time someone is having a meeting, he or she will need a network jack activated.

2. Someone must remember to disable the ports after meetings. If the port it not disabled, anyone who happens to wander by the conference room can use it.

A better solution is to restrict access to a port by MAC address. Most switches support this feature, which will not allow a port on a switch to forward traffic unless it has the mapped MAC address. In general, this is a good security protocol to implement for networks that are relatively static. If users remain primarily plugged into one network jack, then binding a MAC address to a port will prevent an attacker from unplugging someone's machine, and plugging their own in, in hopes of using the active network jack to gain network access.

For areas, such as conference rooms, that have a lot of transient traffic, mapping the MAC address to a port provides a level of security. Only the person who requested access to the port would be able to send data from the port, until the next request comes in and the MAC address changes. This may not be an optimal security solution, but it is a good balance between not allowing any network access to transient areas, and allowing everyone to have network access.

MAC address security is especially important for the core switches. Because that part of the network should be very stable, with very few devices being added or removed, all ports not in use should be disabled, and MAC address security should be enabled on all used ports.

Enabling MAC address security is a relatively simple task. The switch knows the MAC address of the device connected to it, so it can set the address automatically. On a Cisco 5000 switch, it is a couple of lines of code. If you want to use the MAC address that the switch has learned from the network device:

```
Core1> (enable) set port security 2/23 enable
Port 2/23 port security enabled with the learned mac address.
```

Alternatively, if you would prefer to set a MAC address:

```
Core1>(enable)set port security 2/20 enable xx-xx-xx-xx-xx-xx
Port 2/20 port security enabled with xx-xx-xx-xx-xx-xx as the secure
mac address.
```

Before implementing MAC address security, be sure to check with your vendor to see if it is supported on the lower end workgroup switches. A lot of entry level managed switches do not support this feature, which is a shame, because the access level is often where it is most needed.

Enabling port security may have the added benefit of finding out if anyone is using unauthorized equipment on your network. The first 24 bits (three octets) of a MAC address indicate the manufacturer of the network card. If a network is fairly homogenous, then the first 24 bits of all MAC addresses should be the same. If there are discrepancies, it may signal that some employees are using network or company resources for unauthorized purposes.

NOTE

A list of manufacturer codes is maintained by the IEEE and can be found on its website.

Another reason MAC address security is so important is the way in which switches forward traffic. If two network devices with the same MAC address appear on different ports on the same switch, some switches will forward traffic to both ports. Altering a MAC address to mirror another address is a trivial task. If the switch you are using does forward traffic to both ports, then an attacker is not only able to see all traffic destined for the compromised machine, but can also use the information to learn the network topology. The more familiar an attacker is with the network topology, the easier it will be for that attacker to launch a successful break in.

A second flaw in some switch architectures is that a switch will initially act like a hub. Rather than sending traffic directly to its destination port, when a switch is first added to the network, or when the ARP cache is full, the switch will broadcast traffic to all ports, allowing anyone with a sniffer to monitor the traffic being passed across the network. As expected, there are tools available that will allow an attacker to flood a switch with MAC addresses, thus filling the ARP table of the switch, and forcing it to refresh. While the ARP table is refreshing, incoming and outgoing traffic is again broadcast allowing the same attacker with a sniffer to continue to gather data about your network.

Bonding a specific MAC address to a port can stop both of these attacks. MAC address security is commonly overlooked as a way to protect switches from unauthorized access. While there is some administrative overhead associated with this type of security, it is worth it when compared to the possibilities if an attacker gains access to one of your switches.

5.6 ARP Tables

Similar to routers, switches maintain ARP tables that map a logical address, such as an IP address, to a physical address, usually a MAC address. In a switched environment the ARP table is normally very static. The MAC address of a network card does not normally change, and the IP address associated with a machine will also remain relatively constant. Unfortunately, most switches are susceptible to ARP attacks which can render a switch unusable, or be used to gather information about the topology of a network.

In November 2001, Cisco released a security warning about ARP table vulnerabilities in most versions of its IOS software. An ARP request received by a router interface, but with a different MAC address for that interface, would normally be ignored. However, if multiple ARPs were received with the different MAC address, the interface would first attempt to maintain its existing MAC address, but would eventually give up and overwrite its MAC address with the one listed in the ARP. This would effectively shut down the router or the administrative interface of the switch.

This weakness was patched, and new versions of the software were released for all current code trees. This incident highlights some of the security issues associated with ARP tables which can be flooded to force a switch to broadcast traffic; they can also be poisoned with bad information, allowing an attacker to intercept packets.

The basic problem with ARP tables is that they are generated dynamically, which is good and bad. This dynamic generation is what makes ARP tables so useful for generating traffic on the network, and it allows an administrator to use other dynamic protocols, like DHCP, on the network. On the downside, these same ARP tables can be used to disrupt the network, unless they are properly secured.

Another trick attackers sometimes use to gain access to information is called ARP poisoning. An attacker who wants to monitor traffic for another workstation on the network will send that workstation a forged ARP packet. The workstation will receive the ARP packet and direct traffic to the attacker's network device. The attacker intercepts the packet, gathers the necessary information, and passes it on to its original destination.

To get a better idea of how this works, take a look at Figures 5.7 and 5.8.

In Figure 5.7, the attacker sends a forged request to the workstation, representing her machine as the gateway address. The workstation now sends all gateway requests to the attacker's machine. The attacker inspects the packets, and then forwards them on to the real gateway, as in Figure 5.8.

The workstation does not realize that its packets are being intercepted and continues to forward traffic to the attacker for as long as the attacker remains connected to the network.

One way to avoid this is to manually map MAC addresses to an IP address. Because the primary function of the ARP table is to map a logical address to a physical address, if that information is manually entered into the switch configuration, it cannot be overwritten. On a Cisco switch, you can perform this task by typing:

```
Core1(config)# arp 10.10.0.29 xx.xx.xx.xx.xx.xx arpa 0/12
```

This command would map the IP address 10.10.0.29 with MAC address xx.xx.xx.xx.xx.xx to port 0/12 on a switch. The arpa entry indicates the type of traffic; this is the default for IP networks. Extreme, Foundry, and most other managed switches will give you the ability to do this. Check with your vendor for details as to how it is done.

The problem with hard coding MAC addresses, as this is sometimes called, is that it forces administrators to assign static IP addresses to every device on the network. This can open other security holes. Notably, it makes it easier for an attacker to map out network topology. Hard coding MAC addresses is a good

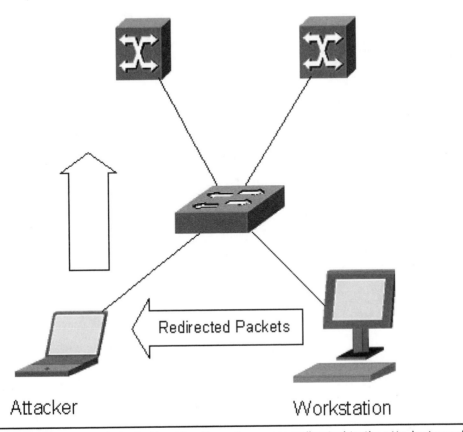

Figure 5.7   Packets destined for the gateway are redirected to the attacker's machine, inspected, and forwarded to the gateway

practice for switches that have network devices with static IP addresses, such as the core switches, or the server access switches. This practice generally does not make a lot of sense for areas where IP addresses are dynamically assigned.

5.7 Restricting Access to Switches

Throughout this chapter ways of securing access and core infrastructures have been discussed, and one common theme has emerged: The best way to secure switching infrastructure is to prevent attackers from gaining access.

The first step to prevent access to switches is to disable unused ports. If an attacker cannot pass traffic while plugged into a network jack, then it is hard to

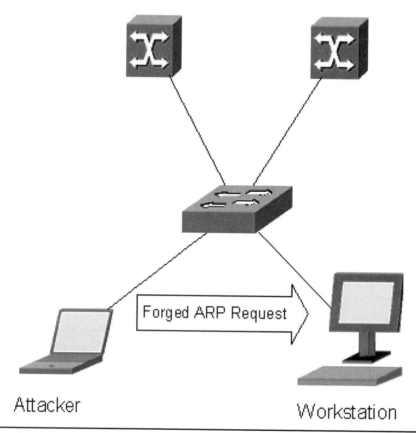

Figure 5.8   An attacker sends a forged ARP request

do damage. Sometimes it is difficult to leave unused ports disabled, as in the conference room example. In cases where a port cannot be disabled, restrict access to that port based on MAC address. To increase security in common areas, consider keeping those rooms locked when not in use. If you use key cards, or some other sort of automated security system to keep areas within your building secure, consider adding conference rooms to the list of secured area. This will require users to scan themselves into the room when they want to access it—hopefully limiting access to authorized personnel, and it generates a log file for network administrators to follow if there is a security breach that originates from one of these common areas.

It is not enough to restrict access to the switch. As with routers, you have to restrict who can access the switch and the methods they can use. To maximize security, start by disabling any HTML interfaces to the switch, unless they allow configuration over an SSL connection (as of this writing there are no switch vendors that allow this). Enable SSH access to the switch, and disable telnet. Foundry and Extreme switches will allow you to use SSH, and Cisco will allow you to use SSH on the Catalyst 2900 and above series. Check with your switch vendor to determine the proper method for setting up SSH on the switches in your network.

Most switches do not have ACLs, like routers, but if you are using multilayer switches in the core of your network you can generally configure ACL-type restrictions on switch ports. Use these restrictions to allow administration of a switch from only a single port.

In fact, many companies use a combination of ACLs and VLANs to create a separate management network. This management network is used to share network updates and topology changes. By isolating this information you are adding an additional layer of security. It also makes it easier to track, log, and isolate network anomalies because you do not have to track every change in the network, only changes that occur within the management VLAN.

Finally, don't forget about passwords. Keep switch passwords secure, and restrict them to as few people as possible. Don't forget to set not only access and superuser passwords, but console passwords as well. If you lock your switches in a secure area, as recommended, it is unlikely that someone will access the switch directly. But, if someone manages to gain access, don't make it easy for them to get into it.

5.8 Summary

Most network administrators give very little thought to the switches in a network. As long as they are forwarding traffic properly, they are generally ignored. As you have seen from this chapter, a switch can be a very powerful tool for securing a network. It can also be a very powerful tool for an attacker.

Because a switch represents an access point into the network, it is important to make it as difficult as possible for an attacker to gain network access through a switch. Of course, this restrictive access has to be coupled with the need legitimate users have to access the network.

Methods for securing a switched network include mapping MAC addresses to a switch port, disabling unused ports, and, where applicable, creating static ARP table entries.

These security measures, used in tandem with other measures discussed throughout this book, will help to keep the network secure.

6

Authentication, Authorization, and Accounting

An important part of network security is authentication, authorization, and accounting, collectively known as AAA. AAA is a framework, similar to the security models discussed in Chapter 2, in which an administrator can maintain access control over network devices.

AAA covers access control over routers, switches, firewalls, servers, and so forth. Just about any network device that is not a workstation, and allows remote access, can fall under AAA policies. AAA is not a protocol in and of itself; instead, it is a set of guidelines promoted by the IETF that outlines how access protocols should behave to optimize their security benefits.

The most commonly used protocols associated with AAA are Kerberos, Remote Authentication Dial-In User Service (RADIUS), and Terminal Access Controller Access Control System+ (TACACS+). These will be discussed shortly.

By providing a framework for access control, AAA offers a network administrator a way to apply a standard policy across all network devices. This type of standard policy has two benefits: It gives the network administrator the ability to centralize all accounting information, and it creates a standard of access that can be applied evenly across the network.

The AAA framework, in networks where it is necessary, allows for the comingling of different types of authentication, not only within the network, but also on the same network interface. AAA, as with any good security model, provides a network administrator with a great deal of flexibility. It fits around an existing network, rather than forcing the network into a rigid security model.

Figure 6.1 demonstrates how an AAA accounting model would fit into the network that is currently being built. AAA services generally reside on remote machines, so if a network device is compromised, and consequently the validity

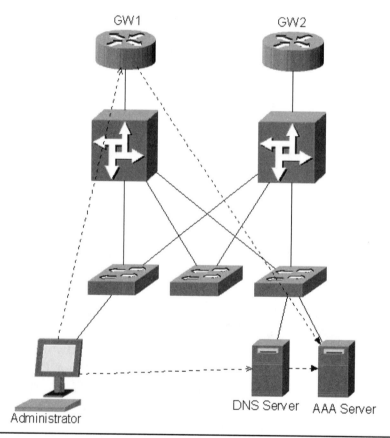

Figure 6.1   A typical network configuration using AAA services

of its own logs are questionable, there is an independent record of access times, and possibly changes made to the device.

The AAA process is somewhat complex, and it allows a network administrator to set multiple levels of control. Referring to Figure 6.1 again, an administrator logs into a router, the router sends a message to the AAA server (either a RADIUS or TACACS+ authentication message) asking the AAA server to authenticate this user. The AAA server authenticates the user and can let the router know what level of access the user has. The router can send updates to the AAA server detailing what changes the administrator makes.

While logged into the router, the administrator decides to log into the DNS server, which sends a message to the AAA server asking it to authenticate the administrator. Even though the DNS server is running on a different platform than the router, because the AAA server relies on standard protocols for authentication, it can perform the same authentication and tracking functions for the DNS server.

It is important to emphasize that the AAA model creates a framework in which protocols like Kerberos, RADIUS, and TACACS+ can develop so they can be standardized and ported to multiple platforms. From an administrator's perspective this framework allows you to standardize on one AAA protocol across the entire network, or select multiple protocols knowing that they will support similar behaviors.

Each aspect of the AAA framework has specific functions and has to meet certain requirements before a protocol can be considered AAA compliant.

Authentication is the process in which a user is identified on a device. This includes the username and password process and the type of encryption—if any—that is used during the authentication process. The purpose of authentication is to restrict access to network devices, so authentication has to occur before a user can gain access to a device. Authentication is defined on a per-interface basis. Multiple forms of authentication are supported on each interface; however, a default authentication can be assigned to all interfaces.

Authorization is the user profile. It is what determines the level of access, or what services to which a user has access. Authorization can be defined in a couple of ways. If the authorization policy for each user is going to be consistent throughout the network, then the authorization policy can be defined on the AAA server. If the authorization policy is going to vary from device to device, then the authorization policy can be defined on the individual network device. For example, a network administrator may want to define different policies for routers and servers, or a web developer may need full access to the web server, but only limited access to the DNS server. Authorization policy does not have to be limited to each user. It can be defined on a per-group basis, with different groups having different privileges.

Controlling who logs in, and what privileges they have when logged in, is not enough. You also have to be able to monitor what they do while logged in, which is where accounting is important. Accounting allows a network administrator to monitor the times an account was logged in, the commands issued while logged in, resources used, and data transferred. Accounting features can add a lot of overhead to your network; however, the additional information can be invaluable when trying to track down either an internal or external attacker as the AAA accounting server has a complete record of the moves an attacker made.

6.1 Kerberos

Kerberos is the protocol most often associated with the AAA framework. Kerberos was originally developed for Unix-based systems and is defined in RFC 1510. Kerberos is an authentication infrastructure used to ensure the identity of users and systems on a network. The current version of Kerberos is 5.0, and there are Kerberos clients for almost every operating system.

Kerberos relies on a combination of key encryption and cryptographic protocols to ensure the authentication of users. The process, outlined in Figure 6.2, is fairly simple; a network administrator sets up an authentication server, known as a Ticket Granting Server (TGS). One or more realms (usually domains) are created on the TCG. A user requesting access to a particular realm must get a ticket from the TGS, by authenticating to the server.

When a user authenticates against the TGS a special ticket is issued. This Ticket Granting Ticket (TGT), is used anytime that user needs access to a service or device in the realm that requires authentication. The user presents the TGT to the TGS, which issues a ticket for that particular device or service.

The user only needs to authenticate against the TGS one time during a session. The rest of the time, the TGS uses the information in the TGT to grant

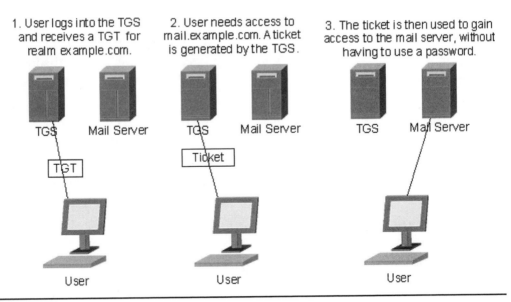

1. User logs into the TGS and receives a TGT for realm example.com.

2. User needs access to mail.example.com. A ticket is generated by the TGS.

3. The ticket is then used to gain access to the mail server, without having to use a password.

TGS   Mail Server

TGS   Mail Server

TGS   Mail Server

TGT

Ticket

User

User

User

Figure 6.2   The Kerberos authentication process

access. Kerberos creates a key based on the user's password to encrypt the TGT packet using the data encryption standard (DES).[1] The user decrypts the packet and uses the ticket to gain access to the desired service or device.

Kerberos Version 4.0 was found to have several security flaws, especially in the area of password authentication. It was especially susceptible to dictionary attacks as it only used a password-based, one-way hash function to generate encryption. Kerberos 5.0 avoids this problem by using the password and the realm to generate the encryption. This makes it much more difficult for an attacker to launch a password attack.

6.2 RADIUS

The RADIUS protocol was originally developed for use with dial-up networks. While it is still primarily used to authenticate dial-up accounts, it has become a popular tool for authenticating other network devices. This growth makes sense, as many administrators do not like the idea of maintaining one AAA server for routers and switches, and another for dial-in users.

---

1. Modern versions of Kerberos actually use 3DES encryption.

RADIUS operates on Port 1812, over UDP transport, and is specified in RFC 2865. The original RADIUS protocol included support for the Point-to-Point Protocol (PPP) and Unix logins; vendors have incorporated support for other types of logins to their versions of RADIUS.

RADIUS authentication is handled through shared secret keys sent over clear text packets; however, passwords are encrypted using MD5. Because RADIUS packets are sent using UDP, there are several fail-safe mechanisms included to help ensure data reaches its intended destination. A RADIUS client can either be set up to resend transmissions at predefined intervals, until a response is received, or it can be set to failover to a second or third RADIUS server in the event of a failure.

Figure 6.3 outlines the process for a successful RADIUS authentication. The router has software, known as a RADIUS client, which interacts with the RADIUS server when it attempts to authenticate a user. The RADIUS server may forward the request to another RADIUS server, or query a Lightweight Directory Access Protocol (LDAP) server to authenticate the information. In cases where the RADIUS server authenticates against another, the RADIUS server acts like the client and forwards the authentication request in an encrypted format.

If it is supported, the RADIUS server may issue an additional challenge-response request from the authentication user. If that is the case, the RADIUS

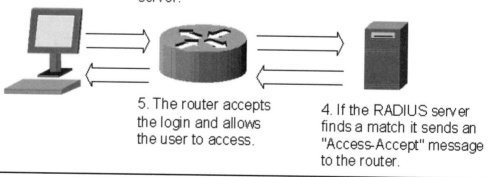

1. User attempts to log into a router.

2. The router encrypts the authentication header and forwards it to the RADIUS server.

3. The RADIUS server looks through its database for a match.

5. The router accepts the login and allows the user to access.

4. If the RADIUS server finds a match it sends an "Access-Accept" message to the router.

Figure 6.3   The RADIUS authentication process

server will issue an "access-challenge" request to the client, which in turn passes it on to the user. The user should reply with an appropriate response to the challenge.

If the RADIUS server is unable to locate the user, or the passwords do not match, the RADIUS server issues an access-reject, along with an error message, to the client, which passes it on to the end user. After the access-reject message is sent, it is discarded.

Because RADIUS transactions are performed across UDP, there is no confirmation between the client and the server that a successful request has been made until the server responds to the client. In order to solve this problem an access-request packet accompanies each request to a RADIUS server. The access-request contains the username and password of the user, as well as the client ID and client port the user is trying to access. The client keeps this information as well and begins counting down. If a response is not received from the RADIUS server within a certain amount of time, the client will either resend the request, or try a secondary RADIUS server—depending on how the RADIUS administrator has configured the client.

The ability to attempt to authenticate logins multiple times against the same server or against multiple RADIUS servers helps to make it a robust protocol that is very resilient in the face of network problems. In fact, RADIUS has to be resilient because its primary use is in dial-up networks. Earthlink, MSN, and AT&T all use RADIUS authentication for their dial-up networks. They have millions of users dialing into their networks simultaneously; if RADIUS were not robust, these providers would experience frequent outages.

6.2.1 RADIUS Security

In March 2002 a security alert was released by CERT detailing two buffer overflow vulnerabilities in most vendor implementations of RADIUS. The first was within the calculation of the MD5 encryption used to secure the authentication process. The second had to do with vendor-specific implementations of RADIUS.

The first vulnerability involved the MD5 encryption. The RADIUS client encrypts the shared secret key without taking into account the size of the RADIUS server buffer. If a large amount of data is sent in this manner, it could cause a buffer overflow, crashing the RADIUS server. This problem is more serious if an attacker actually has access to the shared secret, because at that point the attacker may be able to overflow the buffer and execute a command on the RADIUS server.

The second vulnerability has to do with vendor-specific information. RADIUS allows vendor- or user-specific information to be included in the packets sent between the RADIUS client and server. Some vendors did not enable proper data validation within their implementation of RADIUS. If an attacker were to populate vendor-specific fields, within the packet with a negative value (in this case, any value with a length less than two), it would have the same effect as a DoS attack, rendering the RADIUS server unusable.

The first step in securing RADIUS servers is to ensure that the server has the latest vendor-specific patches. As with anything else in the network, it is important to be aware of any RADIUS vulnerabilities and ensure that the RADIUS vendor is releasing timely patches.

Most RADIUS software will allow you to limit which servers can authenticate against the RADIUS server. This feature should be enabled in order to prevent wayward RADIUS clients from attempting to launch DoS attacks against a RADIUS server and to prevent other RADIUS clients from trying password attacks.

Most RADIUS solutions do a good job of logging information. It is important to log as much data as possible, including IP addresses and phone numbers, if the RADIUS server is being used to handle dial-up connections. In addition to access information, password failures are important to log, and many administrators will disable an account—even temporarily—after three failed attempts to log into the network.

Password protection is also important when dealing with RADIUS servers. If you rely on localized RADIUS authentication, then force users to adhere to the same password policies that are enforced throughout the company. However, it is worth exploring using RADIUS to authenticate against the existing username and password database (Figure 6.4).

Figure 6.4 shows how a network might be set up to take advantage of an existing username and password database. Some RADIUS products, including Funk Software's Steel-Belted RADIUS and Nortel's Shiva Access Manager, have sup-

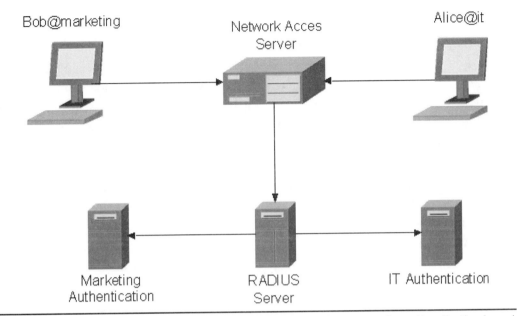

Figure 6.4   Bob and Alice are directed to their respective servers for authentication based on the information in their domain

port for separating users into domains. In our example, Bob is part of the Marketing department, and Alice is part of the IT department. Both connect to the Network Access Server (NAS), which acts as the client, forwarding the authentication request to the RADIUS server. In this case, the username includes not only the login name, but also the domain of the user. The domain tells the RADIUS server where to forward the request. In Bob's case, the domain is marketing, so Bob authenticates to the RADIUS server as bob@marketing. Alice is in the IT department and is part of the IT domain. She connects with the login string Alice@it and is forwarded to a different server for authentication.

The advantage to this type of setup is that a user only needs one username and password to log into the network locally and remotely. This is also a disadvantage, because now an attacker only needs one password to successfully find a way into the network.

This type of access will be discussed in detail in Chapter 7.

6.3 TACACS+

TACACS+ is an AAA protocol similar to RADIUS that was developed by Cisco Systems. TACACS+ is loosely based on two depreciated protocols, TACACS and Extended TACACS (XTACACS)—TACACS+ is incompatible with both TACACS and XTACACS. Because of serious security flaws in the TACACS and XTACACS designs, it is recommended that they not be used in favor of the TACACS+ model.

While TACACS+ was developed by Cisco, the specification for the TACACS+ protocol has been released to the public. Other networking vendors, including Extreme Networks and Foundry Networks, have incorporated TACACS+ into their products.

While TACACS+ performs the same function as RADIUS, its origins are different. TACACS+ was originally developed as a protocol to control AAA for network devices, so the architecture is different than RADIUS, which was originally developed for dial-up networks.

TACACS+ operates over TCP, rather than UDP, and uses Port 49 by default, though TACACS+ can be configured to use any port a network administrator desires. Also unlike RADIUS, TACACS+ encrypts all packet data, not just the password.

The TACACS+ protocol is similar to RADIUS in the way it authenticates users. A user logs into a router or switch interface that is TACACS+-enabled. The network device obtains the username and password prompt from the TACACS+ server that is configured for the interface and passes it to the user attempting to authenticate. The user enters the username and password information, which is encrypted and passed from the network device to the TACACS+ server.

The TACACS+ server will send one of four responses to the network device: ACCEPT, REJECT, ERROR, or CONTINUE. An ACCEPT response indicates that the authentication was successful, and the session can start. If additional authentication information is needed, the user will be prompted for it at this time.

A REJECT message indicates that authentication failed. The user will either have to re-enter the password, or the session will be disconnected. This behavior varies depending on the TACACS+ daemon.

If an ERROR message is returned then there is a problem with the TACACS+ server, the network device making the query, or a problem with the network. If the network device receives the error message it will either try again, or it will try an alternate TACACS+ server, depending on how the network administrator has configured it.

The CONTINUE response is sent when authentication is successful, but additional information is required.

TACACS+ allows for multiple types of authentication. Password authentication is the most commonly used, and the most basic, form of authentication. However, a network administrator is not limited to password authentication; in fact, any form of authentication that is supported by the TACACS+ software can be used. In addition, multiple forms of authentication can be required—as long as the chosen TACACS+ software supports it. For example, if password authentication is not enough, an administrator can configure TACACS+ to require a username/password combination, and an RSA key to gain access. The user would authenticate first by sending the username and password. If that were successful, the TACACS+ server would send an ACCEPT message, followed by a new challenge request, for the RSA key. When both levels of authentication have been completed, the user will be allowed to access the router.

Configuring TACACS+ on a router is a two-part process:

1. Set up a TACACS+ server.
2. Configure the network devices.

Cisco makes the source code for a TACACS+ daemon available on its website, but there are precompiled daemons available for Windows NT and 2000, Solaris, BSD, and Linux. The authentication policy for the network devices is configured on the TACACS+ server. The configuration options available are dependent on the options supported by the TACACS+ server. For example, the Linux version of the TACACS+ server allows an administrator to use pulse amplitude modulation (PAM) authentication to verify network device logins.

In configuring the network devices, it is important to ensure that the same authentication policy is in place across the network. There is very little benefit in defining a default security policy for the edge and core devices but not applying the same policy to the access switches. If TACACS+, or RADIUS for that matter, is going to be deployed, that should be set as the default security policy for all network devices.

The configuration process varies depending on the type of equipment being deployed; for a Cisco router, the process involves several steps. This is an overview of a simple TACACS+ authentication process. Before starting the configuration process, make sure you have console access to the network device you are configuring, so that you can back out of the configuration if something goes wrong.

The first step is to define a new AAA method:

```
gw1(config)#aaa new-model
```

Next, set the TACACS+ host name:

```
gw1(config)#tacacs-server host 192.168.0.40
```

Set TACACS+ as the default authentication policy for the network device:

```
gw1(config)#aaa authentication login default tacacs+
```

Finally, set a secret password that is shared between network devices and the TACACS+ server:

```
gw1(config)#tacacs-server key secretpassword
```

Now, when logging onto the router, the authentication process should be offloaded to the TACACS+ server (Figure 6.5).

Figure 6.5   The router authentication is forwarded to the TACACS+ server

The logs on the TACACS+ server should show the authentication for user allan:

```
Mon Apr 8 22:36:34 2002 [31675]: login query for 'allan' tty2 from
192.168.0.10
1 accepted
```

Using a packet sniffer to monitor the transaction between the router and the TACACS+ server, you would see the information shown in Table 6.1 (in summary format):

192.168.0.101 is the router, and TACACS is the TACACS+ server. When the user allan attempts to login to the router, it sends a message to TACACS, saying it has a TACACS+ request. TACACS responds, saying that it is ready to accept the input. TACACS sends the encrypted information to the router, and the router responds by forwarding the authentication information to TACACS.

Table 6.1   Sniffing TACACS+ Session

PACKET NUMBER	TIME	SOURCE	DESTINATION	PROTOCOL INFORMATION
112	37.072634	192.168.0.101	TACACS	TACACS+ Request
113	37.076789	TACACS	192.168.0.101	TACACS+ Response
114	37.076892	TACACS	192.168.0.101	TCP 49 > 11003 [FIN, ACK] Seq=367679177 Ack=4239449051 Win=5840 Len=0
115	37.080430	192.168.0.101	TACACS	TCP 11003 > 49 [ACK] Seq=4239449051 Ack=367679178 Win=4027 Len=0

6.3.1 TACACS+ Security

To date, no security warnings have been issued against the TACACS+ protocol. In fact, enabling TACACS+ security is a very effective method for preventing problems arising from other security holes.

An example of this is that in June 2001 the CERT/CC issued an advisory concerning the HTTP server that is incorporated into Cisco's IOS software. The advisory related to the authentication process for the HTTP server. CERT/CC recommended using TACACS+ authentication to avoid the problem.

While no security flaws have been found with the TACACS+ protocol, there are some concerns about its design. Communication between the TACACS+ server and the network device is encrypted, but the header information is not. Anyone sitting on the network with sniffing software, as in the example, can track transactions between network devices and the servers. Knowing where the TACACS+ server is may help an attacker determine what software is running on the server, and the attacker may be able to use that information to figure out a way into the core of the network.

The other major security concern revolves around TACACS+ server software. The methods for adding, deleting, and assigning privileges to TACACS+ accounts vary greatly from one TACACS+ program to another. Before deciding on TACACS+ software, check with the vendor to find out what security precautions are taken and the recommended best practices for optimum security.

6.4 Summary

This chapter covered the AAA security model, and how it can be used to control access and authentication processes for network devices. The two protocols most commonly used with the AAA model are RADIUS and TACACS+.

Though Kerberos, RADIUS, and TACACS+ perform the same functions, Kerberos had its roots in server networks; RADIUS grew out of dial-up user authentication; TACACS+ has grown from network device authentication.

AAA, as it relates to VPNs, will be discussed in more detail in Chapter 7. It is important to note that while the default RADIUS protocol may have some serious security problems, many vendors offer enhanced RADIUS solutions, which will dramatically improve the security of RADIUS. That being said, these products are not always compatible with other vendor's solutions. Only use enhanced versions of RADIUS on networks that are running single-vendor solutions.

7

Remote Access and VPNs

Remote access is an important element in enterprise network management. As more employees telecommute, and access to mission-critical services is required 24x7, VPNs are considered an integral part of a network infrastructure.

A VPN is generally defined as a network that uses the public Internet to transfer traffic in a secure manner, using various encryption protocols. That definition is somewhat limiting as a VPN can be run over private lines, wireless networks, and phone lines as well. A broader definition of VPN is the joining of two or more networks—or parts of networks—in different locations, to form a single network. This definition is more inclusive of the types of technologies that may constitute a VPN; it also takes into consideration that not all VPN technologies are encrypted.

From a security perspective, a VPN can be problematic. Network administrators have to go through great pains to keep the network as secure as possible. At the same time, employees have to be allowed remote access from anywhere in the world to the data the administrators are trying to protect. This presents quite a quandary: How do you secure your network from everyone but authorized users, and how do you ensure that the authorized users who access the network remotely are not introducing any potential security holes into the network.

7.1 VPN Solutions

Three broad categories of VPNs are in general use today: dedicated line, dial in, and IP VPN. IP VPN will be the primary focus of this chapter, as it is quickly becoming the VPN type of choice for large corporations.

7.1.1 Dedicated Line VPNs

Dedicated line VPNs have been the type of VPN traditionally associated with large corporations. The process is fairly simple: A company with one or more remote offices contacts either a network provider such as AT&T, Sprint, or WorldCom, or an Incumbent Local Exchange Carrier (ILEC) like Verizon, BellSouth, or Pacific Bell and requests to have point-to-point connections run between offices. These point-to-point connections can either be leased lines or wireless connections, but they have one thing in common: No other traffic is on the network. A point-to-point connection requires a dedicated line to each location; the line runs through the provider's private network to the other locations on the VPN. If the locations on the VPN need to speak to all of the other locations, then a dedicated line has to be run between each connection.

Figure 7.1 shows a typical leased line VPN. Lines are run from the headquarters to Remote Office A and B. A dedicated connection is also run from Remote Office A to Remote Office B. In a perfect world this would not be necessary as the routers located within headquarters could be configured to allow the remote offices to view each other's networks. The reason it is generally not done is that there is no redundancy with a dedicated line network. The company is paying for dedicated transit, so the traffic traveling on the lines never leaves those lines to cross into a public data network. By connecting all of the offices, some redundancy is added to the network, in that there are now two data paths.

Other than the lack of redundancy, the biggest drawback to this type of network is the expense. The cost of maintaining dedicated lines to, and between, each office is prohibitively expensive especially as the number of remote offices grows. Imagine that instead of three offices there were 25. Each time a new office is added to the network, the company has to pay the provider to run the dedicated line from the new office to the headquarters. The farther from the headquarters the office is, the greater the initial cost. This solution generally precludes bringing overseas offices onto the network. Running a cable across the

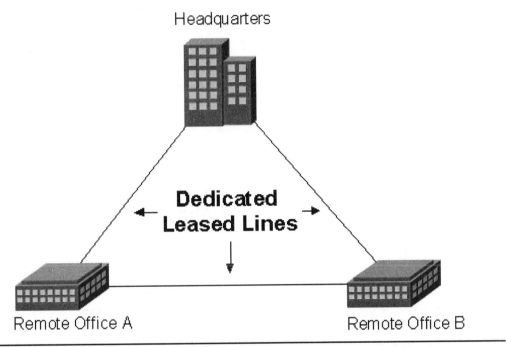

Headquarters

**Dedicated
Leased Lines**

Remote Office A   Remote Office B

Figure 7.1   A typical dedicated line VPN design; each office in the network has a connection to all other offices on the network

ocean is beyond the financial resources of the vast majority of companies. The cost to run that much cable, as well as the monthly costs to the network provider, would be extremely expensive. Of course trying to manage 24 network connections, if the company wanted to run redundant links between each office, would also be an administrative nightmare.

This solution also does not take into account remote users who need access to the network while they are on the road, or working from home. Installing a dedicated connection within the house of every employee is simply not feasible, and still would not help those users who need access to the network from the road.

The positive side to this approach is that it offers the most security. The traffic on these dedicated lines is never shared with anyone else, so there is very little worry that an intruder will be able to sniff traffic as it travels between the various offices. This solution is also nice because it provides an always-on connection that allows all users, at all locations, to be connected to each other simultaneously.

7.1.2 Dial-In VPNs

A second solution is to locate an RAS server in the headquarters, and allow users to dial in to the headquarters to connect to the network. The users connect to the RAS server and have temporary access to the company network. The RAS server acts as a gateway to the rest of the network, allowing the dialed-in user complete access to servers, and other workstations, as if he or she were directly connected. When the user has completed the work, he or she simply disconnects. This solution is less expensive than a dedicated line solution because it makes use of the Public Switched Network (PSTN).

Using the PSTN to transmit data is not as secure as running a dedicated point-to-point connection but it is still a relatively secure connection. When a phone call is made, a temporary dedicated circuit is created and no traffic, aside from the communication between the two parties on that call, will be run across that circuit. Figure 7.2 shows a typical dial-up VPN.

It is still possible for someone to listen in on a phone call, but the government tightly regulates the PSTN. Because of this, providers generally have several layers of security in place to ensure that intruders are unable to easily tamper with telephone calls.

There are some problems with the dial-in model of VPN. The biggest problem is bandwidth; a dial-up connection is simply slow, especially if employees are expected to work while connected to the network.

This problem is further exacerbated when a remote office, with several users, uses a router to initiate the dial-up connection, providing a true VPN, as opposed to a single user from the remote office gaining access to the network. The amount of bandwidth available to the users, generally 53 kilobits per second (Kbps), or less, is significantly slower than a typical network connection.

A second problem is the reliability of a dial-in connection. The PSTN network is very reliable, but it is not designed for long-term conversation, nor is it designed for the type of reliability that is required by a data connection. It is not uncommon to have long lived connections automatically bounced by the LEC.

A dial-in VPN can also be expensive. While generally not as expensive as using dedicated lines, there are some significant costs involved in maintaining a dial-in VPN. The first cost is the phone lines that are needed to support the users. The number of lines will need to be proportional to the number of offices, and remote users accessing the network. If a company has 24 remote offices,

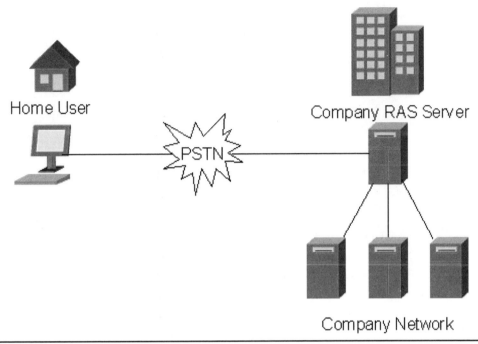

Home User

Company RAS Server

PSTN

Company Network

Figure 7.2   A typical dial-up VPN. A remote user connects into an RAS server and is given access to the rest of the network.

which need continual access to the main network, and averages 20 users accessing the network through the RAS server at any one time, it will need at least 44 phone lines.

In addition to the phone lines, an RAS server with enough modems to support the lines being run in will be needed. If it is only a few modems, then a Windows 2000 or Unix server can be converted to an RAS server. However, if the company has quite a few remote users, it is usually best to use a purpose-built device, such as a Lucent MAX 6000 or a Cyclades PR-4000. Of course, these dedicated devices also require additional training, and maybe even additional staff to manage them.

Another cost involved is long-distance changes. If the remote offices are spread throughout the country they will incur hefty long-distance charges dialing into the corporate LAN several times a day. It is also likely you will have to maintain an 800 number for users to dial into either when they are on the road, or from home, if they live in a different area code.

A dial-in VPN also suffers from the flaw of having several single points of failure. When multiple phone lines are used, the phone company usually provisions a T1 trunk (E1 trunk in Europe). A T1 is equivalent to 24 analog channels (an E1 is 32 analog channels). Each T1 running into your RAS server represents a single point of failure. If you have two T1s (or 48 analog channels) terminating at the same central office (CO), then that CO represents a single point of failure—though the CO itself is designed so that it will generally not experience more than five minutes of downtime a year.[1] The RAS server also represents a single point of failure. The likelihood of failure increases if a company is using a server transformed into an RAS server, instead of a purpose-built machine.

There are several benefits to this solution. The primary benefit is that telephone access is nearly ubiquitous. It is very likely that no matter how far a user is from the main headquarters, he or she will have access to a phone line, and will be able to dial into the network. Despite the costs associated with a dial-in VPN, they are still significantly less than those associated with running dedicated point-to-point connections between offices. Finally, using a dial-in solution means that all employees can connect to the network,[2] giving everyone the access they need, albeit slow access.

Prior to the advent of IP VPNs, it was not uncommon for large corporations to use a combination of dedicated and dial-in VPNs as a way to offer remote network access to their remote offices and employees.

7.1.3 IP VPNs

IP VPNs are the focus of this chapter because they are quickly becoming the standard for remote VPN access. An IP VPN is a VPN that is created using a public network, generally the Internet, as the means of transit.

The appeal of IP VPNs is very apparent: Rather than bear the cost of dedicated point-to-point connections, or phone lines, to allow access into the network, a company only needs to cover the cost of Internet access (Figure 7.3).

IP VPNs allow a company to make use of the existing redundant network infrastructure as a means for remote offices and employees to access the network. Instead of the costs associated with dedicated point-to-point connections,

---

1. Think about it: When was the last time you picked up a phone and got dead air?
2. Discounting busy signals, of course.

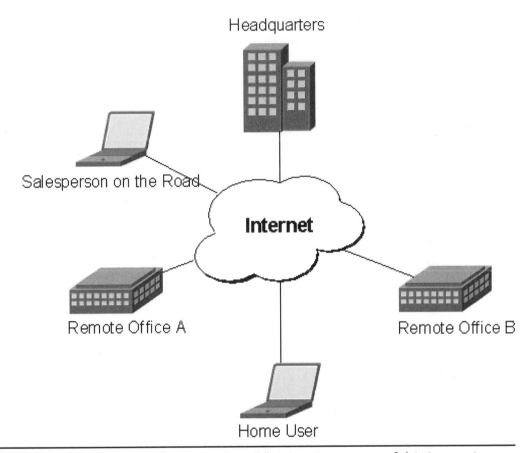

Figure 7.3   An IP-based VPN uses the public Internet as a means of data transport allowing remote offices as well as dial-up users to access the network

or maintaining a dial-up infrastructure, the company simply has to pay for the costs involved to maintain Internet access for the remote offices, and possibly dial-up ISP accounts for employees. Some of these costs the company would have had regardless of the VPN type.

When using the Internet to make a VPN connection, security concerns are paramount. Remote offices and employees may not connect to the same Internet backbone. Even if they do, there is no guarantee that data will not be intercepted between the remote network and the corporate network. It is important to ensure that the data transmitted across the WAN is secured.

Generally, data transmitted across an IP VPN is encrypted and tunneled. There are many types of IP VPNs that incorporate myriad encryption technologies.

VPNs also have a variety of configuration options. An IP VPN can be operated across a firewall or a router, it can be software based, or it can be included as part of dedicated device. Each type of VPN technology, encryption protocol, and network configuration has its own security problems. Before implementing a VPN solution, it is important to be aware of the security considerations associated with the technology used to create the VPN.

Despite a vast array of VPN options, the most commonly deployed VPN solutions are those that allow a single user, with the proper encryption software, or a remote office to connect to the main corporate network across the Internet.

These VPN solutions use varying forms of tunneling protocols to accomplish this connection. A tunneling protocol encapsulates a network packet, encrypts it, and transports it securely across the Internet. In the process of encapsulating and encrypting the packet, the tunneling protocol hides the source and destination IP address of every packet that is being sent across the VPN.

The way an IP VPN usually works is that an NAS is set up within the corporate network, with a publicly available address. Remote users, using a tunneling protocol, make a connection to that NAS device. The NAS device authenticates the user, and the tunnel is established. The user, or office, now has access to the rest of the network through the NAS device. This process is outlined in Figure 7.4. Instead of a home user, a remote office with multiple users could easily be used.

The tunnel can be created using software installed on the remote user's machine, or a VPN router can be used to establish the connection, encrypting all traffic from the remote network to the corporate network and creating the VPN.

The tunnel, once created, is up for as long as the user needs it, or it is terminated at one end or the other. A remote office with a T1 or some other sort of always-on connection can leave the tunneled connection open all the time. Even home users with cable or Digital Subscriber Line (DSL) connections can have a permanent connection to a corporate network.

While IP VPNs are quickly becoming popular because of the cost savings, and relative ease of implementation, there are some serious security concerns that network administrators need to be aware of and prepared to deal with. This will be the primary focus of the rest of the chapter.

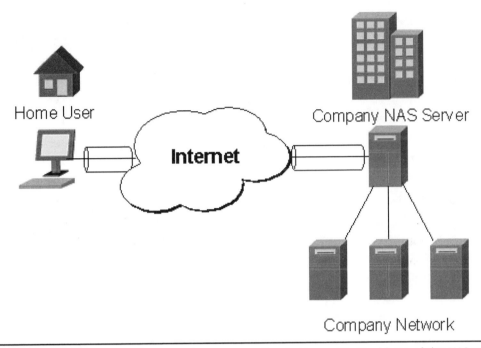

Figure 7.4   A network user makes a connection to the public IP address of the NAS server and establishes the tunnel. Once the tunnel has been established additional traffic is encrypted.

7.2 IP VPN Security

A VPN is a great way to extend a company's network, and to add increased functionality for network users. Many network administrators fail to realize that there are important security considerations associated with this extended network. A lot of control is lost by allowing a remote user access to the core of a corporate network, and there are steps that should be taken to ensure that remote users are not creating security holes in the process of accessing the network.

7.2.1 The Trouble with Passwords

The core of the troubles surrounding VPN access revolves around passwords. Passwords are an adequate form of authentication in a controlled network environment, where the necessary precautions have been taken to hinder the ability of outside intruders to gain access to the network, and to prevent unauthorized users from gaining network access. But passwords are problematic, at best, in the case of remote network access.

Why are passwords problematic? Passwords rely on the ability of a person to memorize them. So, they tend to either be easy to remember, or written down on a Post-It® note attached to a laptop with a label like "Password to Access all the Juicy Corporate Secrets." Either way, it is relatively easy for an attacker, who has managed to access a remote user's system, to determine that user's password and use it to infiltrate the corporate network.

Passwords are also inherently breakable. An attacker with a password checker will eventually be able to crack a password. It may take a while, but because there are only a limited number of characters supported by most password systems the password will eventually be discovered. Of course the same can be said for all encryption schemes. An attacker with enough computer power and unlimited time will eventually be able to crack any encryption system in use today.

Consider that in March 2002, at the Financial Cryptography Conference, Nicko van Someren announced that he and his team had built software that was able to factor a 512-bit encryption key in less than six weeks using standard hardware.

In fact, it is estimated that using currently available hardware, someone could build a computer capable of factoring a 1,024-bit RSA or Diffie-Hellman encryption key in a few minutes. Granted, it would require in excess of $1 billion worth of computer hardware to perform this task, but $1 billion worth of computer hardware is not an inconceivable amount, especially for governments. Until recently 1,024-bit encryption technology was considered unbreakable using current technology.

What do all of these encryption keys have to do with passwords? A password is really just a form of key encryption. Password protection is much weaker than some forms of encryption, but it is also much easier to manage, which is why it is deployed almost ubiquitously.

The other problem associated with passwords is that the longer they are in use, the easier it is to break them. This is true of any type of encryption technology; if it is used for an extended period of time, it is likely that someone will be able to decipher it. It is especially true when dealing with passwords, which is why many security experts recommend a password policy that requires users to change passwords every 15 to 30 days.

Passwords alone do not provide enough security for an IP VPN. A better solution is to require at least one other form of authentication in conjunction with the password authentication. This is known as two-factor authentication. For example, a company may require password authentication combined with a digital certificate. If both levels of authentication are not properly met, the NAS will refuse authentication.

Two-factor authentication greatly improves the security of a VPN, but it usually requires additional infrastructure be added to the network. Certificate authentication requires a certificate server be in place to match public and private keys. This will be discussed further in the encryptions section.

Smart cards are a form of authentication that is becoming more popular. Chances are a company already has some sort of badge system to allow employees access into and around corporate headquarters. These badges can also be used as a form of remote authentication. They are not very secure by themselves, but when combined with a password or a digital certificate, they provide an added layer of security.

Biometrics is another form of authentication. Devices are now available which will plug into a user's machine and allow a company to authenticate based on fingerprints or facial recognition technology.

NOTE

Like other forms of protection, biometric security has its own problems. Fingerprint protection is easy to thwart using items available in your local supermarket. Facial recognition technology is still in very early development, and most forms of facial recognition protection have a 50 percent failure rate.

There are even proprietary methods of authentication. RSA, for instance, has a product called SecurID; it is a hardware token, about the size of a small stopwatch. The token is time synched with an RSA server; based on this synchronization the token generates a new random number every 60 seconds. When a user logs onto the network he or she has to authenticate using a password as well as the number currently displayed on the SecurID token. If the numbers match, and the username and password match, the user is authenticated and allowed access.

VPN authentication security is important, because if the wrong person gains access to a corporate network, the cost to that company could be in excess of millions of dollars. Simple password authentication is not going be enough in the future. In fact most security experts would argue that password authentication is not enough now. If your company is not using a two-factor form of authentication for VPN users, it is something you should seriously consider investigating.

7.2.2 Extending the Security Policy

If a corporate network is going to allow remote users to have access to the network, then the same security policies that apply to users on site must apply to remote users. If there are operating system standards for the company, these standards should be enforced for remote users; if corporate users must run updated virus scanning software, then remote users should as well.

There are myriad examples that can be used to illustrate this point, but the basic rule that should be followed is that any remote user has to follow the same security standards as a local user.

Some companies try to enforce this policy by assigning users laptops that can be used in the home or office. This solution satisfies the basic rule, as long as the purpose of the laptop is understood—in other words, it needs to be clearly explained that it is a corporate-owned machine, and just like any other network device on the corporate network, only approved software and configurations will be supported.

Assigning laptops to all employees who need remote access may not be an option. If that is the case, then guidelines for machines that access the network should be clearly communicated to all employees. Some companies go so far as to have the desktop support group examine machines before allowing the user to access the network remotely. Obviously, this type of control does not scale well, but again, a little preventive maintenance can go a long way toward protecting valuable corporate data.

Equipment security is only one aspect of a corporate security policy. In addition to equipment security the standards for other types of security should be followed as well:

- Users should always log off the VPN when they are finished, or when away from the computer for even a short period of time
- Passwords should never be shared
- A corporate e-mail account should not be used for personal e-mail

Remote users should also not use the corporate network for Internet access while connected to it. There should be no need for this, as the user will already be connected to an ISP and tunneled connections can run simultaneously with nontunneled connections. A tunneled connection that finds its way to the Internet will no longer be tunneled and presents an additional security risk, so all traffic that comes in through a tunneled connection should be directed back through the tunnel to the user who originated the connection.

7.2.3 Logging VPN Connections

All connections that come in through the NAS should be logged, just as any remote connection should be. If there is a security problem network administrators should be able to review the logs and determine from where the connection originated, and the time and date of the connection.

In addition to network logons, as much session information as possible should be logged. If there is a security incident the more information available, the more likely network administrators will be to track down where the break in occurred. More importantly, if proactive monitoring is being conducted on the network any anomalies in the log file, such as a marketing person attempting to access the accounting database, can be spotted sooner, and the attacker may be stopped before a problem can occur. The ability to perform this type of logging is heavily dependent on the features supported by the individual NAS vendors, and the number of security staff.

7.3 Dial-In Security Access

There are two types of dial-up security that a network administrator has to worry about: dial-in VPNs and users who access IP VPNs through a dial-up

ISP. There are different security concerns for each of the dial-in models. For dial-in VPNs, the primary focus is securing the corporate environment, while the security precautions for dial-up IP VPN users focus on securing the remote environment.

7.3.1 Dial-In VPNs

Dial-in VPNs are generally created in one of two ways. Either a network administrator sets up a modem banks with an RAS server, or a user attaches a modem to his or her computer and installs remote access software.

The first type of remote access is fine, and can be an easy way for employees to gain remote access to the network. The second method of remote access should be, to put it mildly, actively discouraged.

Aside from the aforementioned expense associated with dial-in VPNs, the other problem with them is that they have been around, in one form or another, for many years. Remember the movie *WarGames*? *WarGames* took place 20 years ago, and there were already tools available to gain unauthorized access to remote machines via modem. Tools have gotten a lot better since then, and are constantly being improved.

There are two types of attacks used against modem pools: war dialers and demon dialers. A war dialer is a program that dials a string of numbers looking for modem tone. Once modem tone has been detected, a demon dialer will then try username and password combinations in order to gain access.

A properly secured modem bank, with sensible security precautions and a strong password policy, is very resistant to war and demon dialing attacks. That's not what attackers want. They are looking for a single stand-alone modem attached to a device that does not have a password, or has a password that is easy to guess.

Many question the need for a strong modem security policy. Modem access is obsolete, and it is unlikely that anyone will attach a modem to a workstation and leave it connected for an attacker. Remember, unlikely does not mean that it cannot and does not happen often. A prime example where modems are still commonly used is in terminal servers. It is not uncommon for network administrators to set up out-of-band access to routing equipment. If there is a major catastrophe on the edge routers or core switches that takes out the entire network, the administrators need a way to access the equipment—especially if they are at home when it happens. A terminal server with a modem attached is an excellent solution to this problem.

The problem is that terminal servers are often insecure, requiring only a simple password, or even no password to access them. Many terminal servers provide no logging information as well. If an attacker is able to gain access to it, there is often no record of where the call originated, or what commands were issued while the attacker was connected.

This does not mean that a terminal server should not be used as a back door into network routing equipment. Instead, it is important that the same policy that is applied to the primary corporate modem bank should apply to all other modems that are installed on the network. However, the number of modems installed, outside of the primary modem bank, should be limited, and each one should be monitored for potential security breaches.

Modems that are not in use, for instance many laptops come standard with modems, should not be connected to phone lines, and should be removed whenever possible.

7.3.1.1 Dial-In VPN Security

As with anything else on the network, a security policy should be in place for modem services. As previously mentioned, the primary rule in any modem security policy should be no unauthorized modems.

Ideally, all forms of modem access should be forced to authenticate against a RADIUS server, but sometimes that is not possible. If RADIUS authentication is not available for a specific application, consider instituting a minimal rule set for any modem on the network. The rule set should consist of a set of minimally accepted logging standards. It should at least log the incoming phone number and log activities that involve remote access to another device. The modem software should require a password in order to access it and that password should be subject to the same rules as all network passwords.

The modem software should have a lock out feature, so that if an account enters the wrong password more than three times, the account is locked until an administrator reactivates it. Either the modem software, or the device to which it is attached, should allow a network administrator to set policy restricting areas of the network that are allowed to be accessed over a remote connection.

It is important to review the network to ensure there are no unauthorized modems installed. Again, it is becoming less likely that an employee will install a modem for the purpose of remote access, but it still can happen, and when it does network administrators should be aware of it, and remove the unauthorized device.

7.3.2 RADIUS Security

Many of the same security rules that apply to a single modem installation also apply to a modem bank. Fortunately, the RADIUS software that is available today can make it easier to enforce these policies, and give an administrator much more control.

There are many different implementations of RADIUS available on the market such as Steel-Belted Radius, RadiusNT, and GNU Radius. In addition to available software, many RAS devices include their own version of RADIUS. The version of RADIUS is not as important as the security precautions that are taken to secure it.

Starting with the basics, the RADIUS server should be a single use server, with no other services running. Only a limited number of users should have access to the server, and there should not be any unnecessary accounts—this means deleting low-level accounts, such as guest on Windows servers, and the games account on Unix servers.

Whatever version of RADIUS the server is running, the software process should not be owned by the administrator account on the server. RADIUS listens to Port 1812 for UDP connections. Most likely the software will need to be started by the administrative user in order to bind itself to the port, but after that the owner should be changed to a nonprivileged account used just for RADIUS.

One of the limitations of RADIUS is that only the password is encrypted, not the entire packet. On a local network, with proper security precautions in place, this should not be too much of a disadvantage, but it is something to be aware of and monitor.

One of the big debates associated with using RADIUS, or any other remote authentication protocol, is whether or not the RADIUS server should authenticate against the existing network passwords, or if passwords should be created. Using the existing password file is easier from a management standpoint because there are fewer password files to maintain, and fewer username/password combinations for an attacker to guess. Users also prefer a single login to the RADIUS server and network. The downside is that if an attacker does manage to authenticate against the RADIUS server he or she now has full access to the network.

Unfortunately, this problem is compounded by the fact that many remote access tools allow users to save their username and password in the login box. An attacker who manages to get an employee's laptop will have full access to the network. As much of a pain as it may seem, it is generally better to separate the RADIUS username and password from the network authentication username and password combination. It should also be a policy that the two passwords be different.

7.3.3 Dial-Up ISP Security

A remote access VPN creates a whole new set of problems for security administrators, and extends the reach of the security policy. Users accessing the network through a dial-up ISP are the first part of that extension.

Remote users connecting to the network through a dial-up ISP add an element of uncertainty into the network security arena. Network administrators no longer have control over the entire network, and are less able to secure data. There are additional security considerations that need to be taken into account.

First and foremost among these unknowns is the dial-up ISP that remote users are using. Unlike local phone service, the federal government does not heavily regulate dial-up Internet access. The quality of service provided by dial-up ISPs varies greatly from one service to another, and the quality of security varies from ISP to ISP. If possible it is a good idea to select a national ISP, with a solid security reputation, especially if the organization will be contracting with them for many dial-up accounts. A representative from the ISP should be able to answer questions about the steps taken to secure the dial-up network and the data passing across it.

Many large ISPs also provide dial-up services. Providers such as AT&T, Sprint, WorldCom, and Level 3 all have dial-up service as well as high-speed connectivity. If the corporate provider has a dial-up backbone that meets the needs of an organization, signing up through them is usually a good idea—especially because they tend to have a very large dial footprint. While not as safe as a direct connection, knowing that dial-up users will be connecting to the same network as the corporate backbone provides some reassurance that the VPN data will be secure.

In addition to concerns about the security of the dial-up backbone, VPN administrators have to be concerned about the security of the systems connecting to the network. Dial-up ISP users are actually, relatively speaking, more secure than cable or DSL users, but there are precautions that need to be taken.

Many remote VPN users will connect using their company-assigned laptops. This is actually preferred in some ways; it means that the security precautions in place within the organization's network will continue to be in place while the user is dialed into the network. One thing that needs to be communicated very clearly to remote VPN users is that the computer in use still belongs to the organization, and should not be used for any personal activities. It is possible for a remote user to introduce a virus or worm, through the VPN, into the network. Limiting the outside activities the laptop is used for should help keep that from happening.

Some users already have their own computers at home, and would rather use those to access the network remotely. There is nothing inherently wrong with this, but these users should follow the same security precautions that are in place on the corporate network. If, as will be discussed in Chapter 14, there are minimum operating system standards in place in the corporate network, those minimum standards should be applied to remote systems as well.

Generally, this means that a home user should not be connecting to the network using a Windows 98 or Windows XP machine, for example. Home users connecting through dial-up ISPs should also be running an approved antivirus software program and should have the same security patches on their home system that are in place on the network.

A software-based personal firewall would also be useful for dial-up users to have. It may not need to be a requirement, but a program such as BlackICE Defender or ZoneAlarm from Zone Labs should provide ample protection for a dial-up user.

Finally, if possible the machine being used to connect to the corporate network should be a single use machine, or at least a machine used by one person. More households have multiple computers in the house, and with prices for fairly powerful home computers in the $700 price range, it is not an unreasonable request. A machine used by one person, who knows that the machine will be connecting into the corporate network, will be less likely to have viruses and worms that can be spread through the corporate network.

These steps will help bring remote machines into compliance with the security standards of the organization that, combined with the encryption discussed in later in this chapter, should make remote dial-up users as secure as the rest of the network, regardless of where they are connecting from.

7.4 DSL and Cable VPN Security

DSLs and cable modem access account for 20 percent of all home user Internet connections. Over the next few years that number is expected to grow significantly. Users like the speed and always-on connectivity that DSL and cable afford. Unfortunately, the speed and always-on connectivity can be security headaches for network administrators.

When a dial-up user connects, the computer is assigned a dynamic IP address by the dial-up ISP. Dial-up connections tend to be short, and any hidden application designed to use as much bandwidth as possible will cause a noticeable slowdown, causing the user to disconnect. DSL and cable Internet connections are different. Users are often assigned a dynamic IP address—though not always—but the connections are always on, so users stay connected longer, even when they are away from the computer for extended periods of time. Because there is more bandwidth available, users are also less likely to notice an application that is using a lot of bandwidth.

The problem with always-on consumer Internet access services is that subscribers are frequently subject to attacks. These are not attacks against a specific user; instead, the attacks tend to be random, searching for exploitable weaknesses. An attacker will conduct port scans against large blocks of IP addresses known to belong to DSL or cable Internet companies. When the attacker finds a known weakness, he or she will attempt to exploit the weakness, and gain access to the user's computer.

Once the attacker controls the computer, it can be used to launch DoS attacks, or the attacker can monitor activity to see if anything useful, like credit card information, is passed across the WAN. These types of attacks are particularly effective. DSL and cable networks generate so much traffic that ISPs are often unable to detect port scans launched against their networks. Subscribers to

DSL and cable Internet services generally have more money, therefore more powerful computers. Combine this with the high-speed, always-on connection, and you have the perfect launching platform for security attacks.

From a corporate security standpoint it is very important to be aware of these issues. It does not matter how secure the connection to an organization's VPN is if the machine accessing it has been compromised. An attacker sitting at a computer connected to the corporate VPN will be able to access the network as easily as the person using the computer.

As with dial-up ISP users, there are precautions that security and network administrators should take before allowing users to connect to a corporate VPN using a DSL or cable connection. If a user has a laptop issued by the organization, that should be the only machine used to connect to the VPN. Otherwise, users connecting into the network should be using one of the corporate-approved operating systems, with the most current patches installed. The users should also be running one of the approved virus scanners, with up-to-date virus definitions.

In addition to these security precautions, which are identical to the security precautions taken by dial-up ISP users, many organizations require DSL and cable Internet users to have an external firewall device on their home network. Often sold as a combination firewall and gateway router, these network devices generally retail for less than $200 and plug quickly into the network. While not nearly as secure as a full-fledged firewall, personal firewall devices serve as a mask for the computers connected to the DSL or cable ISP. The personal firewall assumes the IP address assigned by the ISP and performs a Network Address Translation (NAT) on all requests from the computers behind it, out to the Internet.

The advantage of this type of system is that these devices are not complex; therefore, they are less susceptible to security problems than an operating system. An attacker launching a port scan against one of these devices will not find any of the traditional operating system security holes and will, generally, not launch an attack against the system. Think of it like a car thief. If there are two identical cars next to each other, a car thief is going to choose the one that is unlocked with the keys in the ignition.

While personal firewalls are not a cure-all solution for problems facing DSL and cable Internet users, when combined with a fully patched system and updated virus software they provide a good level of security. These three layers of security should be enough assurance that DSL and cable Internet users are properly secured for VPN access to the network.

7.5 Encrypting Remote Sessions

Encryption is an integral part of the IP VPN process. While there are many ways to encrypt traffic over a VPN, there are three methods that are generally used. These methods—PPTP, L2TP, and IPSec—are considered standards, and all are extensively documented.

That being said, IP VPN is a growing area, and there are still lots of compatibility problems between different vendor implementations of these protocols. Before deciding on an IP VPN solution, ensure that all possible connectivity combinations have been thoroughly tested. If compatibility problems are found, report them to the respective vendors and ask for a resolution. In order for IP VPN to gain mass acceptance, it will be necessary for vendor interoperability to grow.

7.5.1 PPTP

The Point-to-Point Tunneling Protocol (PPTP) was specifically designed for the dial-up ISP market. Microsoft, in conjunction with Ascend, 3Com, ECI Telematics, and US Robotics, introduced PPTP in 1996 as a way for dial-up users to securely connect to a remote network.

PPTP runs over a PPP connection. A user connects to any ISP that accepts PPP connections, which is the currently accepted dial access standard protocol. Once the PPP connection has been established to the ISP, a connection is then made to the PPTP NAS located on the corporate network. Data can then be transmitted across the PPTP connection. PPTP will transport TCP, IPX, and NetBEUI packets across the VPN.

The official PPTP specification, outlined in RFC 1171/2637, uses TCP port 1723, and IANA assigned IP ID 47 for Generic Routing Encapsulation (GRE) protocol. PPTP clients are available for just about every major operating system including Windows, MacOS, Linux, Solaris, and BSD.

When PPTP was first introduced it came under a lot of fire. Bruce Schneier, president of Counterpane Systems, released a paper detailing some of the flaws with Microsoft's implementation of PPTP. Because Microsoft was the only major operating system vendor with a PPTP implementation at the time, security experts often derided the protocol. However, PPTP's ease of use and its ubiquity made it very popular with small businesses and network administrators. The problem with PPTP, in general, is that the specification does not outline minimum security precautions that a vendor should follow in order to implement it.

Microsoft is not the only company in which PPTP security weaknesses were found. In July 2001 Cisco issued a security warning indicating that it was possible to crash Cisco routers by issues malformed by PPTP packets. This bug is present in all versions of IOS 12.1, 12.2, and earlier. Routers are only susceptible to the attacks if PPTP is enabled, which it is not by default.

PPTP is a tunneling, not a transport, protocol. To transport data, PPTP uses GRE. GRE is defined in RFC 1701, RFC 1702, and RFC 2784. It can be used in conjunction with any protocol as a means of encapsulating data for transport, though PPTP is the most common association. PPTP is used to establish the tunnel, then PPP data packets are used to transmit the GRE encapsulated data.

PPTP has gained wide acceptance because of the support of Microsoft. A PPTP client has been bundled with all versions of Windows since Windows 98; a client was even made available for Windows 95. Unfortunately, the security vulnerabilities associated with the protocol have caused concern among security experts, who have largely abandoned it in favor of L2TP or IPSec.

7.5.2 L2TP

Cisco, Microsoft, Ascend Communications, and Redback Networks released the Layer 2 Tunneling Protocol (L2TP) as RFC 2661 in 1999. Like PPTP, L2TP was designed as a way to tunnel information across an Internet connection. Data is encrypted, and the destination address is hidden by the encryption, creating a secure connection.

The significant advantage that L2TP provides over PPTP is that L2TP can be used to encrypt traffic across ATM, SONET, Ethernet, and other means of data transport. L2TP is not limited to PPP connections only. L2TP uses UDP Port 1701 to send data across the tunnel. As with PPTP, L2TP is capable of encapsulating and tunneling non-IP packets, such as AppleTalk or

IPX. This makes L2TP very useful for joining disparate networks with different protocols.

L2TP, as with PPTP, is encryption agnostic. Tunnel traffic can be encrypted in any manner that is agreed upon by the user opening the tunnel and the tunnel terminator. While remaining encryption agnostic, both Microsoft and Cisco are pushing for tunnel encryption using IPSec. In November 2001, they released RFC 3193, which details the process of encrypting L2TP sessions using IPSec.

7.5.3 IPSec

IPSec is often lumped with PPTP and L2TP as a VLAN tunneling protocol. IPSec is not really a tunneling protocol; instead, it is a suite of protocols designed to extend the security of IP-based networks using authentication and encryption. One of the ways in which IPSec secures IP packets is through the use of the Encapsulation Security Payload (ESP) part of the IPSec header. ESP can act as a means to tunnel data, hence the confusion many people have with regard to IPSec and tunneling protocols.

IPSec gives vendors a wide range of security options; unfortunately, this also leads to interoperability problems between vendors. The IETF IPSec working group has set minimum standards of security for each aspect of the IPSec suite. The minimum levels of security do not provide enough protection for an enterprise environment. Most implementations of the IPSec suite should be able to negotiate security levels, but when dealing with different vendors this negotiation, and therefore the connection, may fail.

An IPSec packet consists of three portions:

1. IP header
2. Authentication header (AH)
3. ESP

The IP header is the same as a standard IP header, which allows IPSec packets to traverse the same equipment as traditional IP packets, without having to make any changes to the equipment.

An IPSec packet header will look similar to Figure 7.5. It is constructed the same way as a standard IP packet header. The fragment offset field is used to indicate the start of the ESP, and the protocol field lists ESP, instead of the usual TCP or UDP.

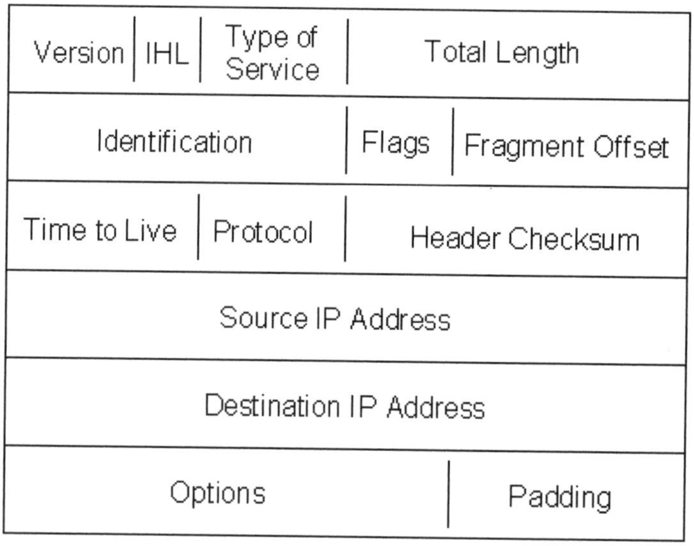

Figure 7.5   A typical IP packet header

The AH follows the IP header. The AH is used to authenticate information about the packet itself; it does not encrypt the data. The AH can be used with ESP, in tunneling mode, or by itself. It is optional.

The AH consists of six fields (outlined in Figure 7.6): They are: next header, payload length, reserved, security parameters index, sequence number, and authentication data. The purpose of each field is outlined in Table 7.1.

Table 7.1   Authentication Header Fields

FIELD	FUNCTION
Next Header	Indicates the protocol that follows the AH
Payload Length	The length of the AH
Reserved	Future use; currently set to 0
Security Parameters Index	Security parameter used in the datastream
Sequence Number	Used to keep packets in order
Authentication Data	Key, or other form of authentication

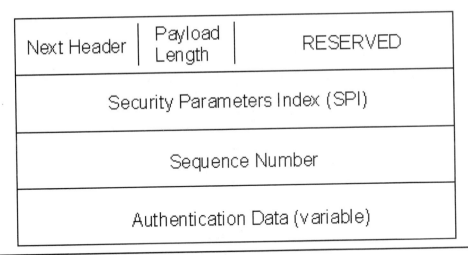

Next Header	Payload Length	RESERVED
Security Parameters Index (SPI)		
Sequence Number		
Authentication Data (variable)		

Figure 7.6   IPSec authentication header

The authentication header uses either SHA-1 or MD5 one-way hash algorithm for protection of the data. The next header field refers to either a TCP or UDP protocol, or ESP, when AH is used in conjunction with ESP.

The ESP will either follow the AH or it will come directly after the IP header if there is no AH. The ESP contains the data being transmitted, as well as the protocol information (TCP or UDP).

There are two levels of security with the ESP. The entire payload is authenticated in the same manner as the AH and the payload data is encrypted, providing two layers of data integrity protection within the payload. There are seven fields within the ESP: SPI, sequence number, payload data, padding, pad length, next header, and authentication data.

The SPI, sequence number, and authentication data function in the same manner as they do in the AH. The only difference is that the authentication data field in the ESP is optional, whereas it is required within the AH.

The payload data is a variable-length field that contains the data information. As mentioned previously, this field is encrypted. Encryption information for the data is found in the SPI.

Padding, pad length, and next header are all optional fields that are used for encryption. Up to 255 bytes of padding can be added to the ESP to fill space left

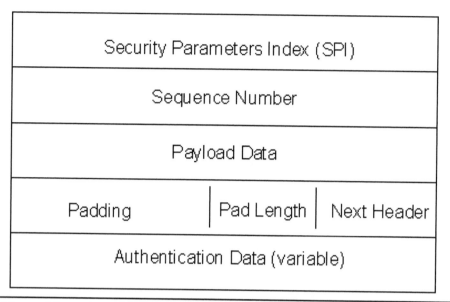

Figure 7.7   The IPSec ESP

over by the payload data. It can be used to either align the authentication data to a four-byte boundary or to create additional space when an encryption algorithm requires that plain text be the multiple of some number of bytes. The breakdown of these fields is shown in Figure 7.7.

IPSec can be used for tunneling in one of two ways:

1. The ESP allows a tunnel to be created simply using the IPSec suite. The ESP transmits encrypted data while encapsulating the original source and destination IP address within the payload data.

2. IPSec can be used as the encryption protocol for other protocols, such as L2TP and PPTP.

As vendor interoperability improves, IPSec will most likely become the default VPN protocol.

7.6 The VPN on the Network

There is some debate about the best place to terminate a VPN. Part of the debate originates from the fact that there are so many devices available for VPN termination. There are three common termination points for VPNs: router, firewall, and dedicated VPN device.

Each one has advantages and disadvantages. The right method of VPN termination is largely dependent on available resources, network design, and comfort level.

7.6.1 Terminating the VPN on the Router

Terminating the VPN on the router is not very common for enterprise networks. As already demonstrated, routers have notoriously bad logging facilities, and rely on external logging sources to log information. Adding the burden of encrypting and decrypting VPN information may overwhelm some routers.

For example, Cisco has introduced a VPN module for its 2600 series routers. The 2600 router, generally used for terminating T1s, with the VPN module requires a minimum of 128 megabytes (MB) of random access memory (RAM).

A second problem is with the firewall rule set. Additional rules will need to be added to the firewall to allow VPN terminated traffic into the network. This may raise security concerns.

Some vendors have resolved this problem by incorporating the VPN, firewall, and router into a single device. This type of access device may work well for small networks, but they are generally underpowered for large networks. In addition, having all three services in the same device removes two layers of security. If a hole into the network is found, there is not another layer of protection.

As previously mentioned, VPN termination to a router requires that the router be equipped to handle VPN terminations. This involves encrypting and decrypting connections, and, depending on the number of VPN connections, can put a significant drain on CPU and memory resources.

Shown in Figure 7.8, the VPN terminates at the edge router. The authentication request is forwarded to a NAS server, similar to the way TACACS+ or RADIUS works. The NAS server authenticates the user, and the user is granted access to the network.

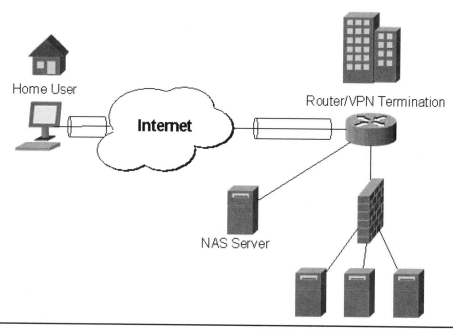

Figure 7.8   VPN termination at the edge router. A VPN connection is made to the router, which forwards the request onto the NAS. The NAS authenticates the user, who is now allowed access to the network.

Figure 7.8 also illustrates the biggest problem with this approach: The user now has to get past the firewall. Unfortunately, there is not always an easy way to allow this, without creating rule sets that are so broad that they are essentially useless.

Again, terminating the VPN at the router may be a good idea for a small network, or a home user—who does not want to use a VPN client—but for an enterprise network router, terminated VPNs are generally not a good idea.

7.6.2 Terminating the VPN on the Firewall

Firewall termination of VPNs has become very popular recently. Cisco PIX, Check Point, and NetScreen all have products that allow their firewalls to become VPN terminating devices.

The pairing of VPN and firewalls makes sense for several reasons. The firewall already performs extensive logging of network connections; adding the

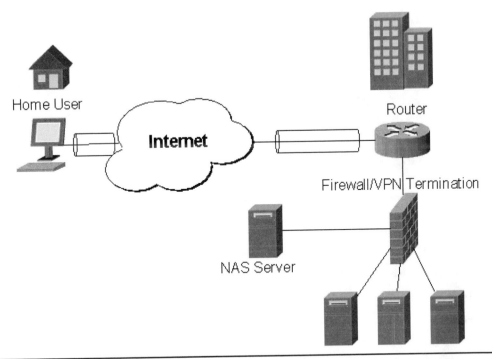

Figure 7.9   The VPN from the user into the company network is terminated at the firewall. The firewall receives the authentication request and forwards it to the NAS server, which handles the actual authentication process.

additional logging of VPN connections should not create an excessively large load. Firewalls are also the entry point to the network; having a VPN terminate at the firewall means that users can have network access without having to open additional holes in the firewall rule set.

The termination of a VPN at the firewall level operates in much the same way as the termination of a VPN at the router level. A user makes a connection to the firewall. The firewall forwards the authentication to a NAS server. The NAS server authenticates the user, and the firewall grants the user access to the network. This process is outlined in Figure 7.9.

Firewall termination gives a network administrator much more control. Users terminated at the firewall can be restricted to only a certain part of the network, and firewall termination means that no holes have to be opened in the firewall for users already authenticated.

One of the downsides that plagues this type of connection is the same problem that router terminated VPN connections have: The VPN encryption/decryption process uses significant system resources. A firewall that is already burdened, especially one with an active DMZ, may be crushed under the weight of managing hundreds of simultaneous VPN tunnels.

A firewall-terminated VPN solution is appropriate for an enterprise organization. However traffic patterns should be monitored closely to ensure the firewall is not being overloaded with VPN tunnels.

7.6.3 Terminating the VPN to a Dedicated Device

Some companies prefer to use a dedicated VPN device, rather than a combination VPN and router, or a VPN and firewall device. Cisco, Nortel, AppGate, Lucent, and Check Point—among others—all make dedicated VPN devices or software that can run on a dedicated VPN device.

Dedicated devices have several advantages, the primary one being that they take the load of managing the VPN off the router and the firewall. A purpose-built device is now handling the encryption and decryption process, so even if it does become overburdened by too many connections, it will not impact the rest of the network.

A second advantage is that it creates another layer of security in the VPN process. Rather than risk having tunnels terminated at the router or firewall, they are terminated within the network, where administrators have more control (Figure 7.10). Termination inside the network gives network administrators the ability to restrict traffic to certain parts of the network, limiting the damage an attacker can do should the VPN be breached.

Figure 7.10 illustrates the process of terminating a VPN to a dedicated device. The user authenticates against the dedicated device. The VPN device can either handle the authentication process, or forward the request to a NAS. If the authentication of the user is successful, the user has access to the network. Again, the part of the network the user has access to can be controlled by the network administrators.

While VPN devices provide a lot of benefits, there are minuses. The chief concern is that it is another network device that has to be managed, and monitored, for software upgrades and potential security holes. Security holes in a VPN device are of particular concern, because if they can be exploited they

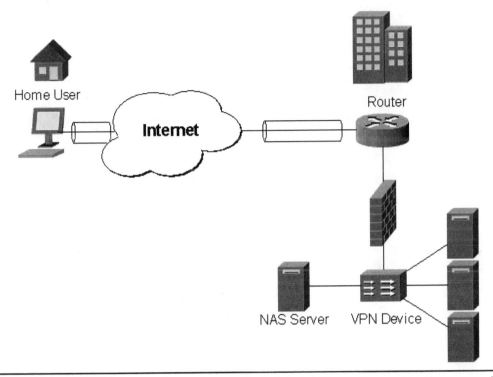

Figure 7.10   VPN is terminated to a dedicated device. Depending on the placement of the device within the network, the user can be restricted to certain areas once authenticated.

may give an attacker access to an entire network. In addition, there may be software management involved. Most of these dedicated devices include software that can be used to create the tunnels. This software has to be distributed and installed on machines of users who will connect to the VPN. Upgrades and patch installations of the software will also have to be maintained. This can often be avoided by taking advantage of the tunneling software bundled with an operating system. However, if there are connectivity problems between a user and a VPN device, the user may be forced to use the vendor-supplied tunneling software.

Dedicated VPN devices also require creating additional holes in the corporate firewall. Ports have to be opened to allow either PPTP or L2TP tunnels through the firewall and into the network. While this does not pose much of a security concern, any time additional traffic has to be allowed through the firewall should be cause for concern.

Finally, there is the cost factor associated with dedicated VPN devices. A VPN device that can maintain the number of connections required by an enterprise network can cost in excess of $10,000, double that number if redundancy is desired. That cost will increase as the popularity of the corporate VPN increases.

A dedicated VPN solution does offer an excellent solution for organizations that desire a robust and scalable solution, which will not impact the rest of the network. As with any other decision, it is important to explore all options and assess potential traffic patterns thoroughly before making a decision.

7.7 Summary

As the popularity of IP VPNs increases, and they become more commonplace in the network, the security issues surrounding them are going to take on increased importance. A VPN can extend the reach of a network and increase productivity.

Unfortunately, a VPN also increases the security risk to an organization. For a VPN to be properly implemented, the security policy of an organization has to be adjusted to take into account the machines of home users, as well as the method by which the users connect to the VPN. A single tunneling protocol should be chosen and standardized across the organization.

Finally, the placement of the VPN on the network has to be taken into consideration as well as what device will handle the VPN termination.

8

Wireless
Wide Area Networks

Wireless networks have become very popular in recent years, with good reason: They are usually less expensive than traditional wired networks to implement, plus a wireless network can be quickly deployed anywhere, making it attractive to companies with a mobile or rapidly expanding workforce.

As with wired networks, there are two types of wireless networks: LAN and WAN. This chapter covers some of the security issues related to WANs, and the next chapter covers potential security problems with wireless LANs. It is important to understand that wireless networking technologies are rapidly evolving. Some of the concerns raised in these two chapters will undoubtedly be addressed in the near future. As with any other technology, it is important to discuss security concerns with your vendor before implementing a wireless network.

Wireless WAN technology has two primary uses:

1. Connecting to the Internet
2. Connecting offices that are dispersed throughout a city

Wireless WANs have emerged as a low-cost alternative to a traditional methods of Internet access. Wireless WAN connections can offer the same amount of bandwidth as a T1, at a fraction of the cost. Wireless connections are also being deployed in areas where cable and DSL access is not available.

From a service provider perspective wireless access is especially nice, because the service provider has end-to-end control of the deployment process. Setting up a DSL account for a customer can involve more than a month of waiting for the ILEC to install and test the line, then direct that line to the service provider's equipment. In addition, if there is a problem, there is often a lot of finger pointing between the service provider and the ILEC as to where the problem lies.

DSL can also be significantly more expensive to deploy than wireless access and provides less reach. When a service provider offers DSL, equipment has to be provisioned in every CO that serves the area in which the provider wants to offer service. Even after installing the equipment, DSL can realistically only be offered to homes and offices within 21,000 feet of the CO. Generally this is enough to serve about 70 percent of the people within the area.

Wireless access, on the other hand, has a much greater service area. Depending on the terrain, and the type of service offered, a receiver placed on a high enough tower could serve a radius of 35 miles, often more than the area covered by four or five COs. This allows a provider to cover the same area with wireless access for one-fifth the cost of deploying DSL.

The contrast is even more apparent when comparing wireless access to a traditional T1. In addition to higher costs associated with T1s in general, there is the local loop charge that has to be paid to the ILEC. Local loop charges can be more than $300 over the cost of the actual T1. With wireless connections the ILEC is out of the picture, so there are no local loop charges. In addition to the lower cost, customers of the service provider benefit from the fact that they only have to deal with one company in the event of a failure. As with DSL, the ISP owns every aspect of the connectivity, so if there is a problem, there is only one point of contact.

The other use of wireless networking is connecting offices that are dispersed throughout a city. It is not uncommon for a company to outgrow its existing office and look for additional space. Often the company does not want to interrupt business by moving everyone, or the company is unable to find enough space in a single location to accommodate all employees. The company may also be unable to get out of their existing lease. Whatever the reasons, a company may find itself with three or four offices spread throughout a relatively small area.

In situations like this, you still want the employees in the remote office to have access to the servers and facilities in the main office, where server administrators reside. Creating a VPN, as discussed in Chapter 7, is the generally accepted way to do this. Unfortunately, with a VPN and three offices, you are generally paying for three Internet connections, maintaining three firewalls, and administering three routers. Alternatively the company has to pay a monthly fee for two private lines to the main headquarters.

Wireless connectivity can be especially useful in this situation. Rather than paying a monthly fee for private lines, a company can run its own wireless connections, which bypass both the ILEC and the ISP. This type of VPN often has a higher initial cost, but because there are no recurring monthly costs to outside organizations—assuming the company has the in-house expertise to manage the wireless network devices—the overall cost savings is substantial.

Wireless networks do have their problems; the most notable and often talked about is their inability to function in severe weather conditions. Depending on the technology used, wireless networks have a tendency to fail, or significantly reduce their capacity and distance capabilities during rain, fog, or snow. The second most commonly mentioned problem is their lack of compatibility, and how quickly the architecture is progressing. The speed and distance capabilities of wireless WANs have increased dramatically in the last couple of years, and growth is expected to continue. Unfortunately, this often means buying new equipment every couple of years to keep pace with the new technology. Contrast this with Ethernet, or frame relay, both of which have remained relatively constant.

Given the importance of an interoffice VPN, or a company's Internet connection, a wireless network may not be the best solution. Check with your wireless equipment vendor, and follow up with independent sources to determine how their equipment will perform during extreme weather conditions, how it interoperates with other equipment, and what sort of upgrade paths the vendor offers to avoid equipment obsolescence after a couple of years.

8.1 Wireless WAN Security Issues

Securing wireless WANs poses problems that are unique in some ways, but essentially the same as those network administrators face when trying to secure landline connections. The security issues that surround wireless WANs are:

- Transmission
- Equipment

These are the same issues that have been faced throughout the book; the only difference is the medium. Because wireless transmissions are broadcast over airwaves, it is possible for anyone to monitor transmissions, without physical access to any part of your network. This is an important distinction. Up until this point, for an attacker to gain access to your data, he or she had to have physical access to either a machine on your network or a machine on the backbone of your ISP. That barrier no longer exists. An attacker with a wireless network card and some rudimentary knowledge of how a wireless system is deployed may be able to monitor all traffic traversing the network.

Before delving into fixed wireless Internet access, it is important to understand how the technology works. Most forms of fixed wireless Internet access use the radio frequency (RF) spectrum to communicate. The RF spectrum is actually a broad range of microwave frequencies, ranging from 500 KHz to 300 GHz. Some common devices that use RF spectrum are cellular phones, cordless phones, televisions, AM and FM radios, and microwave ovens.

Frequencies within the RF spectrum are licensed by the Federal Communications Commission (FCC) in the United States, and by the International Telecommunications Union (ITU) for the rest of the world. This disparity often leads to devices in the United States operating at different frequencies than the same devices in the rest of the world.

Not all frequencies within the RF spectrum require licensing. Some frequencies have been set aside as license free, the most common of which is the Industrial, Scientific, and Medical (ISM) band. ISM frequencies (Table 8.1) are the ones most commonly used by fixed wireless Internet access equipment.

The two most common forms of fixed wireless Internet access are Multichannel Multipoint Distribution Services (MMDS) and Local Multipoint Distribution Services (LMDS). MMDS and LMDS can both operate in the licensed or

Table 8.1   ISM Frequency Bands

ISM Start Frequency	ISM End Frequency
902 MHz	928 MHz
2.4 GHz	2.4835 GHz
5.725 GHz	5.85 GHz

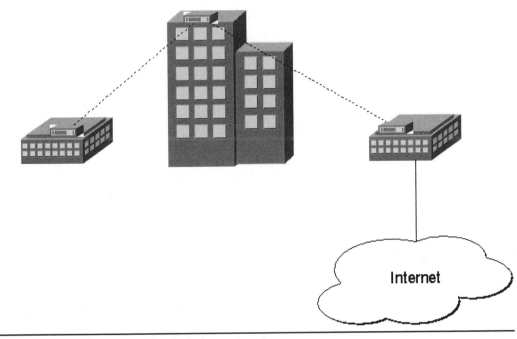

Figure 8.1   A typical fixed wireless network

the unlicensed ISM frequencies, though most providers operate them in the unlicensed frequencies.

MMDS and LMDS fixed wireless Internet connections generally operate in the same way. An antenna is placed on the roof of an office, or on a pole outside of an office. That antenna is pointed to either a tower or the roof of a tall building, where the ISP has stored a WMTS. The WMTS forwards data to another WMTS on the roof of the ISP's building. The WMTS is connected to a router, which forwards traffic out to the Internet (Figure 8.1).

8.1.1 MMDS Technology

MMDS was originally developed in the 1980s as a way to serve wireless cable television customers. The first use of MMDS technology was in 1984, in Bessemer, Michigan. Wireless cable distribution never really took off in the United States; the total number of MMDS cable subscribers never surpassed much more than 250,000. MMDS television delivery has had more success in other countries.

The television roots of MMDS are important for understanding how the technology involved into Internet-access use. When MMDS was initially developed, the FCC allocated eight channels, distributed in blocks of four. This meant that a wireless cable company was only able to deliver four channels of programming to its subscribers. Because more is better in the cable TV industry, MMDS-based cable companies petitioned the FCC for more channel allocation, leading to the current frequency distribution, which can support up to 31 channels.

MMDS television was most popular in rural areas not served by cable television companies, which helps to explain why MMDS Internet access has its roots in rural areas. In 1996, when the Telecommunications Act passed, many companies began acquiring MMDS licenses to offer phone and data services in these rural areas. While MMDS still has not caught on as a phone service, it is becoming a predominant force in the fixed wireless industry with support from both WorldCom and Sprint.

MMDS operates in the 2.5–2.7 GHz frequencies. The receivers are generally omni-directional, allowing connections from all sides, and because MMDS operates at a relatively low frequency, it is fairly resistant to atmospheric conditions and a single antenna can serve a large area—up to a 35-mile radius.

The big drawback to MMDS technology is the bandwidth. MMDS is generally limited to 1.5 megabits of download, about the speed of a T1. MMDS is also asymmetrical, which means that the upload speeds are generally slower than the download speeds. While a company may get 1.5 megabits of download throughput, upload throughput is often capped at 128 kilobits—the equivalent of a bonded ISDN line.

Companies support MMDS for a wireless system because it is relatively cheap to deploy. A single antenna, placed high enough, can serve a large area, minimizing the initial cost of deployment. MMDS antennas can also be linked. An ISP can route a connection through multiple antennas before sending it out on the Internet. This allows the ISP to save on bandwidth costs, by having a single backbone connection support several antennas. It also allows an ISP to set up redundant connectivity for its customers. A ring of wireless antennas can be created to serve an area, providing fault tolerance for the data transmission, and even multiple points of connectivity for the ISP's customers. Figure 8.2 demonstrates this ring.

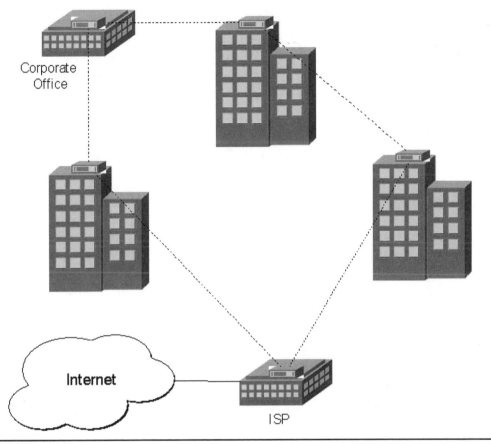

Figure 8.2   Using multiple MMDS antennas to provide network redundancy

8.1.2 LMDS Technology

Like MMDS, LMDS is a fixed wireless solution. This means that the two communicating devices—the antennas—are stationary, as opposed to a mobile wireless solution. Despite the fact that it is a fixed wireless solution, the technology behind LMDS is similar to cellular technology, though it also was originally designed for wireless cable television.

LMDS operates in the 28–31 GHz frequencies and was originally licensed by the FCC in 1998 to companies that planned to use the spectrum to provide two-way communications, such as telephone, television, and Internet access.

LMDS has a smaller range than MMDS, offering only a five-mile radius of communication, and only about 2.5 miles of full bandwidth capabilities. It is also much more susceptible to weather and other disruptions than MMDS.

The advantages that LMDS provides over MMDS are generally a lower cost per access antenna to deploy and the higher frequencies allow a provider to offer more bandwidth per user. LMDS providers can offer 10 megabits of download and two megabits of upload throughput.

Because of the limited reach of LMDS, and strict line of sight requirements, LMDS tends to be deployed in urban, or business areas, where there is a high concentration of potential customers.

8.1.3 Wireless Encryption

By default, fixed wireless transmissions are secured using spread spectrum technology (SST). Spread spectrum technology, discussed in detail in the next section, has one serious limitation: It does not encrypt the data. Of course, the majority of Internet traffic is not encrypted over wire line connections.

The difference is that data over a wire line connection is transmitted over a closed connection. Assuming that your ISP has taken reasonable security steps[1] data should be secure while it transmits across the ISP's backbone. At the very least, it is relatively difficult for an attacker to gain access to an ISP's backbone and sniff traffic.

A wireless connection, on the other hand, can be sniffed by anyone with an antenna. Because wireless connections are transmitted across a spectrum of frequencies, just like FM signals, it is possible for an attacker with an antenna and a similar network device to "tune in" to a site and sniff transmissions from a device to the WMTS.

The best way to enhance transmission security between a corporate site and the WMTS is to encrypt it. Fortunately, wireless manufacturers have developed a system based on the cable security standard Data Over Cable Service Interface Specification (DOCSIS), called DOCSIS+ or wireless DOCSIS.

Using DOCSIS+, an ISP can force encrypted traffic between the WMTS and the user's modem. DOCSIS+ supports several different types of key management encryption including X.509 digital certificates, RSA public key

---

1. If it has not, you should find a different ISP.

encryption, and 3-DES encryption. The WMTS sets the encryption policy; the end-user modems are forced to comply, or the WMTS will not the accept data. This serves two purposes: (1) it prevents attackers from being able to view data and (2) it prevents unauthorized users from attempting to use the WMTS to gain unauthorized access to the ISP's backbone.

The limitation of the DOCSIS+ protocol is that it is not currently interoperable between equipment. An Alvarion access point may not necessarily be able to send DOCSIS+ encrypted data to a Cisco WMTS. As the DOCSIS+ protocol becomes more developed, interoperability should improve.

8.2 Spread Spectrum Technology

As mentioned previously, the most common form of security provided for fixed wireless Internet access is SST. SST was originally developed for the military so that wireless military transmissions could be broadcast without fear of an enemy deciphering the communication or jamming the signal.

SST is a wideband RF technology. It converts the narrowband fixed wireless signal and outputs a wideband signal. The WMTS receives the wideband signal and converts it back to a narrowband and pieces the information back together. When the narrowband signal is distributed over a wideband signal, it scrambles the data, making it difficult for any device that does not have the conversion information to piece it back together.

Because of the way SST divides the signal, a random observer would see a modem-to-WMTS transmission as noise. In other words, it makes it difficult for someone to randomly pick up on transmissions. Instead, an attacker has to make a conscious effort to track down and decode your signal.

To get an idea of how SST works, imagine a 20-page report. Each page of that report is a data packet. Now, run the 20-page report through a wood chipper.[2] The wood chipper provides the same function as SST; it cuts up the document and spreads it out over the yard. On the other side of your yard, you have a reverse wood chipper; it catches the debris from your report and restores it to its original shape. This function is performed by the WMTS in a wireless transaction.

---

2. Warning: Do not actually do this unless you have a backup of the report.

SST does a great job of scrambling the data, and makes it very difficult for an attacker to sniff data through the air, because the attacker has to know how the wireless modem distributed the data, in order to start piecing it back together. Understand, that with enough equipment, and some information about the make and model of your wireless networking equipment, it is very possible for an attacker to do just that. Once the SST has been decoded it is possible for the attacker to intercept all unencrypted transmissions, without the knowledge of the network administrators.

Three types of SST are commonly deployed:

1. Frequency-hopping spread spectrum (FHSS)
2. Direct-sequence spread spectrum (DSSS)
3. Code-Division Multiple Access (CDMA)

When FHSS is deployed, a signal will hop from frequency to frequency over a period of time. The current standard is that the signal will switch frequencies at no longer than 400 millisecond intervals. Current standards also dictate that a signal must hop between at least 75 different frequencies. The WMTS must know the intervals at which the origination modem will be hopping frequencies, and the set of frequencies that will be used, so data can be pieced back together properly.

DSSS accomplishes the same thing as FHSS, but in a different manner. With DHSS the signal from the originating modem is joined with a higher rate bit sequence, sometimes called a chirping code. This chirping code is then spread across the spectrum in a manner similar to FHSS. The chirping code provides redundant information about the data, making the transmission less susceptible to atmospheric interference and providing an extra level of redundancy. DSSS technology is generally used for high-speed fixed wireless connections, while FHSS technology is used for lower speed connections.

CDMA is most often associated with the cellular telephone industry. In fact, CDMA is so common within the cellular industry that it is often thought of as synonymous with SST. CDMA converts data in the same manner that FHSS and DSSS do, but it spreads the signal through far fewer frequencies than FHSS and DSSS. To compensate for the smaller signal distribution CDMA generates fake noise. The signal is still distributed along the narrower band, but extra noise is added to the band, making the signal more difficult to detect than the signals from FHSS and DSSS devices. In addition to the enhanced security CDMA also digitizes the data, allowing for a mostly digital transmission from the modem to the WMTS. These two enhancements allow modem manufacturers to squeeze more bandwidth from a CDMA-enabled modem.

The different types of SST are useful for different types of fixed wireless connections. While CDMA is increasingly becoming more popular, it is not a fully accepted standard. If your company is deploying a fixed wireless Internet solution, find out from your provider what type of equipment is in use, and what type of SST is supported.

8.3 Location

Location is very important in fixed wireless environments for two reasons: accessibility and security. It is important to keep both of these objectives in mind when determining where to place both the antenna and the wireless modem.

Accessibility is generally the primary concern of fixed wireless Internet users, especially those using LMDS technology. If the antenna does not have clear line of sight to the ISP's WMTS, the connection is rendered useless.

Oftentimes, the need for line of sight access to the WMTS means that the antenna will have to be placed on the roof of the building, or on a pole several feet from the building. When the antenna is placed in remote areas like this, a cable is usually run to the modem, which is stored somewhere inside the building. In order to maximize accessibility, it is a good idea to work with the manufacturer of the wireless modem to determine the maximum distance that the modem can be from the antenna before unacceptable signal degradation begins to occur.[3] Obviously, it is not very effective to have a clear line of sight, but have the modem placed so far away that the signal fades.

NOTE

One way to improve wireless network performance is through the use of better cabling. Using better cabling, such as LMR-400 coaxial cable, can help reduce the signal degradation experienced.

---

3. Signal degradation begins the moment the signal travels through the coupler to the RF cable.

A second concern is equipment security. Whenever possible, a wireless modem should be locked in the same closet as other routing equipment. As with routers and switches, an attacker who has direct access to a wireless modem can either sniff traffic directly from the modem, or can use the modem manufacturer's information to develop strategies for sniffing data.

Some companies will store the modem in the same location as the antenna, generally on a rooftop, as a way to keep the signal strength strong. From the roof, an Ethernet cable is run to the network. There is nothing inherently wrong with this, as long as proper security precautions are taken. The modem itself should be locked up in such a way that it is protected from both atmospheric conditions and from potential attackers. Someone lurking on the rooftop should not be able to determine the equipment manufacturer, and if possible, a fence should be built to enclose both the modem and the antenna.

As with any other piece of network equipment, default passwords on the modem should be changed, and the number of employees who have access to it should be limited.

8.4 Summary

Fixed wireless Internet access is growing in popularity because it is generally less expensive and quicker to deploy than similar landline technologies. Fixed wireless technologies are improving at a very fast rate, making them attractive to cost-conscious companies.

It is important to remember that while there are some special concerns with fixed wireless Internet access, they are really no different than the concerns for landline access. If the same precautions that are followed for landline connectivity are followed for wireless connectivity, fixed wireless Internet access can be as secure as landline Internet access.

9

Wireless
Local Area Networks

Wireless LANs as part of an enterprise network are increasing in popularity. Users enjoy the freedom of being able to use a laptop anywhere in a building or on campus. It doesn't hurt that a WLAN can be very cost effective. Of course, there are serious security issues associated with WLANs. The freedom that a WLAN provides users can also become an easy way for an attacker to gain access to an organization's network. Attackers often target WLANs because, like routers, network administrators deploy them without considering the security implications. Even worse, a network user may deploy an unauthorized access point—sometimes called a rogue access point—without informing network administrators.

The generally accepted standard for WLAN connections, as defined by IEEE, is 802.11. The 802.11 specification only defines the physical layer and MAC address portion of wireless Ethernet. It is based on the IEEE Ethernet Standard, 802.3, so WLANs are designed to be an extension of a network, although even a peer-to-peer WLAN will support any protocol that normally runs over Ethernet. As with most standards, the interoperability of network devices does not always work as advertised, but as the technology matures, the level of communication between network devices is improving.

There are three important physical layer series within the 802.11 protocol: 802.11b, 802.11a, and 802.11g. Series are different ways of implementing the 802.11 standard. Wireless network cards have to conform to these individual series in order to speak with other WLAN network interfaces in the same series.

Table 9.1   802.11 Spectrum by Region

REGION	SPECTRUM
Europe	2.4000–2.4835 GHz
France	2.4465–2.4835 GHz
Japan	2.4710–2.4970 GHz
Spain	2.4450–2.4750 GHz
United States	2.4000–2.4835 GHz

802.11b is, by far, the market leader. It operates at 11 megabits per second (Mps) and uses the 2.4 GHz spectrum, though the bands within the spectrum vary depending on the region in which the WLAN is deployed. 802.11 protocols use DSSS and FHSS to communicate in the ISM unlicensed 2.4 GHz spectrum. The actual spectrum used depends on where the equipment is being deployed. Each country can define certain frequencies within the 2.4 GHz frequency for use in wireless networks. Table 9.1 lists the bands by region.

The 802.11a standard was ratified in 1999; however, products did not begin shipping in volume until 2002. The 802.11a series operates in the 5 GHz spectrum, and has 8 available radio channels for data to travel on. 802.11a compliant cards support data rates up to 54 Mbs. Because 802.11a and 802.11b cards operate in different spectrums, they are not compatible.

A third series, 802.11g, operates in both the 2.4 GHz and 5.0 GHz spectrums. It is backward compatible with the 802.11b series, but operates at speeds up to 54 Mbs, just like 802.11a.

NOTE

The Wireless Ethernet Compatibility Alliance (WECA) was formed to test the interoperability of WLAN devices. As WECA continues to perform tests and certify products, expect compatibility between devices to improve and prices to fall.

WLAN design is fairly simple. Users with wireless network cards using compatible protocols can either connect to each other in a flat network, or plug into an access port. If the users are tied into an access point, they can connect to it as long as they are within 300 feet—farther with an antenna. In a large building or campus, multiple access points can be strategically placed to provide continuous network connectivity throughout the organization.

In cases where an access point is used, it acts as a bridge between the WLAN devices and the network. The access point emits a signal from an omnidirectional antenna attached to it. WLAN devices using the same 802.11 series pick up the signal and make a connection to the access point. The access point can either assign an IP address from its pool or forward the request to a network-based DHCP server. The WLAN device accepts the IP address and begins transmitting clear-text data to the access point. The access point, acting as any bridge, forwards the data to the network and returns any responses to the originating network devices.

The basic security problem facing WLANs is the same one facing wireless WANs: An attacker no longer has to be within the premises to launch an attack. With a traditional wired network an attacker either has to be inside the building to connect to a network port or to figure out a way to bypass router, firewall, and server security to break into the network remotely. A wireless attack, sometimes known as a "drive-by hacking," doesn't involve being on the physical premises and it doesn't involve bypassing the network edge security measures. Instead, the attacker launches the attack from within the network, where there tend to be fewer obstacles to a successful attack, because security is generally lighter inside the trusted network.

NOTE

An unofficial survey conducted by Ziff-Davis reporters in April 2002 revealed that 61 percent of all wireless networks had little to no security protection enabled.

Wireless attacks work in this fashion because a wireless access point broadcasts its signal in a radius. WLAN technologies do not require line of sight, unlike LMDS or MMDS, so the signal spreads out irrespective of any walls,

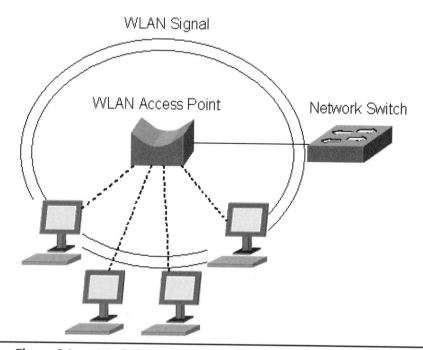

Figure 9.1   A typical WLAN design. Multiple workstations connect to an access point, which plugs into the network. The access point forwards traffic to and from the workstations and the rest of the network.

floors, or ceilings that may be in its path. This means an attacker standing outside of the office building, with the right equipment, may be able to receive the wireless signal and use that information to gain access to the network.

In fact, there are tools, such as AirSnort, that have been developed to scan for wireless network signals. These tools allow a remote computer to listen to particular channels for WLAN signals (Figure 9.1). Once a signal is located, AirSnort will collect the data as it is transmitted through the air. A WLAN sniffer is different than a normal network sniffer in that the attacker does not have to belong to the network in order to use it. In other words, normally an attacker attempting to sniff a network would have to be attached to that network, either by being plugged directly into a switch or by compromising a server on the network. Someone attempting to sniff a WLAN does not have the same constraints. In a manner similar to reporters who monitor police channels, an attacker can monitor WLAN traffic without participants of the WLAN knowing.

NOTE

AirSnort is available for Linux platform and can be downloaded from the AirSnort website: *airsnort.shmoo.com/*

Figure 9.2 illustrates how an attacker could monitor WLAN network traffic, using a laptop, with a wireless network card. To increase the reach of the laptop, the attacker can attach an omni-directional antenna to extend signal strength up to three times the normal reach of an access point. Remember—and this is very important—an attacker does not have to be part of the network in order to monitor it. This is especially important to keep in mind when plan-

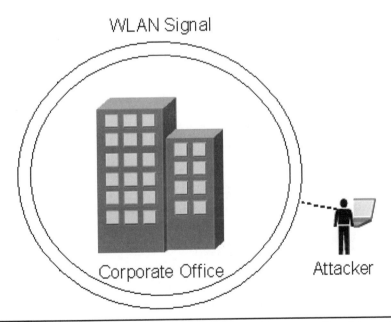

Figure 9.2   An attacker is able to use a WLAN sniffer to monitor data on the wireless network, even though the attacker is not attached to the network

ning the security of the WLAN. Truthfully, an attacker does not even need a laptop. There are programs available that will convert either a Palm or a Pocket PC handheld computer into a wireless network sniffer. These tools are designed to help administrators secure a WLAN, but attackers can use them just as effectively.

9.1 Access Point Security

WLAN security starts with the access point. The remainder of this chapter discusses ways of securing communications between the end users and the network, but those steps are pointless if an attacker can easily compromise the access point.

Location is the first step that needs to be taken to secure an access point, or a series of access points. The access point has to be physically secured, so that it is not easily accessible by an attacker. If possible, access points should be mounted within the ceiling and stored inside a locked cage to prevent unauthorized direct access and removal.

Access points should be located toward the center of a building, so the signal weakens by the time it gets to the perimeter. If an organization has multiple buildings and is trying to set up a WLAN throughout the campus, it may be difficult to limit the signal to the interior of the buildings. In cases like this, steps should be taken to ensure the security of the campus itself, preventing unauthorized users from accessing the grounds.[1]

Proximity and physical security are not enough. If keys and other filters are to be stored on the access points, access to them should be limited. This presents a real problem for most WLAN administrators, because many access points ship with management tools that are inherently insecure. Access points generally rely on one of three methods for configuration: HTTP, Telnet, and SNMP. The security flaws in Telnet and HTTP are well known: All data is sent clear text. SNMP suffers from many of the same security problems as Telnet and HTTP; SNMP will be discussed in Chapter 16.

Whenever possible HTTP, Telnet, and SNMP should be disabled on access points, and other methods of access should be used (e.g., HTTPS or SSH). If a vendor does not support a secure method of control for an access point, then

---

1. Especially unknown users carrying a laptop and several high-gain antennas.

connections to the access points should be made only over the wired network segment, as opposed to the wireless segment. The risk still exists that an attacker has compromised the network and is scanning for password, however, if that is the case, wireless access points are going to be a very low priority target.

Finally a scan should be periodically made of all access points to look for unauthorized traffic, and, more importantly, unauthorized access points. Occasionally a user, or a group within an organization, will set up a WLAN without informing the IT department. These may be set up in a lab, or as a way to add more computers to the network; there are many reasons. Chances are these users are not aware of the steps necessary to fully secure a WLAN, and may inadvertently be allowing unauthorized traffic into the network.

Oftentimes, security measures in place on the wired network will prevent an unauthorized access point from bridging a rogue WLAN to the network, but it is still possible that one may have slipped through. Software products from IBM (Wireless Security Auditor) and Netaphor Software (PDAlert) can be installed on handheld devices equipped with an 802.11b-compliant LAN card and used to monitor network activity. These software packages are specifically designed to audit WLAN networks and alert administrators to potential security holes.

This type of network audit will help WLAN administrators determine where security holes are and hopefully use that information to rectify the security problem. The information can also be used to determine how the problem was allowed to occur, so it can be prevented from recurring.

9.2 SSID

WLAN security, like other types of security, involves many layers of protection. Some of these layers are optional, but because of the inherent insecurity involved in WLANs it is a good idea to implement as many layers as possible.

The first layer of security is the Service Set Identifier (SSID), basically a password that has to be transmitted by the clients connecting to an access point. If the SSID sent by the client matches that enabled on the access point, a connection is established and communication can begin.

An SSID is also a good way to segment a wireless network. If a campus network is designed so that users should only have access to certain parts of the network, then different SSIDs can be used in different areas, restricting the access of users to certain parts of the network.

Table 9.2   Well-Known SSIDs

MANUFACTURER	MODEL	SSID
Cisco	BR1000	2 or tsunami
Compaq	WL–100	Compaq
DLink	DL–713	WLAN
INTEL	2011	Intel, xlan, or 101
SMC	SMC2652W	WLAN

SSID has several security problems associated with it, the biggest of which is that the default for most access points is to broadcast the SSID. Broadcasting the SSID obviously defeats the purpose of having it. Essentially, the access point is broadcasting its password to any devices with the same 802.11 standard enabled, defeating the purpose of having the SSID in the first place.

Even with SSID broadcast disabled on the access point, the SSID is still sent in plain text by the network device. If no encryption is enabled on the network, then an attacker with a WLAN scanning program will be able to sniff the password from devices configured to use it. Table 9-2 lists access point manufacturers and their well-known SSID.

Many network administrators do not change the SSID when a new access point is deployed, so the default SSID of the access point remains in place. As long as the same manufacturer makes the access point and WLAN Ethernet cards, the SSID will be the same for both, or the cards will be configured to accept a broadcast SSID.

9.3 WEP

SSID by itself does not provide enough security for most administrators. To further secure a WLAN, many administrators will enable Wired Equivalent Privacy (WEP). WEP is a form of encapsulation that is part of the 802.11 standard.

WEP uses symmetric key encryption to secure data between an end user and an access point. It cannot be used to secure traffic between end users in a peer-to-peer network. The WEP standard specifies the RC4 (a stream cipher designed by Ronald Rivest) pseudorandom number generator (PRNG) algorithm to encrypt key transmissions between the two devices. The key is stored on both the WLAN network card and the access point, and all data sent between the network card and the access point is encrypted using the key. The 802.11 standard does not have provisions for a key management system, so all keys are managed manually.

The WEP standard does not allow for multiple keys bound to an access point. So, all users have the same key bound to their network card, and each access point only has one key. The WEP key can be used in a manner similar to SSID, allowing administrators to limit which users can gain entrance to the network using certain access points.

WEP uses a 24-bit initialization value to create the key. There are two types of encryption: (1) a 40-bit encryption key and 64-bit encryption and (2) 104-bit encryption key and 128-bit encryption. Obviously, the more encryption the better, but not all manufacturers support 128-bit encryption, and the 802.11 standard requires only a 64-bit key.

WEP encapsulation is known to have severe security flaws. An attacker using a program like AirSnort can sniff enough information to break WEP encapsulation with only 500 MB of data.

NOTE

In October 2000, Jesse Walker from Intel Corporation released a document titled "Unsafe at any Key Size: An analysis of the WEP encapsulation." The document detailed the vulnerabilities in WEP.

In addition to known flaws in the WEP encryption algorithm, another problem associated with WEP security is key management. Different keys can be associated with different access points or groups of access points, but all users who are authorized to use an access point have to have the same key enabled on their WLAN network card.

If an organization has a security policy that requires passwords to be changed within certain periods of time, then WEP keys will have to be changed often enough to comply with the policy. This means not just updating the key on the access point, but all users who use the access point will have to change the key on their WLAN network cards.

Since all users of an access point have the same key on their systems, the new key will need to be communicated to everyone who is supposed to have it. That creates an additional problem for network administrators: The updated keys have to be communicated in a manner that is secure, but practical.

WEP key updates should be communicated to users verbally or through encrypted mail messages. After the new keys have been put in place, communications containing the key should be deleted.

WEP does not provide enough security to serve as a stand-alone method of data protection. WEP encryption used in conjunction with a nonbroadcasted SSID provides a better level of security. However, even the combined protocols do not provide adequate security for an enterprise network. If WEP and SSID protection are to be used on the network, it should be with the understanding that they are simply better than no protection.

9.4 MAC Address Filtering

Another layer of security used on WLANs is MAC address filtering. Just as an administrator can filter MAC addresses on a switched network, they can also be filtered on a WLAN network.

MAC address filtering makes sense in small WLAN networks, where an administrator can maintain tight security. In a large WLAN network, especially one with access points segmented by SSID or WEP, MAC address filtering can be an administrative nightmare.

An access point can usually manage a maximum of 255 MAC addresses. For large WLAN installations, this may not be enough. Even in smaller networks multiple lists, which have to be managed manually, can be an excessive amount of work for an overburdened administrative staff.

MAC addresses can also be spoofed. Remember, unlike a traditional network, where an attacker has to be physically attached to monitor traffic, on a WLAN an attacker can monitor traffic without having authenticated to the access point. Even with encrypted data, the MAC address of a machine connected to the network will be sent in clear text. Someone sniffing the network will be able to find allowed MAC addresses and change the MAC address of the card they are using, gaining quick entrance into the network.

Current best practices, as advocated by the IEEE, recommend the use of a combination of SSID, with broadcast disabled, WEP, and MAC address filtering to secure WLANs. Even these steps are not enough to provide the level of security that can be provided to a wired network, but they should be adequate for smaller networks. Using these three layers of security should be enough to dissuade an attacker searching for a random access point. They will not, however, be enough to stop an attacker intent on breaking into a specific network.

There are steps, described in the next sections, which a network administrator can take to further enhance WLAN network security. Enhanced security for WLANs may not be required depending on other security measures in place within the network. If enhanced security measures are not going to be taken, it is important to be aware of the risks involved in using the security measures described thus far.

9.5 RADIUS Authentication

Configuring access points to use RADIUS to authenticate users can further enhance wireless network security. RADIUS authentication gives network administrators much more granular control over network access through WLAN access points.

RADIUS authentication is not supported by all access points and is not required as part of the 802.11 standard. However, the security risks inherent in the 802.11 standard have encouraged many vendors to include RADIUS support. Access points from vendors such as Cisco, Linksys, Lucent, and Proxim include RADIUS capabilities, and RADIUS software from Funk Software, and others, includes special extensions to support wireless RADIUS authentication.

The authentication process with RADIUS is outlined in Figure 9.3. A user connects to an access point and the network card authenticates using SSID, WEP, or both. A RADIUS request is then forwarded from the access point to a RADIUS server. The RADIUS server authenticates the user, who is now able to pass traffic across the network. For redundancy a second RADIUS server can be added to the access point. If the primary server fails, users will be automatically forwarded to the secondary server.

As expected, if a user is unable to authenticate to the RADIUS server, he or she is not granted access to the network. RADIUS authentication prevents

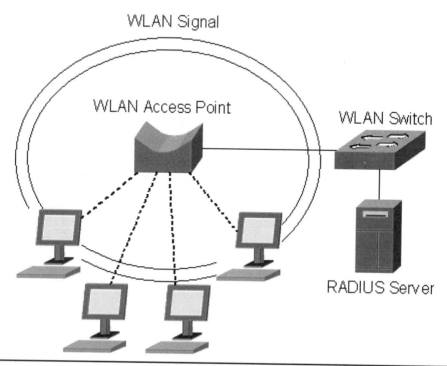

Figure 9.3   A WLAN network using RADIUS authentication. The RADIUS server forces WLAN users to authenticate before gaining network access.

unauthorized users from gaining network access through the WLAN. It also puts WLAN users on the same level as other users on the network; they have to log into the network in the same manner as everyone else.

RADIUS authentication, when used in conjunction with a strong password policy, helps to deter unauthorized users from gaining access to network resources. Unfortunately, RADIUS authentication will not solve the problem of attackers scanning the wireless spectrum looking for data, because RADIUS does not encrypt data. RADIUS authentication is generally used when authentication is more of a concern than encryption.

It is not a good idea to use RADIUS authentication as the only form of WLAN security. Administrators sometimes enable WLAN RADIUS and then disable the existing security functions. This makes it easier for users to log into the network, but it lessens WLAN security. Even though WEP security is severely flawed, it is still better than broadcasting data in clear text.

RADIUS should generally be used in conjunction with WEP, and, if possible, MAC address filtering. WLAN traffic should also be segmented. If possible, all access points plug into the same switch or group of switches. Keeping WLAN traffic segmented in this manner helps to limit the damage an attacker can do, if the WLAN security is breached.

9.6 WLAN VPN

Unlike RADIUS authentication, adding VPN tunneling to a WLAN provides both authentication and encryption. Requiring access to a WLAN through a VPN is a relatively new method of security, but one that is gaining a lot of support.

A WLAN VPN is implemented by adding a NAS server between the network and the access point, as shown in Figure 9.4. A WLAN user connects to the access point, and the request is forwarded to the NAS. The NAS handles the authentication and encryption of data and creates the tunnel. Once a user has been successfully authenticated against the NAS server, a tunnel is created and encrypted data is freely transmitted between the user and the network.

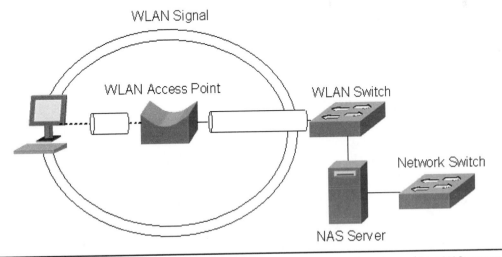

Figure 9.4 Securing a WLAN using a VPN. The WLAN user creates a tunnel to a NAS server, encrypting all traffic sent between the user and the network.

VLAN VPNs are nice because they are, generally, neutral so whatever VPN protocol is enabled on the network can also be used for WLAN users. Similar to a dial-up ISP, the access point serves simply as a transit to the VPN, with no regard for the protocols used to encrypt the data.

The other advantage to the WLAN VPN method is that most operating systems either include, or have readily available, clients for the most common forms of VPN tunneling: PPTP, L2TP, and IPSec. WLAN VPNs make the 802.11 security standards, SSID, WEP, and MAC address filtering, redundant. They can be disabled on all access points, because without authenticating to the VPN NAS, a user will not be allowed onto the network. WEP is not needed because the WLAN VPN will take care of the encryption process using much stronger encryption algorithms.

As WLAN VPNs continue to grow in popularity, expect additional enhancements in the service. Colubris Networks, for example, introduced an access point that terminates VPNs directly. This enhances security by bringing the VPN termination to the edge of the network, rather than allowing packets into the network, then authenticating and encrypting them.

While WLAN VPN technology is a good idea, and many would argue essential for enterprise networks, there are some downsides. The first is the additional CPU overhead that the tunnels will create on both the NAS server and the end user machines. If a VPN is already heavily used, and an additional 20–30 people or more are going to be accessing it simultaneously, serious performance degradation may be experienced. If a VPN does not already exist in a network, the time and expense involved in setting up a new one could be prohibitively expensive.

9.7 802.11i

The IEEE is painfully aware of the security holes that have cropped up as the popularity of the 802.11a and 802.11b series has increased. To that end, a new series, 802.11i, has been introduced. 802.11i is not a physical specification as much as it is a security specification. This series is designed to help vendors develop compatible best practice security standards, which will allow secure communication between devices on a WLAN network.

The migration to more secure WLAN networks will occur in gradual phases. As new standards are introduced, they will need to be tested for backward compatibility with older 802.11a and 802.11b devices. Part of the reason that 802.11x products have enjoyed so much success recently is that they have become much more compatible, thanks in large part to the work of the WECA. To introduce a new standard that breaks compatibility would be a mistake.

9.7.1 TKIP

To that end, the first step in advancing security issued by the 802.11i task force was to introduce a new security protocol. The protocol was originally supposed to be called WEP2, but the name was changed to Temporal Key Integrity Protocol (TKIP). TKIP is designed to be backward compatible with WEP, and it allows vendors to provide firmware updates to their hardware products. This means companies will be able to run TKIP on existing equipment, rather than having to purchase all new hardware. TKIP is also a requirement for 802.11 standards compliance.

TKIP is actually a means of encapsulating WEP session information. TKIP addresses four security concerns associated with WEP:

1. Forged packets
2. Replay attacks
3. Weak encryption keys
4. Rekeying

TKIP uses message authentication codes to tag data and to prevent forged packets from being accepted by the access point. Message authentication codes use keys, which are encrypted, provided by the WLAN device and the access point and combine them using a tagging algorithm. If the result of the tagging algorithm attached to the message is what the receiver expects, the message is accepted. Otherwise, the message is dropped.

NOTE

The acronym for message authentication code is MAC. Because the IEEE already uses the acronym MAC for media access control, the 802.11i working group has opted to label this tagging message integrity code (MIC).

Replay attacks occur when an attacker captures a valid packet and resends it to the access point. The data being sent back passes the security requirements that the message authentication code tests for, but it is still a forged packet.

To address the issue of replay attacks, TKIP introduces initialization value sequence enforcement. Each packet sent between a WLAN device and the access point has a sequence number associated with its TKIP encryption key. Whenever a new TKIP encryption key is initialized, the sequence number is reset. An attacker with the old data will be attempting to send an out-of-sequence number and the access point will drop the packet.

To deal with the problems associated with the weak keys generated by WEP, which uses an algorithm to combine the base key with a key based on the initialization value, a new method of per-packet keying has been developed for TKIP. TKIP uses a two-phase key process. The first phase involves combining the MAC address of the WLAN network card with a temporal key to create an intermediate key. In the second phase the packet sequence number, under the intermediate key, is encrypted creating a 128-bit key for each packet. Because temporal keys have a low Time to Live (TTL), the encryption is only used for a short period of time before the process is restarted, making it very difficult for an attacker to decrypt the keys.

The last step in the TKIP process is management of the encryption keys. The TKIP process uses three different keys: temporal, key encryption, and master. Because each has to be reset whenever a WLAN device and an access point connect, or re-connect, to monitor this process, TKIP uses rekey key messages. The rekey key message ensures that neither the WLAN device nor the access point attempts to regenerate keys that have been used in previous communications.

TKIP provides the level of encryption that is needed for data on an enterprise network. Because TKIP is also designed to be backward compatible with existing WEP-enabled 802.11a and 802.11b devices, it should be deployed within the network. It may take a year or more for WECA to certify all TKIP-enabled devices to ensure interoperability; however, if a network is running with equipment from a single vendor, there is no reason not to upgrade to TKIP.

9.7.2 AES

The second type of encapsulation the 802.11i working group is developing is based on the Advanced Encryption Standard (AES). Because there is significantly more overhead involved in AES encryption, it is not compatible with most existing equipment. When the standard is finalized, sometime in late 2003, it will most likely require the purchase of new equipment to implement, as opposed to a simple firmware upgrade.

AES is the encryption standard adopted by the Unites States Government. It replaced the old standard, DES, in November 2001. AES on WLAN devices meets the same standards of security as TKIP, and provides even greater levels of encryption.

AES, like TKIP, is a symmetric key block cipher, which means the same key is used for encryption and decryption. AES supports encryption keys that are up to 256 bits in length, double the length supported by TKIP.

Block ciphers encrypt data in blocks, as opposed to a byte-by-byte basis—like RC4 encryption. AES encrypts data in 128-bit blocks, filling in packets with white space when they are not a multiple of 128.

At this time the 802.11i working group has not determined a standard for AES encapsulation, but AES will figure more prominently in future 802.11 standards.

9.8 Summary

Wireless security is an area that has increased in importance as the popularity of wireless networks has increased. The current state of security within the 802.11 standard is insufficient, at best.

Network administrators have adopted other means of securing wireless networks, such as RADIUS authentication and VPN encryption, to bypass the weak security protection associated with the 802.11 standard. These methods of security provide the protection necessary for an enterprise network.

The 802.11i working group is actively developing better security protection for wireless networks. Some of the security protections will be backward compatible with existing systems; other standards, like AES, will require new equipment.

Wireless networks will continue to evolve at a rapid pace. Learning from earlier mistakes, vendors will undoubtedly ensure that tight security standards are in place within these new wireless protocols.

10

Firewalls and Intrusion Detection Systems

Firewalls are an integral part of any enterprise network design. Firewalls can tremendously enhance the security of a network and provide detailed information about traffic patterns from the core to the edge of the network, and vice versa. Firewalls can also be a security risk. The complexity that many organizations require from their firewalls can create unforeseen security holes and allow unwanted traffic through.

Before deploying a firewall it is important to map exactly what purpose the firewall will serve, and what benefits it will bring to the network. If a firewall exists on the network, then it is a good idea to audit it periodically to see if it is fulfilling its design goals.

Too many administrators assume they are well protected because a firewall is in place; sometimes this is simply not the case. A firewall is only as good as the rule sets provided to it. If bad data is entered into the firewall, it will do a poor job of guarding the network. Many security consultants will sometimes recommend against the use of a firewall, especially if it is going to be used as a security panacea. With no firewall an organization is forced to secure the rest of the network and follow good security practices.

A firewall is an excellent tool, when used as part of an overall security strategy. But it should be viewed as just that: one part of a network security strategy. In a layered security design, no one layer of the security infrastructure is more important than any other. So, while firewalls may get all of the attention, they should not be viewed as the primary security strategy, and the firewall should most definitely not be the only security strategy for an organization.[1]

Before delving into firewall network design, it is important to understand the purpose of a firewall, what a firewall cannot do, and the different types of firewalls. This type of information will help security administrators design a more complete security plan for firewall deployment, management, and monitoring. The more detailed the information included in the firewall security plan, the easier it will be to implement the firewall and perform tests against that plan.

10.1 The Purpose of the Firewall

There are several different types of firewalls and each will be discussed in detail later in this chapter, but all serve the same purpose: to separate the public and private networks, and to prevent unwanted traffic from reaching the private network.

NOTE

Firewall was originally used to describe a barrier put between connected homes and apartments to reduce noise and protect neighbors from fires in neighboring units.

To understand what this means it is important to understand the structure of a firewall. A firewall consists of at least two interfaces: public and private. The public interface, generally the Internet, is the side of the firewall to which everyone has access. The private interface is the side that contains the protected data. There can be multiple private interfaces to a firewall, depending on the number of network segments that need to be isolated. The firewall uses a set of rules, applied to each interface, to determine the type of traffic that can be passed from the public to the private networks. All traffic not explicitly allowed by the rules is denied.

Firewalls can also do a lot more, which has advantages and disadvantages. There is a temptation to save money by having the firewall act as a VPN terminator, IDS, authentication server, and DNS server, as well as perform firewall

---

1. Despite claims to the contrary from vendors.

services. Just like any other network device, the more services run, the greater the security risk. A firewall should not be used to run multiple services. As critical as the firewall is to the security infrastructure, anything that increases the risk of a security breach should be avoided at all costs.

NOTE

A possible exception to limiting the number of services on a firewall is many companies prefer to have VPNs terminated on the firewall. Check Point, Cisco, and NetScreen—the three largest firewall vendors—support this combination, and there is some justification for it.

A firewall is the second layer of protection within the network (illustrated in Figure 10.1), the first being the router. The deeper a packet travels into the network, the more specific the protection gets. At the router level the concentration is on which IP addresses are going to be allowed or denied, and looking for malformed packets. The firewall is going to look at what ports are going to be allowed and denied. In addition, the firewall determines to which devices those rules apply. Firewalls are also sometimes useful for blocking smaller network segments, or individual IP addresses.

Because routers are often overworked, using the router to filter out a single IP address, or a small block, can create unnecessary load. In certain cases filtering at the router level makes sense, such as when filtering RFC 1918 IP blocks. But if it is a single host that needs to be stopped, it is usually better to do it at the firewall level.

Firewalls are useful for protecting networks from unwanted traffic. If a network has no public servers on it, then a firewall is a great tool for denying all incoming traffic that was not originated from a machine behind the firewall. A firewall can also be configured to deny all traffic except for port 53 traffic destined to the DNS server.

The strength of a firewall lies in its ability to filter traffic based on a set of rules, called a rule set, entered by the administrator. This can also be the biggest weakness of firewalls; bad or incomplete rule sets can leave openings for attackers, leaving the network insecure. Fortunately, most firewalls make it difficult—though certainly not impossible—to design bad rule sets.

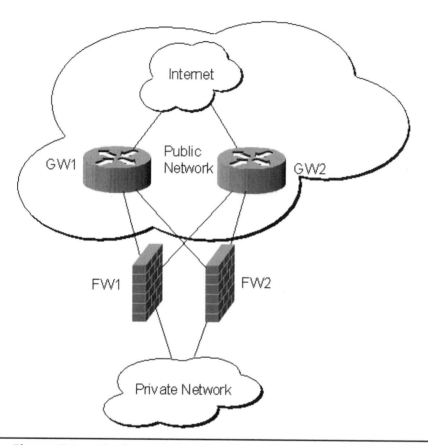

Figure 10.1   The firewall is the second layer of protection on the network. It is used to separate the public and private networks, and filter unwanted traffic.

Many administrators don't think about the firewall acting as a multiple network device. There is a lot of concern about keeping unwanted traffic from reaching the private network, but not a lot of time is devoted to keeping unwanted traffic from reaching the public network. Attention should be paid to both types of rule sets. If an attacker manages to break into a server, he or she should not be able to use that server to launch attacks against remote network devices. It is important to ensure the traffic leaving the network is as secure as the traffic entering the network.

Another consideration often overlooked by network administrators is running multiple firewalls on a network. It is important to protect traffic entering and exiting the network, but it is equally important to protect traffic traveling within the network. To protect and further segment internal traffic, administrators will often run two sets of firewalls, the first set to protect the entire network, and the second set to protect different network segments.

NOTE

When using multiple layers of firewalls on a network, it is usually a good idea to use different types of firewalls. For example, if the primary firewall, or pair of firewalls, is Check Point the internal firewalls should be NetScreen or PIX. This way, if an attacker manages to exploit vulnerability in one firewall the second will still provide a layer of protection.

Multiple firewall layers also allow security administrators to better control the flow of information, especially in and out of departments that deal with sensitive information (Figure 10.2). Activities that may be permitted on the rest of the network can be restricted in more sensitive areas, without placing an undue burden on the primary firewall.

10.2 What a Firewall Cannot Do

As mentioned in the beginning of this chapter, a firewall often becomes the focal point of network security. This is not necessarily a bad thing as long as this focus is accompanied by a strong network security plan. If the firewall is going to be the only security plan, then the network will be extremely vulnerable to attacks.

To make the best use of a firewall it is important to understand its weaknesses. Firewalls are good at blocking ports and IP blocks, or addresses. They can also be good at detecting and dropping malformed packets.

Firewalls are not good at doing a detailed examination of packets. If the problem is in the packet header, such as a spoofing or a smurf attack, a firewall can be an effective tool. On the other hand, attacks that involve sending bad informa-

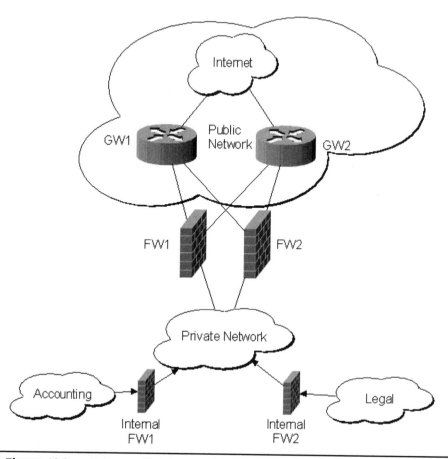

Figure 10.2 Using multiple layers of firewalls on a network helps to increase security. By adding an extra layer of protection to departments that have sensitive data, administrators can help ensure the security of company information.

tion within a packet—such a virus or worm—are much more difficult to stop with a firewall.

Firewalls also cannot defend against attacks that do not go through the firewall. War dialing and attacks that use employee-created back doors into the network will not be stopped by the firewall. While some dial-up connections cannot be avoided, there should be no back doors into a network. All traffic entering the network should pass through the firewall. This makes sense, as an attacker who does a network scan of an IP block is going to find those back entrances anyway, and use them to breach the network.

Firewalls also cannot tell a security administrator when the firewall rules are inadequate. Most firewalls start with a secure rule set, but because the security needs of each organization are different, it is possible to create a rule set that is insecure. Most security experts recommend having at least one person on staff who is certified in the use of the firewall. That person should be able to verify the firewall rule set and ensure the rules are logical, and within the realm of the security policy.

NOTE

Because even the best security experts make mistakes, it is a good idea to have the firewall rule set audited by a third party. Many organizations pay third parties to perform a security audit on their network after the firewall—and other measures—have been put in place.

A firewall is also not a network-monitoring tool. Many firewalls are capable of notifying administrators when an attack occurs, but there is some debate as to the prudence of that because the purpose of a firewall is to stop attacks. An IDS is more capable of identifying security violation patterns and notifying administrators. Firewalls also do not monitor the network to determine whether or not servers are available. Separate monitoring servers and software are required for that.

The most important thing to remember about firewalls is that they cannot stop the most common type of attack: internal. Network security breaches caused by employees, or people posing as employees, are the most common type of network attack. These events generally occur behind the firewall and are therefore below the perimeter of the firewall.

This returns to the original point: A firewall is an important part of network security, but it should not be the only security precaution taken. A firewall that is used as part of an overall network security policy is going to be much more effective than one that is the network security policy.

10.3 Types of Firewalls

Firewall is really a generic term that covers many different types of devices used to separate network traffic. Most firewalls are simply a server, with a hardened operating system, and a software-based firewall providing the protection. Some firewalls, known as embedded firewalls, have the operating system and firewall programmed directly onto the system CPU.

Three types of firewalls will be covered in this section:

1. Packet filtering
2. Stateful packet filtering
3. Application proxy

The most basic type is the packet filtering firewall. A packet filtering firewall sits between the public and the private network, as shown in Figure 10.1. All network traffic, both ingress and egress, has to pass through the firewall.

The firewall determines what happens to packets based on one of four criteria: source IP address, destination IP address, source port, and destination port. The four criteria can be combined in the firewall rule set to determine what type of traffic will be allowed through.

For example, if an organization maintains a primary DNS server on the private network, UDP and TCP traffic destined for Port 53 has to be allowed for that server, but it should not be allowed to any other device on the network. This is shown in Figure 10.3. Packets destined for the DNS server are allowed, while the same packets destined for the web server are denied.

Generally, destination IP address and destination port are the criteria used by administrators to filter. Unless all external traffic is being denied by the firewall—such as on the private side of a DMZ—firewall administrators have the most control over these two criteria. Most of the time when a hole is opened through the firewall, it is to grant access to a public server. DNS, web, and mail servers are the most common examples of public servers. Because these servers are public, any IP address may connect to them. Rather than try to filter a source IP address, or addresses, it is easier to deny all traffic unless it is destined to the IP address of a server running the public service.

The same process applies to the source port. When an HTTP, DNS, or SMTP request is made, the source port is usually one of the higher, unreserved

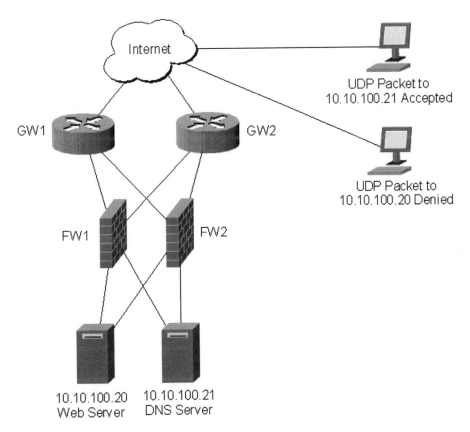

Firewall configured to only allow TCP/UDP on
port 53 if they are destined to 10.10.100.21

Figure 10.3   Packet filter firewalls can be configured to allow/deny traffic based on
source or destination IP address, as well as source and destination port

ports. The destination should always be the same, Port 80 for HTTP, Port 53
for DNS, and Port 25 for SMTP. An administrator cannot filter out the higher
ports, so it makes more sense to deny based on the destination port.

This type of strategy makes configuring the firewall a lot easier, and it makes
the rule set simpler. For most firewalls, this is the default policy: Deny all services, except for those explicitly allowed.

Stateful packet filters offer the same features as packet filtering firewalls, with
some expended functionality. A stateful packet filtering firewall keeps track of

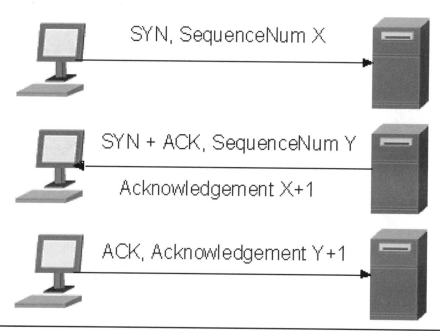

Figure 10.4   A TCP session initiates with a three-way handshake

session information between two devices. Specifically, the stateful packet filter tracks the current session state of all transactions.

As shown in Figure 10.4, all TCP sessions initiate with a three-way hand-shake. The device initiating the connection sends a request with a sequence number. This is known as a SYN request. The device on the other end of the connection responds with a SYN/ACK. It acknowledges the request, increases the value of the initial sequence number by one, and sends its own sequence number (independent of the original sequence number). The device that origi-nally initiated the session responds to the SYN/ACK with an ACK. The ACK contains the sequence number of the remote device, incremented by one.

Attackers will often attempt to trick servers, and other machines, by sending packets that have the incorrect bit set. This is especially common when port scanning: An attacker attempts to see what ports are open on a server by sending packets that have the ACK bit set, tricking the server into thinking that it is an open session.

A stateful packet filtering firewall maintains a state table. The state table is simply a database that tracks current connections, and what state they are in. If the firewall receives a packet in an unexpected state, the packet is dropped.

Another common ploy used to bypass a regular packet filtering firewall is to forge a response packet to a machine behind the firewall. Even though the machine did not initiate the request, the firewall will allow it through, giving an attacker access to the internal network.

A stateful packet filtering firewall does not understand the application that the two devices are using to communicate; it only understands the packet structure, so it won't filter based on any information other than packet structure. This can still leave a network vulnerable to some types of attacks.

The third type of firewall, the application proxy, sits between the client and the server and responds to all requests. This is different from a packet filtering firewall, which simply forwards requests between the two devices, in the same manner that a router would.

An application proxy firewall responds to all requests, as if it were the device to which the request is made. For example, if a proxy firewall was placed, logically, in front of a web server, as in Figure 10.5, a client would make a request to the web server. The proxy firewall would intercept the request, and then make the request of the web server on behalf of the client. The web server responds to the proxy firewall, which then forwards the request to the client.

As you can imagine, application proxy firewalls are very powerful, and are able to probe much deeper into a packet than packet filtering firewalls can. Application proxy firewalls can do pattern matching within the packet, looking for matches that might indicate an attack is in progress. If a match is spotted, the packet is dropped, and the server never knows there was a problem.

This power comes with a steep price; application proxy firewalls require a lot of CPU resources and, especially on busy networks, they can often be ineffective in dealing with a large amount of traffic. Some security experts argue that application proxy firewalls don't always live up to their potential—and don't stop as many attacks as they could. Again, the problem arises that many security administrators who use application proxy firewalls feel that they have a complete security solution and do not take steps to secure the rest of the network.

Determining the type of firewall that best suits a network depends largely on the experience of the staff that will be administering the firewall, and other

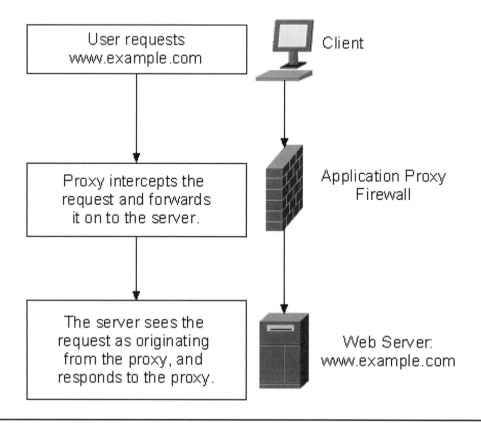

Figure 10.5   A proxy firewall intercepts incoming requests, examines the packet, and forwards those requests onto their intended destination. If there is a problem with the incoming packet, it is dropped.

security precautions that are available within the network. Many firewalls can run in all three modes, giving administrators a wide range of options when selecting the firewall that best meets the needs of the network.

10.4 Layer 2 Firewalls

A relatively new type of firewall has emerged over the last couple of years: Layer 2. Layer 2 firewalls are "invisible"; they sit on the network and watch packets and filter out bad packets, but they are never seen.

The disadvantage to a typical firewall is that it is a destination on the network. A traditional firewall has a public and a private network, so it has addresses that can be attacked. A frustrated intruder, who is unable to bypass the security mechanisms, can attempt to launch a DoS attack against the firewall directly. Many firewalls are set up so that if the firewall application crashes, the server underneath simply becomes a router—directing traffic from the public to the private network.[2]

Obviously, this can be a serious security problem. If an attacker successfully launches a DoS attack against the firewall, and is able to crash the application, that attacker now has full access to the network.

Many firewall companies, including Check Point and NetScreen, allow their firewalls to be configured in "invisible" mode, which is the same as a Layer 2 firewall. The firewall acts like a bridge joining different network segments, without performing any routing.

Layer 2 firewalls offer several advantages over a traditional firewall:

- Because the firewall does not provide an attacker with an IP address it is more difficult to build a network map—therefore more difficult to find vulnerable devices on the network.

- The lack of a public IP address also makes it more difficult for an attacker to determine the type of firewall in place—making it hard to exploit weaknesses in the firewall.

- It is easier to add a firewall to an existing network; Layer 2 firewalls do not require any change in network settings.

A typical network design using a Layer 2 firewall is shown in Figure 10.6. The firewall is placed at the head of the network, just like a typical firewall, but rather than have the firewall act as the gateway for the network, the gateway is pushed to the router, and the firewall simply forwards traffic, similar to a bridge. While a Layer 2 firewall design can be elegant, it can also have problems. Because the network is no longer being broken up into subnets, it is important to carefully architect various segments of the network to prevent sensitive traffic from spilling into areas where it should not be seen.

Layer 2 firewalls can also make network troubleshooting difficult. Having a device on the network that is directly impacting traffic, but does not show up as a network node, can sometimes create confusion and make spotting network problems more difficult.

---

2. Thankfully, this is becoming less common.

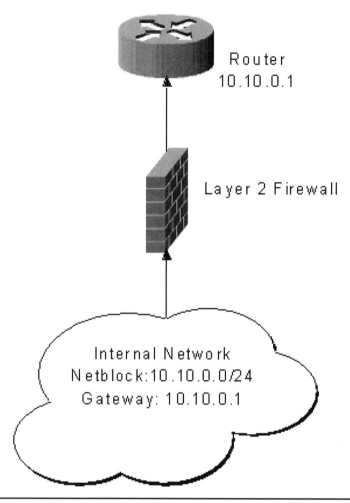

Router
10.10.0.1

Layer 2 Firewall

Internal Network
Netblock:10.10.0.0/24
Gateway: 10.10.0.1

Figure 10.6 A Layer 2 firewall sits in the same place on the network as a typical firewall, but it does not perform any routing on the network, making it invisible to a casual attacker

10.5 Intrusion Detection Systems

IDSs are increasingly popular additions to network security. An IDS is used to search for patterns that may indicate an attack on a network. Unlike firewalls, which are designed to block suspect information, an IDS only issues a warning.

Generally, an IDS is placed at the edge of the network (Figure 10.7), so it can monitor all traffic in and out of the WAN. This is known as a network IDS (NIDS). An IDS installed on a server that is used to monitor connections to that server only is known as a host-based IDS. Most networks use a combination of host-based IDS and NIDS, because a single NIDS on the edge of the network may have trouble processing all of the incoming traffic. The NIDS is used to get the state of the network in a big picture fashion, while the host-based IDS are used on critical servers to watch for potential problems on those servers.

How does an NIDS work? The NIDS is placed between the routers and firewalls, usually plugged into a Layer 2 switch, or even a hub. If a switch is used, the port mirroring needs to be set up on the switch to allow traffic from the monitored ports, or VLANs, to be mirrored on the port the NIDS is plugged into. On a Cisco 2900 switch port mirroring can be accomplished in a manner similar to this:

```
Core1(config)#int fa0/24
Core1(config-if)#port monitor fastEthernet 0/1
Core1(config-if)#port monitor fastEthernet 0/2
Core1(config-if)#port monitor fastEthernet 0/3
Core1(config-if)#port monitor fastEthernet 0/4
```

This will allow Fast Ethernet Port 24 to monitor all traffic coming through Ports 1, 2, 3, and 4. Different vendors and even different product lines within the same vendor have different ways of configuring port mirroring. Information about how to configure port mirroring should be included on the vendor website, or in its documentation.

NOTE

While hubs can be used, and some people prefer them because there are no configuration requirements—they are just plug and play—hubs do not have the processing power that switches do. It is possible to flood a hub on an enterprise network and slow down traffic.

Port mirroring is how network intrusion detection is accomplished from a design perspective, but the more important question is, how do NIDS process data. An NIDS is, basically, a packet sniffer. It sorts through the traffic on the

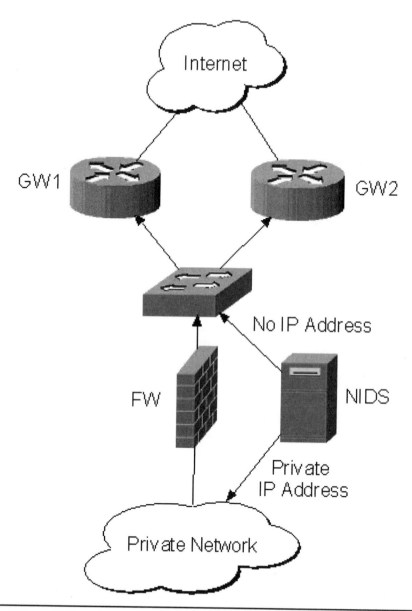

Figure 10.7   A typical NIDS design. The public side of the NIDS does not have an IP address and is plugged into the same switch as the firewall. The switch is configured for port-mirroring; all alerts gathered by the NIDS are sent to a device on the private network.

network looking for patterns, which may be representative of an attack. These patterns are called signatures. A signature is a set of events indicative of a network attack—the events may not actually be an attack, but there is a preponderance of evidence to suggest it is. The way signatures are matched against network traffic depends on the type of NIDS in use.

Based on how the problem of detecting attacks is approached, there are two types of NIDS systems: signature and anomaly. These types of NIDS can be broken into smaller categories, but the NIDS in each category all follow the same architecture. Signature-based NIDSs rely on internal databases with common attack patterns. If one of these patterns is matched, a flag is set off alerting administrators. Anomaly-based NIDSs rely on changes in traffic patterns to determine whether an attack is occurring.

NOTE

To increase the level of network security, most administrators do not assign an IP address to the port on the NIDS that is doing the sniffing. That interface is often outside the firewall, so there is nothing to protect it—if there is no IP address it is much more difficult for an attacker to detect and compromise the NIDS.

10.5.1 Signature-Based NIDS

Most commercial NIDSs are signature-based. It requires a great deal of effort to keep databases current with the latest security information, so the attack patterns can be included in the database. While this is not outside the realm of possibility for an open-source project, to date it has not been done. There are three types of signature-based NIDSs: pattern matching, stateful pattern matching, and protocol decode.

Pattern matching is the simplest of NIDSs; it is a basic pattern-matching system. The database consists of a series of rules, and the NIDS inspects each packet looking for a match. When a match, or series of matches, is found they will be reported.

Pattern-matching rules are very simple; they usually consist of the protocol, port, and the actual pattern. Some pattern-matching NIDSs also allow administrators to include things like source and destination IP address. The following is an example of a typical signature, prepared for the SNORT database:

```
alert UDP $EXTERNAL any -> $INTERNAL 53 (msg:
"IDS489/dns_named-exploit-tsig-lsd"; content: "|3F 909090 EB3B 31DB
5F 83EF7C 8D7710 897704 8D4F20|"; classtype: system-attempt;
reference: arachnids,489;)
```

This is based on the BIND transaction signature vulnerability (CVE CAN-2001-0010) in BIND Version 8.0. An attacker exploiting this vulnerability would be able to gain root access to the DNS server. If a match to this pattern were found, the NIDS would alert administrators to a potential problem.

Administrators have to be careful with simple pattern-matching NIDSs. If a pattern is too general, the NIDS will generate a lot of false positives from normal traffic. If a pattern is too specific, it may not catch all attempts.

The problem with pattern-matching NIDSs is that they are too rigid. If a packet does not match the information in the database exactly, it will not be reported. This can be problematic, especially when attackers can change small portions of an attack. For example, if an attack is based on buffer overflow vulnerabilities in PHP, an attacker may construct an attack that makes an HTTP request:

```
POST http://www.example.com/script.php?efffff7d2b9bfff
```

Obviously, that is not a fully formed HTTP request, but it will do for example purposes. In fact, there is a security hole in PHP, with a pattern that looks a lot like this:

```
alert TCP $EXTERNAL any -> $INTERNAL 80 (msg:
"IDS431/web-cgi_http-php_strings_exploit-atstake"; flags: A+;
content: "|ba49feffff f7d2 b9bfffffff f7d1|";)
```

If a signature match based on the pattern in the example is added to the NIDS database, there is nothing stopping the attacker from changing the attack to:

```
POST http://www.example.com/script.php?efffff7d2b9bfff16932
```

Especially in the case of HTTP-based attacks, it is relatively simple to adjust the attack to avoid matching an entry in the NIDS database. So, while pattern-matching NIDSs are great because of their simplicity and the relatively low number of incidences of false positives, they are too easy for a savvy attacker to fool. Simple pattern matching can also be problematic when dealing with streaming protocols, such as HTTP. Because simple pattern matching inspects each packet individually, it does not take into account attacks that span across several packets, so these attacks may be missed.

Stateful pattern-matching NIDSs have a different approach to signature tracking. These NIDSs search for the same information, but they track session streams, not just individual packets. By maintaining session information, stateful pattern-matching NIDSs can track much more complex attacks, and return fewer false positives and fewer false negatives.

To understand the benefits of stateful pattern matching, look at the PHP exploit in the previous example. Suppose an attacker were able to separate the query into two packets; the first packet contains ba49feffff f7d2, while the second has b9bfffffff f7d1. A simple pattern-matching NIDS will return a false negative, because the data is in two packets, neither of which matches the database entry. A stateful pattern-matching NIDS will spot the match and report it, even across multiple packets.

The benefits to this type of pattern matching are obvious and, if managed properly, a stateful pattern-matching NIDS will report fewer false negatives than a simple pattern-matching NIDS. While this type of pattern matching is an improvement, it is still susceptible to alterations in the attacks. If the details of an attack are altered, it is no longer a match for the information in the database, and it can evade detection.

10.5.2 Anomaly-Based NIDS

An anomaly-based NIDS is an IDS that baselines normal traffic patterns and generates alerts when that pattern alters significantly. Rather than monitor for specific types of traffic, the NIDS looks at changes in the behavior of the network.

Anomaly-based NIDS offer the advantage of not relying on existing signatures, so they are less susceptible to new attacks than signature-based NIDSs. If a new attack is launched on the network, the NIDS will detect the change in traffic patterns—assuming the attack is different enough to generate an alarm—and alert administrators to the problem.

Anomaly-based NIDSs work best when used in conjunction with a signature-based NIDS. The signature-based NIDSs should catch known attacks, while the anomaly-based NIDS will report suspicious activity.

One of the best-known anomaly-based NIDSs is the Statistical Packet Anomaly Detection Engine (SPADE), a plug-in for SNORT that was developed by Silicon Defense (*www.silicondefense.com/*). SPADE is a preprocessor for SNORT; it monitors the network for anomalous packets. If a suspect packet is discovered SPADE logs the packet, then generates an alert using the standard SNORT mechanisms.

Anomaly-based NIDSs require a good deal more time to set up than signature-based NIDSs. It takes a while to examine the traffic patterns of a network and determine when to generate alarms. It can often take several weeks, or even months, to set the triggers in an anomaly-based NIDS so that it is not generating alarms to frequently, or infrequently.

10.6 Summary

Firewalls and intrusion detection systems make an excellent perimeter protection combination. Each has different strengths that, when combined, can make a powerful warning system for the network.

Unfortunately, both devices require a lot of maintenance to make sure they are performing at peak efficiency, and that they are behaving in a manner that aligns with the expectations of the network administrators. A bad firewall rule or a missed signature can leave a network open to attack.

It is important to avoid the trap of over reliance on these two devices as the sole means of network protection. Firewalls and intrusion detection systems should be part of a strong security plan that includes regular audits; and it should not be the entire security plan.

11

The DMZ

A common design used to enhance network security is the DMZ, also known as a perimeter network. A DMZ is a way of separating sensitive information from that designed to be publicly available. Servers in the DMZ have to be available to all users, but they still need some level of protection. Servers most commonly placed within a DMZ are web, DNS, and mail servers.

The DMZ is a good example of layered security design. By isolating the public servers into a segmented network there is little chance that data between the two networks will be shared. This isolation prevents an attacker who manages to gain access to one of the servers within the DMZ from further penetrating into the network. That is the purpose of the DMZ: to isolate and limit the damage an attacker can do by gaining access to a server.

The most common use of a DMZ is to isolate servers that require public access. However, that is not the only purpose that DMZs can serve. A DMZ can be used to isolate servers on a network, limiting who can access them. It can also be used to isolate whole networks from the rest of the organization; this is especially true in cases where extreme privacy is required.

While there are many uses for the DMZ, the primary use is to isolate public servers. Of course, like most aspects of security, there is some debate about the best way to implement a DMZ. There is also debate about whether a single DMZ or multiple DMZs is the most efficient design. The truth is that what is considered the best DMZ design will vary from network to network, and will be dependent largely on the security needs as well as the budget that is available to the network.

NOTE

A DMZ increases network overhead, and there is usually a performance dip at the server level when a DMZ is activated. It is not a large performance decrease, but it is something to note and expect.

11.1 DMZ Network Design

Traditionally, the DMZ network design was done at the router level. A separate interface was added to the router, and a network segment was set aside strictly for the public servers. This network segment is connected directly through a router interface, and none of the traffic destined for the servers is routed through the firewall (Figure 11.1).

The problem with this traditional design is that it does not adequately take into account the security needs for these public servers. The only protection, aside from the security precautions taken for any server, afforded the servers in the DMZ would be the router ACL. In most instances, this would clearly not provide the desired level of security.

A second solution is to segment the DMZ on the firewall. Rather than terminate the network to the router, terminate it at a second interface on the firewall. This is shown in Figure 11.2. This type of DMZ makes a lot more sense. The servers can be protected by the firewall, and certain traffic can be allowed through the firewall, to the servers. In most cases, allowing traffic destined to the web server IP address on Ports 80 and 443, the DNS server IP address on Port 53, and the mail server IP address on Port 25 is sufficient.

Another benefit to this solution is that it allows administrators to make use of the existing network infrastructure, rather than having to create a whole new one. On the private side of the firewall the traffic to the servers will be isolated to a single VLAN, preventing information from being shared between the DMZ and the rest of the network.

There are still problems with this design. The most notable is that there is no way to securely update information on the servers. There are also no facilities in place to secure the database transactions between the web server and the data-

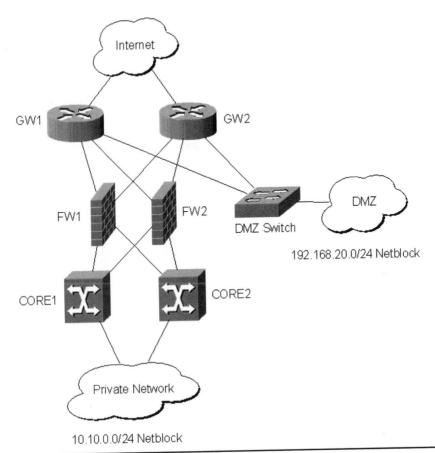

Figure 11.1   A traditional DMZ design: The DMZ network terminates at the router, and none of the DMZ servers are protected by the firewall

base server, or any of the backend servers. The common resolution to this problem is to put secondary network cards in the servers and assign them IP addresses from the private network. The servers can be plugged into the switch and connected to the private network through the backend, allowing updates from the private network through the secondary interfaces. This is shown in Figure 11.3. It also has the negative consequence of destroying any security put in place by the firewall.

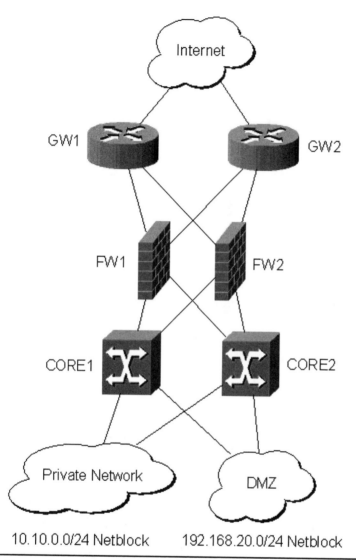

Figure 11.2   A DMZ design using the firewall as the terminating point for the network. The firewall secures and isolates the DMZ traffic, which travels within a separate VLAN from the private network.

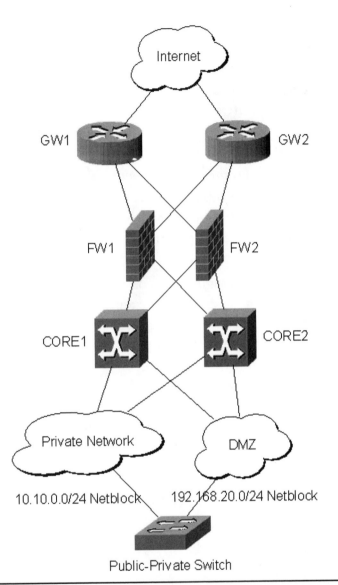

Figure 11.3 A switch is used to facilitate communication between the public and private networks, creating a large security hole, and negating the purpose of the firewall and DMZ

Think about it. The purpose of the DMZ is to isolate the network. Rather than isolate the network, this design joins the two networks, making it very easy for an attacker to gain access to the rest of the network. A big red X should go through Figure 11.3 so it is never implemented.

A better way to enhance the security of the DMZ and facilitate communication between the machines in the private network is to add a second firewall. This is where some of the debate starts, although the premise is fairly simple:

1. Create a DMZ off the primary firewall for the public servers.
2. Add a second network card to the public servers. The second network card terminates to a secondary firewall, which allows access from the internal network to the servers, and from the web server to the database server, or any other specific queries that are required.

The debate originates in how this design should be implemented. There are two ways it can be done. The first method is to create an isolated network, as in Figure 11.4. The first firewall is connected to the edge routers on the public side.

Only the public servers exist on the private side of the first firewall. Each server has two network interface cards as well. The public interface connects to the first firewall, and the private interface connects to a secondary one.

The secondary firewall connects to the private interface of the public servers and to the private network. The two firewalls have different purposes. The front firewall provides access to the public server, but is very restrictive otherwise. The secondary firewall is even more restrictive. It allows certain types of queries from the public servers to the private network, and it acts as a gateway for the private network. It also allows the private network to communicate with the public network in a secure fashion.

What this creates is an additional layer of network security. An attacker has to go through two firewalls to get to the private network. Even if the target is a server on the public network, the information gathered on the public network is relatively limited, unless the attacker can get through two firewalls as well as the security precautions set up on the server.

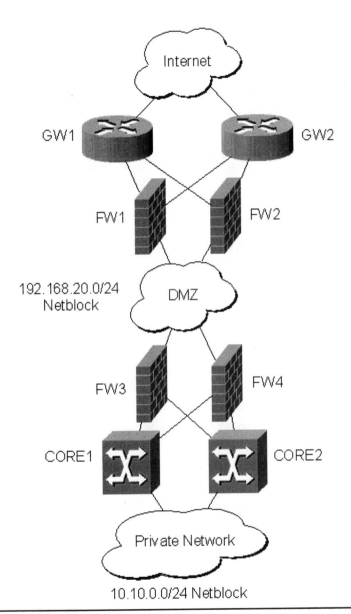

Figure 11.4 Increase network security by adding a second firewall and creating a DMZ that is truly isolated from the network

NOTE

Most security experts recommend using two different types of firewalls for the DMZ; if an attacker is able to exploit a security hole in one firewall, the secondary firewall will most likely not be susceptible.

In some ways, this makes managing security policy less complicated. If a DMZ contains just a web server, the first firewall has to allow through-only traffic destined for Port 80 or 443. All other traffic can be dropped—unless the request originated from behind the firewall. The second firewall is even more specific. It only needs to allow traffic from the web server to the database, or application, server on the private network. Because the same administrator controls both servers, a very precise hole can be punched into the firewall.

A second way in which this design can be accomplished is to have the secondary firewall back up to a management network. This is shown in Figure 11.5. The front firewall is configured in the same manner as Figure 11.2, with the DMZ and private networks being assigned different interfaces on that firewall. The secondary firewall connects to a management network, rather than directly to the private network. The management network, detailed in Chapter 17, is a separate private network used only by administrators to manage servers.

Connecting the secondary firewall to a management network, rather than the primary private network, removes the advantage of the multiple-layer firewall design. It compensates for the loss, but it simplifies the firewall rule sets even further, making it easier to manage the firewalls.

Unlike the previous design, the secondary firewall only needs to allow certain traffic to the private interfaces of the server. The secondary firewall does not have to worry about general Internet access, as it will not be used for that purpose. This allows administrators to tighten the security on that firewall and severely limit the amount of traffic that is passed through. Alternatively, rules can be put in place to allow server management to the public interfaces of the servers. This is not recommended, but it can serve to increase the security on the second firewall even further.

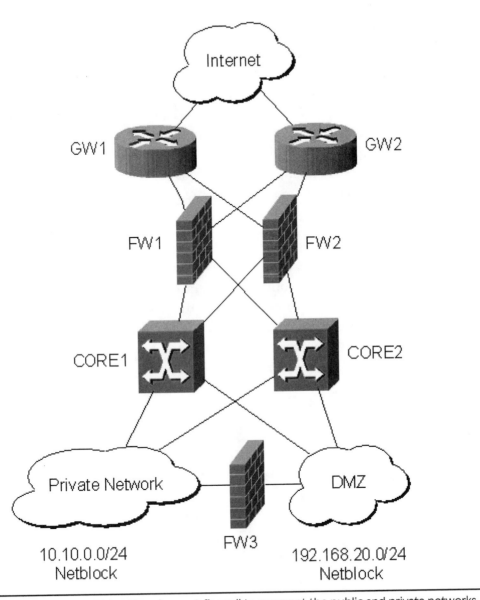

Figure 11.5   This network uses a firewall to segment the public and private networks, and a secondary firewall to secure data exchange between the two networks

11.2 Multiple DMZ Design

The multiple firewall design can be extended even further, creating multiple DMZs to protect corporate data. A multiple DMZ design allows administrators to further isolate public servers by placing each server inside a separate DMZ. Many security experts argue that a multiple DMZ design provides very few benefits,[1] and the added capital expenditure combined with the increased network complexity negate any benefits that are gained.

There are two types of multiple DMZ designs that are generally implemented:

1. One which adds more layers to the current design.
2. One which isolates each of the public servers into their own DMZ.

The first, an extension of Figure 11.4, simply adds more layers to the current design. This type of design, illustrated in Figure 11.6, is most useful when a public server needs to query a private server. In Figure 11.6 the web server has to query the database server. Rather than put the database server on the private network, it is moved to a separate network, sandwiched between two firewalls.

The same types of rules that were used in the original DMZ design apply here. The first set of firewalls allows traffic from any source to the web server on

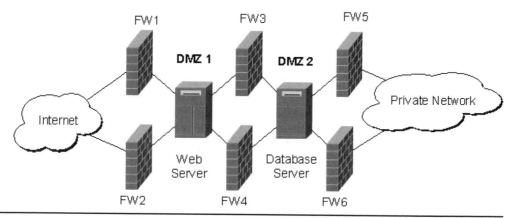

Figure 11.6   A multiple DMZ network, in which the database server is isolated from the private network. To ensure the integrity of the database server, a separate set of firewalls is added, and a DMZ is created.

---

1. Except to firewall manufacturers

Ports 80 and 443. The second firewall only allows traffic from the web server to the database server, on Port 3306 (the MySQL port). The third firewall is used to connect to the private network. Again, the third firewall is configured so that it will only allow certain types of connections from the database server through to the private network.

This design makes individual firewall management simpler, by only needing one rule for the second and third firewalls. Overall, it can make network management more difficult by increasing the complexity of the network. The more devices added to a network, the better the chance of a security breach.

A different type of multiple-DMZ design is to isolate each of the public servers into their own DMZ. Rather than use multiple firewalls, this design (Figure 11-7) relies on multiple interfaces on the same firewall. This type of multiple DMZ design isolates the public servers into private networks. Because the firewall terminates each of the networks, a DMZ is created for every server. The argument for this type of design is that, if an attacker gains access to an organization's web server, this design prevents the attacker from gaining access to any of the other public servers.

Of course, if the public servers are secured properly, the attacker should not be able to gain access to them anyway. Creating a multiple DMZ network design in this manner adds complexity to the firewall rule sets, and can make the firewall more difficult to monitor and maintain. In some cases, particularly when dealing with sensitive information—such as a VPN—using a secondary interface to create a DMZ makes sense. However, any new firewall or network complexities should be weighed carefully against the level of security benefit that may be achieved.

11.3 DMZ Rule Sets

Depending on the types of services offered within the DMZ, the firewall rule sets might be very simple, or very complex. In a typical design, where only a web server, mail server, and DNS server are placed in the DMZ, the rule set is relatively simple. Traffic destined for the appropriate ports on the appropriate servers should be allowed, and everything else denied.

The secondary firewall is a little more complex. Obviously, administrators do not want mail stored on a server in the DMZ, and certainly users should not be

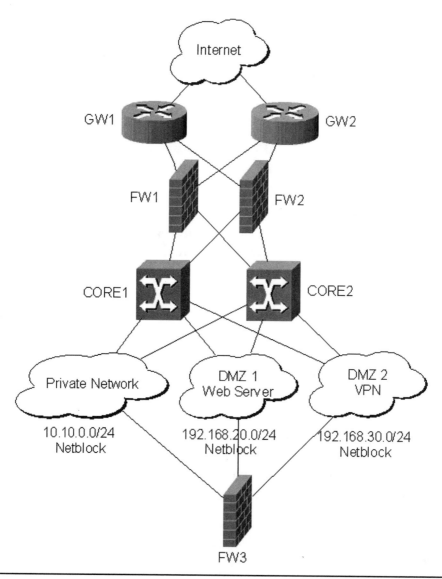

Figure 11.7   Rather than create an additional physical DMZ, this design uses additional interfaces on the firewall to isolate the networks

checking mail on a server in the DMZ, so the mail server in the DMZ is really a dummy. It simply relays all incoming mail to a mail server on the private network. To accomplish this, the secondary firewall has to allow Port 25 traffic from the public mail server IP address to the private mail server IP address.

Unless the network is using a multiple DMZ design, the web server IP address has to be allowed to query the database server on the private network, so that a port or ports will need to be allowed. If the DNS administrators are running a split-DNS design, the public DNS server will need to query the private DNS server on Port 53. To simplify the rule set, the source port of the public DNS server will need to be set to Port 53.

Various employees will need to be able to access the servers for monitoring and management purposes. Traffic from the internal network should be allowed to the private interfaces of the servers, but no traffic should be allowed past the private server interfaces. Remember, it is just as important to filter private to public traffic as it is to filter public to private traffic.

11.4 Summary

A DMZ, or even a multiple DMZ network, can be a useful way to isolate traffic to public servers, while still offering a level of protection through the firewall. It is important to remember, especially when dealing with DMZs, that a firewall is no substitute for good server security. A DMZ is an excellent layer of security, but it should not be the only one.

There are many different types of DMZ design. It is important to plan the DMZ carefully; otherwise, it is very easy to wind up with a gaping hole in the network design. Careful planning prior to DMZ deployment can increase the level of security that the DMZ provides. This planning may involve the use of a multiple DMZ design. Multiple DMZs increase the complexity of the network, and can make managing the firewall rule sets more complex, but they can also increase the level of network security on the network.

12

Server Security

Servers are the last layer of defense against attackers. If an attacker does manage to bypass the security restrictions in place on the routers and firewalls, the servers have to be hardened enough to keep the attacker from gaining unauthorized access to information on the network.

The server security problem is complicated by the fact that some servers are, by nature, public servers, so everyone—even people outside the organization—has to be allowed access. Even if all the servers on your network are private, security measures still need to be put in place to prevent unauthorized users from gaining access. This includes access from unauthorized employees.

A server is any machine to which multiple network users must connect in order to perform their jobs. Generally these machines have more memory, storage capacity, and faster processors (or multiple processors) than end user machines, also called workstations. Servers usually run different operating systems than workstations, though not always. Microsoft, for example, has created Windows 2000 Professional and Windows XP Professional for workstations and Windows 2000 Server, Windows 2000 Advanced Server, and Windows 2000 Datacenter Server for servers. In a similar manner Red Hat Linux 8.0 Professional is designed for workstations, while Red Hat Linux Advanced Server is designed for servers. On the other hand, Sun Solaris and FreeBSD use the same operating system for both servers and workstations.

That is not to say that all these server operating systems should be in use on the network, simultaneously. Running several different operating systems within the network can actually be detrimental to network security. Chances are the company's server administrative staff has a core expertise with one or two operating systems. If a third or fourth server operating system is added to the network—for whatever reason—there may not be enough staff members who have the knowledge to secure it properly.

For this reason, many security experts recommend using no more than two server operating systems on a network. There are, of course, exceptions to this guideline. If an organization has separate administrative staff for different servers, then the staff will presumably have expertise in the server operating system. For example, if the administrators for the web farm have experience with FreeBSD then running FreeBSD poses no security problems, even if it is not in use anywhere else in the network. This guideline applies primarily to organizations where server management is centralized in one group.

There is a lot of debate about operating system security within organizations, and over the Internet.[1] The truth is that all server operating systems can be properly secured when managed by an administrator who understands the operating system and how to secure it. No server operating system is inherently more secure than any other, but some are more secure out of the box, making the security process easier.

If an administrator does not know what he or she is doing, it is very easy to weaken the security of a server, especially a public server. That's why it is so important to ensure that all members of the server administration staff within an organization are properly trained on good server operating system security procedures. These procedures should be operating system specific, and organization specific. General guidelines, such as those present in this book, are a good start for forming internal best practices for server security, but each organization has specific needs, and the internal documents should reflect them.

Remember, too, open source does not automatically equate to less secure. There is a lot of misinformation about the security of open-source projects, but it basically boils down to same mantra: Because everyone has access to the source code, anyone can find security holes and exploit them.

The people who point this out usually forget to mention the opposite: Because everyone has access to the source code, anyone can find security holes and fix them. The vast majority of developers fall into the latter category. Open-

---

1. Debate is the nice way of saying "flame war."

source projects like Apache, Sendmail, BIND, and Linux have been tested, reviewed, picked over, and beaten on by so many developers that they are both stable and secure. Do security holes still arise? Absolutely, but those holes are quickly patched and the code updated. More importantly, long-standing open-source projects, like the ones mentioned, do not report security incidents more frequently than their closed-source counterparts.

This is not to suggest that an enterprise network should dump all closed-source products in favor of open-source solutions. There are open-source products that have abysmal security records. Instead, organizations should not be afraid to evaluate open-source products alongside closed-source products for use in the network. If an open-source product can meet the security requirements of an organization there is no reason not to use it. If the product cannot meet the security requirements, let the developers know about the problems experienced, and maybe the next time an evaluation is performed, it will be able to meet the requirements.

The first section of this chapter covers general guidelines for server security, including some operating-system-specific guidelines. The other sections focus on different types of servers. Web, mail, file, and other servers are all discussed in general and specific terms.

12.1 General Server Security Guidelines

There are two goals in the security process of any server: Allow authorized users to access the information they need, while preventing unauthorized users from gaining information they should not have. These goals seem to be almost polar opposites; an administrator has to let a user access his or her files, at the same time an attacker has to be prevented from accessing them. Considering that an attacker may be another employee who does have legitimate access to the server, it is easy to understand why server administrators are sometimes grumpy.

12.1.1 Server Construction

The first place to start with server security is the server itself. Remember, redundancy, scalability, and availability are critical components of security. A server should be constructed with these features in mind.

Most large organizations do not build their own servers, relying instead on servers from companies such as Dell, IBM or Hewlett-Packard. Fortunately, these companies will allow organizations to configure servers to fit their needs. Take advantage of this by selecting equipment that is designed for availability, and configuring as much redundancy into the system as practical.

Server components most likely to fail are those that have moving parts: power supplies, hard drives, fans, CD-ROMs, and floppy drives. Power supplies, hard drives, and fans are crucial to a functioning server; CD-ROMs and floppy drives are not as critical as the server can generally run without a working CD-ROM or floppy drive until it can be replaced.

To ensure continual performance, all servers on the network should be equipped with dual power supplies. Both power supplies should be plugged in. The server will only use the primary power supply, switching to the secondary if the primary fails (the reason for keeping both power supplies plugged in).

Power failures are especially dangerous, not only because they take the server offline, but also some server operating systems are particularly sensitive to data corruption that can be caused by incorrectly shutting down the server. Databases and other applications that are continuously writing to the disk are also sensitive to corruption by incorrectly shutting down the server.

Failover from one power supply to another should be instantaneous, meaning there is no interruption in service if the power supply fails. One thing to bear in mind is that it is not enough just to have the dual power supplies. The server has to have a way of notifying administrators when the power supply fails. If there is no notification, then there is no way to know that the power supply needs to be replaced. Server vendors should provide information about the notification process; if not, ask.

NOTE

Many servers do not have power buttons. This is to prevent an unknowing administrator from inadvertently destroying a server by using the power button to turn the server off. Unfortunately, this does not stop the same novice administrator from pulling the power cord—yet another reason for dual power supplies.

Hard drives are equally important to component availability. After all, the reason for the server's existence is the information located on the server. The information on the server is crucial to the existence of an organization, and should be protected as such. Hardware experts recommend Small Computer System Interface (SCSI) hard drives over Integrated Device Electronics (IDE) hard drives. SCSI drives are faster, at 10,000 to 15,000 revolutions per minute, than IDE drives, at 7,200 to 10,000 revolutions per minute, and SCSI drives are designed to last longer, with a longer mean time between failures (MTBF). Some SCSI manufacturers claim up to 1.2 million hours MTBF for their drives, while IDE drives generally have claims in the 100,000 hours MTBF range.

In addition to a quality hard drive, drives should be deployed in a redundant fashion. This is accomplished using a redundant array of independent disks (RAID). The most common RAID configuration is to deploy the drives in a redundant fashion. All data written to Disk 1 is also written to Disk 2, also known as a RAID 1. A second type of RAID configuration is RAID 0, which treats the string of disks as a single large disk. This increases the amount of storage available, but does not provide data redundancy.

The third type of RAID configuration is RAID 5. In this configuration, data is striped across multiple disks in a redundant fashion, giving the best of both worlds: It allows an administrator to create a single large storage area from several smaller disks, and it still allows for redundant data.

SCSI drives arranged in a RAID configuration often run very hot, so they require additional cooling, and sometimes even a separate case for the drives. Server cooling is usually handled through small fans placed throughout the case to optimize the cooling effect. Server fans have small motors, which can fail. Server cases usually have four or more fans placed in the server; if one fails, the others will continue to cool the inside of the case.

Unfortunately because the motors in the fans are so small, they do not usually have a way of alerting the system if there is a failure. Instead many server motherboards now include thermostats. If the temperature inside the case starts to rise an alert is generated, and the administrator of the server can take a look during the next maintenance window (unless the temperature gets too high, in which case the server may shut down).

12.1.2 Server Placement

Where the server is placed is just as important as its components. Two aspects of server placement have to be considered:

1. Physical location
2. Network placement

With regard to physical placement, the ideal location would be in a data center environment. Servers should be in a separate room, which is locked at all times, and to which only certain employees have access. Servers should be rack mountable, and they should be fully mounted. That sounds obvious, but many times rack mountable servers are simply stacked on top of each other within the rack. This makes it very easy for anyone who has access to the server room to walk off with a server.[2] In addition to physical security, rack mounting servers does increase availability. Computer racks are generally designed with air circulation in mind. If the servers are properly mounted, it will be easier for air to circulate through the rack, and assist in keeping the server temperature cooler.

The room should have a separate cooling and filtering unit. The HVAC unit should recycle the air at least every five minutes to keep dust and other contaminants out of the room. Dust is the biggest small-scale natural threat to computers. If dust begins to collect in the servers it can degrade the performance and decrease the life expectancy. The temperature of the data center should hover around 70 degrees Fahrenheit, or 21 degrees Celsius.

The room should also be equipped with FM200 fire suppression conduits, rather than traditional sprinkler systems. FM200, chemically known as heptafluoropropane, is a foam-like fire suppressant that can, unlike water, douse fires that occur in the data center without necessarily destroying the servers, or the data on the servers. Fires that occur as a result of overheated computers are extremely rare, but still possible, so good fire suppression is necessary for a data center environment.

Finally, the data center should have some form of backup power. The most common form of backup power used is an uninterruptible power supply. APC and Liebert are two manufacturers most often associated with data-center-wide UPS.

---

2. If you doubt this try unmounting a server that is fully mounted in less than 10 minutes.

The two most important considerations when deciding on a backup power supply are the amount of power needed and the length of time the data center needs to stay up. The amount of power needed is based on the number of network devices in the data center and the amount of power they consume. The length of time that the data center needs to remain online will depend on what types of servers are housed there, and who needs to access them.

If the data center is used primarily for on-site employees to access information, then the backup power supply should need to provide power for only an hour or two. This should be ample time to contact the power company and determine when the power will be restored. A one- or two-hour window also gives the administrative staff time to shut down the servers.

On the other hand if there are public servers, or servers that employees from other locations need to access, located within the data center, then additional backup power requirements may needed. Generally, a UPS should not be used to provide more than six hours of backup power. If more time is required a generator should be used. Generators require special wiring to ensure that power will flip over to the generator in the event of a power failure. Before installing one check with building management to ensure that there are no restrictions against generators.

NOTE

If power outages are common in your area, make sure there is gas in the generator. Many companies have procedures in place to deal with power outages, but nothing in the procedures addresses what to do when the power returns. Either make refueling the generator part of the power outage procedure, or make it standard to check the generator once a month to make sure it has fuel.

Physically securing servers is not enough; servers have to be placed on the network in a manner that will ensure their security and availability.

Network administrators will often segment servers into a separate VLAN, as shown in Figure 12.1. This makes sense at one level because it makes the management and monitoring of the servers simpler. It can also make network security easier by isolating the servers and creating more restrictive security policies for those switches.

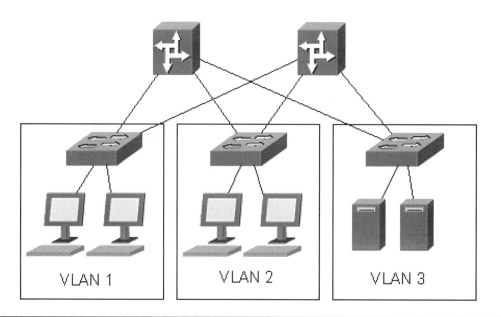

Figure 12.1   A traditional network design. Each switch block is segmented into different VLANs, creating an unnecessary load on the network.

The downside is it increases network traffic. Requests from the workstations have to be routed to the servers and back. A better solution for servers that are workgroup specific is to include the server as part of the workgroup VLAN.

This network design does not work for all servers, only servers that need to be accessed by a specific workgroup. For example department-specific file servers, DHCP servers, or domain controllers can be isolated in this manner.

As Figure 12.2 shows, a server that is used by the workgroup associated with VLAN 1 is also placed in VLAN 1. Traffic going from the workstations to the server, and vice versa, needs only to be switched, not routed. This decreases the load on the core switches or routers, and makes more efficient use of bandwidth within the network.

Of course this won't work for all servers. web, mail, and DNS servers—among others—need to be accessed by all employees, as well as users outside the network. As discussed in Chapter 11, public servers should be placed on a switch that is only used for public servers.

Having each server in a separate VLAN might seem like it would make it more difficult to effectively manage and monitor those servers. It will not if a separate network, a management network, is created.

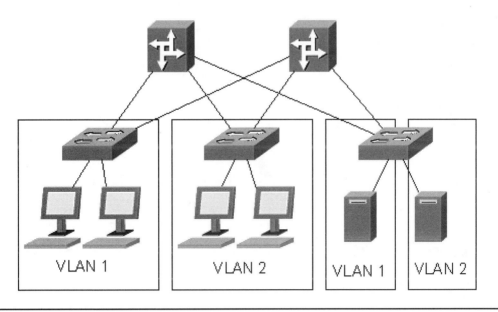

Figure 12.2   Segmenting servers into VLANs associated with different networks can decrease the load on routers

A management network, sometimes referred to as a backnet, is an isolated network that can be used to manage the servers. This management network is designed to facilitate server upgrades, backups, configuration, and monitoring. The most important aspect of a management network is that it has to be isolated. There should be no traffic, aside from management traffic, that traverses the backnet.

Figure 12.3 illustrates the typical setup of a management network. Each server on the backnet has a primary IP address in a separate VLAN. The backnet interfaces are all part of the same VLAN, and they are part of a separate network. A separate network infrastructure is in place to support the management network. Again, this is to keep management traffic apart from the rest of the network traffic.

There are two advantages to installing a management network in this manner:
- It isolates management traffic which improves overall network performance.
- It keeps management passwords, monitoring information, and other tools used to keep tabs on the network isolated from attackers and prying eyes.

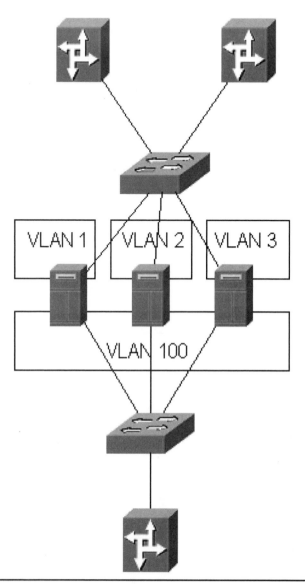

Figure 12.3 Using a management network to control the type of traffic that is sent to the main server IP address and to better manage network traffic

In fact, many organizations with a management network in place will only allow human connections to be made through a VPN, further enhancing the security of the information shared across this network.

A backnet will not work well in all network environments, but it does make a great additional layer of security when it can be used.

12.1.3 Server Security

The servers have now been physically secured and isolated on the network. The next step is to secure access to the servers. Because the most damaging network attacks require gaining access to a server, it is important to restrict access as much as possible to all servers.

Start by limiting servers to single-use machines. The web server should be used only to serve websites, the mail server should only be used for mail, and so on. It is easier to manage security on individual servers if an administrator can limit the number of services running on them.

A good example of this is the X-Windows management system that is installed on many Unix systems by default. Because Unix servers are generally managed through the command line, keeping the X-Windows system installed only leaves unnecessary accounts installed and potential security holes open.

Of course in order for this strategy to work, it is also important to follow through and disable any services that are unused. Not only should unnecessary services be disabled, but whenever possible they should be removed, or not installed in the first place.

Services should never be run as the administrative user. It may be necessary to start the service using the administrative user account to bind it to the port, but the service should continue to run as a nonprivileged user. If the service is run as a nonprivileged user then if the service is compromised it is less likely that an attacker will be able to cause any further damage to the network.

In addition to running services as nonprivileged users, unnecessary accounts should be removed from servers, or at a minimum, renamed. The Windows guest account is an example of an unnecessary account that should be deleted. The same goes for the Unix games, bin, and sys accounts as well as other well-known accounts. If the accounts cannot be removed entirely they should be configured with no login capabilities and a very restrictive password. All accounts on all network devices, but especially on servers, should have passwords.

Accounts created on the server should be subject to the same password policy as the rest of the network. This means that the passwords should be changed at regular intervals, and they should be sufficiently difficult to crack using password cracking tools.

Whenever possible information about user accounts should be stored in a centralized database. This helps decrease the likelihood that a wayward account will be created on a server. It also makes it easier for employees to hop from server to server, as long as they have permission to access the server. In cases where a centralized user database is in use, the authentication from the servers to the user database should use some sort of encryption. Kerberos is the type of authentication most often associated with this type of server management. Kerberos is also nice, because Unix operating systems, and Windows 2000, support it, making it possible for a user to authenticate against both types of servers, if necessary.

This does not mean that users should have the run of the network; servers should be configured so that only specific groups have access to specific servers. Users in the accounting group should not need access to the sales server, and so on. Again, limiting who has access to a server will limit the amount of damage an attacker who gains access to one of the servers can do.

Files on the system should be restricted as well. A common way of enforcing file security is to create separate partitions on the server. One partition should be used for system files, while a separate partition can be used for user files. This is a common practice on Unix servers, which are generally broken into /, /usr, /etc, /opt, and others, depending on the needs of the server administrator. This is a less common practice on Windows-based servers, but one that should be followed, even if it is as simple as putting the system files on a C:\ and user files on an F:\ partition.

Partitioning servers has two effects:

1. It separates system information in a logical manner. If something happens to one of the partitions, data on the second partition is usually safe.

2. It creates a separate root directory for users. Users on the F:\ partition, or in the /usr partition see F:\ and /usr, respectively, as their root directories, and are unable to access the system files on the other partitions. While this is not perfect security, it does make the job of an attacker more difficult.

Cording off partitions is not enough; servers should have file systems that are as restrictive as possible. No users should have executable access on file servers, and, ideally, the user should only be able to access files in his or her own directory. In other words, the user should not be able to browse the directories or files of other users. This is done by giving the user's directory read and write permissions, but no other user—except the administrative user—should have access to the user's directory. Figures 12.4 and 12.5 show the best practices file permissions for Unix and Windows 2000 servers. These permissions assume the server will be used solely for storing data, and no programs will need to be run directly on the server.

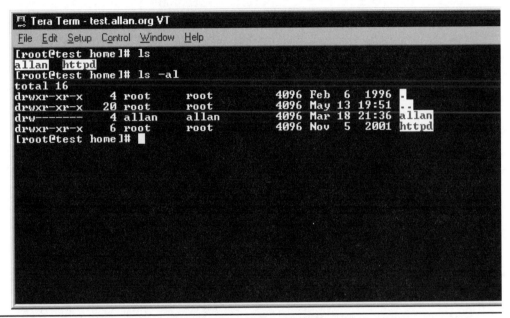

Figure 12.4   Unix system file permissions. User Allan has read and write access to the directory allan; no other groups have read or write access.

System files should always be owned by the administrative user, and should be viewable or executable only by the administrator. This may mean tightening default permissions on some operating systems. This change is necessary especially when dealing with configuration files. Configuration files are often plain text, so if one has weak permissions, it can be used by an attacker to gather more information about a server and increase the amount of damage an attacker is capable of inflicting on the server.

On Windows servers, the group "Everyone" should be removed from the server, or used sparingly. The "Everyone" group allows all users on a server to have access to a file or directory, including the guest user. Since the "Everyone" group defeats the purpose of restricting file systems, there is no point in using it on the server. Instead only groups that need access to the server should be installed on it.

If each department has its own dedicated server, the task of restricting access is a lot simpler. It is easier to restrict access to a group and then assign permission to individual folders. In some environments, especially within workgroups that are more collaborative in nature, it is acceptable to restrict individual folder access to the group, instead of the individual user. This will allow group members to access files in each other's folders, share information, and still keep the data protected from outside users. Group permission is 660 (rw-rw----) on a Unix system and Read and Change on a Windows server.

Giving group access to an individual's folder can have negative consequences. If an employee's password is compromised the attacker will now have access to all files on the server, and can delete the files, make changes, or even copy them and use them against an organization. Many organizations have opted to use intranets to facilitate group collaboration. With an intranet, files that need to be shared with group members can be posted publicly, while files that are private, or still in development, can be left in the user's directory, keeping them segregated from other members in the group.

NOTE

Because servers, especially web servers, are susceptible to attacks, Unix administrators often install chkrootkit (*www.chkrootkit.org/*), or a similar program. These programs look for signs of known rootkits on the server and report any suspicious findings.

Another good practice is to monitor file permissions on the server. A task that looks for inappropriate file permissions can be scheduled to run nightly. Usually a report is generated, then permissions can be automatically changed, or e-mail can be sent to the offending users, explaining what needs to be done to correct the problem. Of course, this process should be monitored closely to ensure the users are actually making the permission changes.

On Unix systems, another method of file system security is to create a special environment using chroot. Chroot is a way to create a jailed environment for

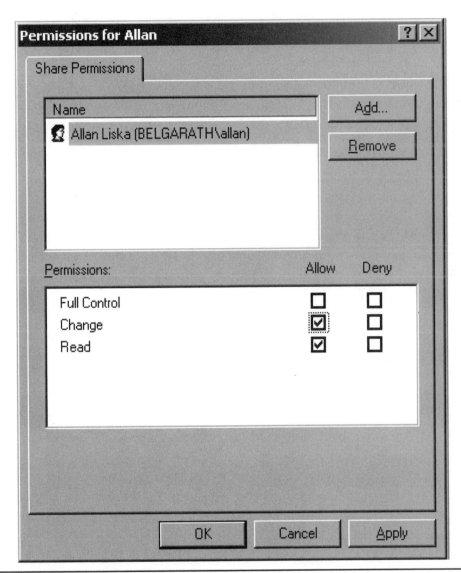

Figure 12.5   Windows 2000 file permissions. The user Allan is the only person, aside from the Administrator, who has access to the folder allan.

users. The jail limits the directories to which a user has access. For example, a typical Unix user's home directory might be /home/users/allan/. The directory /home is already a partition; however, an administrator may want to create an environment in which the user Allan sees the root directory as being /allan. This forces the user to stay within the home directory, and prevents users from searching through other files.

An environment protected by chroot is still vulnerable to attacks, so it should not be used as a single solution for securing file systems. However, when used in conjunction with other security precautions, chroot can add an extra level of security to a server.

12.1.4 The Administrative User

The administrative user is the one user who can cause the most damage on a server. The administrator has access to the entire server and is able manipulate any file on the server. Limiting the capabilities of the administrative user is not a good idea; instead, it is better to restrict server access, making it difficult to become the administrative user.

Windows and Unix operating systems approach the administrative user in two distinct fashions, although the user performs the same tasks. The administrative user is known as administrator, which on a Windows server is a username that can be changed. In fact, many Windows security experts recommend changing administrator to an account name that is less obvious. This is another example of security through obscurity, which is not the recommended approach to securing a server, but it is a good idea when used in conjunction with other security measures.

Windows servers require that many services run as administrator, opening the possibility for root exploits. If an attacker is able to compromise one of these services remotely, the username is known, so it is just a matter of determining the password. If the attacker has to determine the username and password, breaking into the server is that much more difficult.

For the name change to be effective, the administrator account should be renamed to something non-obvious. Renaming it to root, or another common name, is very ineffective, and still leaves the server easily exploitable.

Different users can have administrative access to a server, and a user can be made the administrator of a single server, but not necessarily an entire server farm. However, if a user is logged in as a non-administrative user, that person has to log out and login as an administrator to gain server control.

This contrasts greatly with Unix, which allows users to login as one user and switch to the administrative user, known as root, using the substitute user (su) command. The obvious downside to su is that, in its most basic implementation, it allows any user to become root. To limit the security risks posed by allowing any user to become root, most administrators create a wheel group. The wheel group is a special Unix group which allows an administrator to control the users that have access to becoming root.

Unix, like Windows, allows users to belong to multiple groups, making it possible to give different users root access to different servers. For example, if the company webmaster needs root access on the web server, but no other servers, then the webmaster's account can be added to the wheel group on the web server, but not on any other servers. An administrator has the ability to add individual users to the wheel group, while leaving other users in the same group unaffected. Using the example of a web server, it is common to have a group of users maintain a website. These users are most likely part of the same group; the webmaster will also be part of this group. An administrator can give the webmaster the capability of becoming root, without giving the other users in the group root access.

Unlike Windows-based servers, it is not recommended that administrators change the root user to a different name. There are too many services that rely on having access to the root user in order to start. In addition, Unix has built-in tools that allow administrators to limit how root is accessed.

One recommendation commonly made by security experts is to limit console and TTY access, so only the root user can login from the console. Within the server, limit the range of IP addresses that are able to access the server remotely, and log all connection attempts, as well as any attempts to change to the root user. Some security experts also recommend disabling remote root access. This forces administrators to log into the server, then su to root, in order to become the administrative user. The argument for this security step is that it forces a potential attacker to try to crack two passwords instead of one.

Finally, on Unix systems it is possible to give certain users permission to execute commands as the root user. The most common way to do this is using the superuser do (sudo) suite of commands.

Sudo has become a very popular method of delegating security on Unix servers. Using sudo allows the administrator to tightly restrict who has root access, while still giving users the ability to run commands necessary to perform their jobs. Sudo also has several security enhancements, including extensive logging facilities, creating a detailed trail whenever a command is executed through sudo.

The way sudo works is that a server administrator can assign permissions so that a process is owned by root, but a user, or group, is able to run it as well. The user or group runs the process without having to actually su to the root user, and the administrator can still restrict permissions on the file so that it is owned by root. Referring to the webmaster example, a webmaster should not need access to most system files; however, it is not uncommon for a webmaster to have to restart web services. Rather than make the webmaster part of the wheel group for this one task, an administrator can delegate the web server processes to the webmaster allowing him or her to start and stop web services as needed, but with no other administrative rights on the server.

Taking proper precautions to restrict access to the administrative access to the server can increase server security exponentially and can help protect against the most common system attacks.

12.2 Backups

A common mistake made by administrators is to assume that installing RAID controllers on a server is the same as backing up data. It is not. The purpose of RAID is to provide failover in the event of a hard drive failure. Backing up data involves making a copy of existing information on a separate device. Backups are especially important in a server environment, as the purpose of a server is to store information.

Data backups are an inherent part of good network security. If a server, or another network device, is compromised, restoring proper data quickly is just as important as responding to an attack.

There are three different types of backups:

1. Full
2. Partial
3. Image

Full and partial backup combinations are the most popular. Initially a full backup of a system is created. Subsequent backups only copy files that have changed. If there is no change, the file does not need to be copied. Periodically, usually once every week or two weeks, a full backup is again completed, and the cycle restarts. A disk image is a sector-by-sector duplication of a disk that is stored as an image. The image can then be transferred to other media, or restored at a later date.

Backed-up data can be stored in several different ways. It can be stored to tape, or on multiple tapes using a tape jukebox, or data can be stored within a Storage Area Network (SAN). The two methods of storage are not mutually exclusive; tape servers can be included as part of a SAN, and, in fact, this is very common.

Using a SAN is the recommended method of performing backups. A SAN is a network of mass-storage devices that is isolated on a private network, segmenting SAN traffic from the rest of the network. Because SANs involve a lot of data, high-speed connections are used to connect devices on the network. Usually, this involves fiber optic connections between the devices.

The private network, combined with the fast connectivity between devices, has quickly catapulted SAN as the preferred backup technology, which makes sense, because backups are useless if they have been corrupted. So, it is important to secure backup data, just as you would any other communication.

Obviously, backup security would be enhanced if the data were encrypted, but the load on the network and the servers would be too great for a midsized network. Instead, by isolating the traffic, at least some level of security is achieved.

The backup process starts with the frequency and times of backup. Server backups should be performed on a daily basis, unless the information on the server does not change often, in which case every few days may be acceptable. No server should go more than a week without being backed up. Router, switch, and firewall configurations should also be backed up on a daily basis, or at least several times a week.

If an organization is run in a traditional manner, where employees access servers between 9:00 A.M. and 5:00 P.M., then anytime overnight is fine to perform backups. As more organizations more toward a 24x7 operation, it becomes increasingly difficult to set a time to do backups. In cases like this, it is important to monitor server and network traffic to determine the best time to perform backups. There is no rule that says all backups have to be performed at the same time; in fact, in many cases it helps to spread out the backups throughout the day.

Backups to a tape, or writable CD-ROM, are preferred as it is more difficult to write over, or corrupt, those mediums than it is a hard drive sitting on a server. In addition, whenever possible, backups should be encrypted. The backup process does not have to be carried out over an encrypted connection. Once the data is backed up it should be encrypted; this helps to prevent an attacker from tampering with data that should be safe.

Backups should be tested on a regular basis. Not only should they be tested to ensure that the data was successfully backed up, but restores should be tested as well. Backup software will sometimes report corrupted data as a successful backup, so everything looks fine in the log file, but the data is actually worthless. This is especially common when a bad tape or CD-ROM is used. Taking a few minutes a week to spot check backups by attempting to restore a file, or directory, is a good practice and may provide warning signs that a failure is about to occur.

Test restores of data can also help server administrators determine how long a restore will take. The most commonly asked question when a server fails is when it will be back online. The better answer administrators can provide to that question the happier network users will be. Practicing helps to ensure that the data will be restored in a timely manner.

Backup mediums should also be rotated to offsite facilities. Companies such as Archive Away, StorNet, and Storage Networks offer organizations ways to store backups in a separate facility, away from the corporate network. Data can either be transferred to these facilities across the WAN, using a private VPN, or even physically sent to the location.

A good rule of thumb is to keep two weeks of backup on site, and at least two or three months of backups at a remote location. In some instances, especially where financial or legal records are involved, this length of time may not be adequate. If this is the case, local or federal laws may govern the length of time the backups have to be stored.

12.2.1 Disaster Recovery

Offsite backups are a critical part of a disaster recovery plan. Disaster recovery is the ability of an organization to recover and continue doing business, with minimal interruption, in the face of a catastrophic disaster.

As awareness of security network problems has increased so has the interest in disaster recovery. To address the problems associated with a catastrophic failure, a disaster recovery plan should be developed within an organization.

Such a plan outlines the steps necessary to bring an organization to a fully operational status in the event a disaster occurs. Disasters generally fall into one of four categories:

1. Accidental
2. Internal
3. Natural
4. Terrorism/Civil unrest

These categories are intentionally broad. Similar to a security plan, it is up to each individual organization to determine what constitutes a disaster (what would cause a business interruption) and what steps need to be taken to restore business operations.

While the categories have some leeway in terms of interpretation, there are guidelines as to what makes up each. An accidental disaster is a complete loss of power, a train derailment or other transportation accident, or an employee who accidentally destroys valuable corporate data.

Internal disasters include things like employee sabotage, theft, or even workplace violence. The difference between accidental disasters that involve employees and internal disasters is that with an internal disaster the action is intentional. Natural disasters include floods, hurricanes, heavy rain, blizzards, and other catastrophes initiated without human intervention.

Many offsite storage organizations also offer disaster recovery solutions. These solutions are mirrors of existing data that are activated in the event of a complete network failure at the primary location. If that is not an option, then determining the fastest way to recover data from an offsite location should be considered as part of a disaster recovery plan.

Disaster recovery is not inexpensive. In fact it can often seem to be excessively priced. However, the cost pales in comparison to the cost of hours, or days, of downtime, which is why many organizations opt to participate in some form of disaster recovery.

12.3 Web Server Security

An organization's web server is an attacker's most common point of entry into the network. A web server is, almost by definition, a public server, so it makes an attractive target to attackers. In addition, depending on the nature of the website, breaking into the web server may give an attacker access to valuable customer information. Because web servers are such attractive targets, special steps need to be taken to secure the web server against attackers.

The web server should be a single-use server, and should have a very restricted access policy; only personnel who absolutely need access should have it. In fact, a staging server is commonly used as a means of further restricting access to the actual web server.

A staging server is a replica of the web server. It should have the same operating system, same patches, same file structure, and all of the same software as the web server. Content destined for the web server is loaded to the staging server and the pushed to the web server using software like RedDot Solution's Content Management Server (CMS). Different users, or departments, are given accounts on the staging server; the accounts are used to upload content to the staging server. The content is pushed from the staging server to the actual web server using a separate account to which the users do not have access. The web server is configured to only allow the staging account access from the IP address of the staging server.

As shown in Figure 12.6, the staging server should be placed on a separate VLAN than the web server. The staging server should be part of a private VLAN that is not accessible through the firewall. This will prevent an attacker who does gain access to the web server from getting to the staging server and using it to launch additional attacks.

Because the staging server is the only machine that will send content to the web server, an administrator can restrict the ways of accessing the server. Depending on the type of server, content can be uploaded using either Secure Copy (SCP) or Secure FTP (SFTP), and standard FTP ports can be disabled on the server. If other forms of access are required, they should only be allowed from the staging server, and those ports should be blocked to the server through the firewall.

NOTE

If FTP is required to run on the server, it is critical that anonymous FTP be disabled on all servers—except servers that have files available for general download. An increasingly common attack is to scan for servers that have anonymous FTP enabled, with very loose file permissions. These servers are then used to store pirated software, and other files, leaving a company open to lawsuits and increasing the amount of bandwidth used exponentially.

Content on the web server should be stored on a separate partition from the operating system files. Programs installed to assist in serving web pages, such as Apache, Internet Information Server, and ColdFusion should have any sample files included as part of the default install deleted.

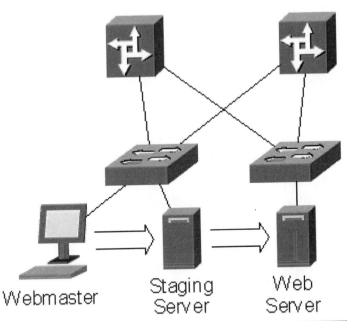

Webmaster   Staging   Web
                 Server   Server

Figure 12.6   A staging server is used as an added measure of web server security. Content is uploaded to the staging server then pushed to the web server.

NOTE

A common practice among attackers is to look for sample files that programs like ColdFusion install by default, and exploit weaknesses in those default installs.

Within the content partition, file permissions should be as restrictive as possible. This probably sounds like an oxymoron; files on a web server have to be world-readable because anyone can visit a website. The difficulty is finding a balance between making the website user experience enjoyable and keeping the web server secure.

If the content of a website is largely static, consider using strict HTML pages, and setting the file permissions so they are world-readable but not writable, and certainly not executable. On the other hand, if website content is dynamic and database driven, the files will have to be world-readable and executable, but they should not be writable. Windows-based web servers have a special scripting permission separate from executable permissions; that permission should be used for dynamic content.

In cases where executable permissions are required, security precautions should be taken to secure the scripting software. Whether the site uses Perl, PHP, Java, VBScript, or ColdFusion, there are vendor-recommended practices that a server administrator can follow, like running PHP in safe mode, to increase the security of scripts on the server.

Outlining security steps for all of the commonly used scripting languages is beyond the scope of this book. There is plenty of excellent information available for locking down each language.

There are three general guidelines that all scripts in use on a website should follow to ensure security:

1. A script should never accept unchecked data.

2. All input should be validated.

3. Scripts should not rely on path information gleaned from the server.

Whether it is a form, database query, or some other type of user input, any data that is processed by a script should be validated. The data has to be checked to ensure it is not passing malicious information to the script.

All input being passed to another program on the server should be validated. While Rule 2 sounds similar to the first rule, the implications are different. In the first instance, the script is checking for potentially damaging input before processing it. This applies to information that is generally damaging to the server. For example, an attacker loads the command:

```
ls -al
```

into a feedback form, and is able to get a directory listing of the root web directory. In this case, information that is being passed to a specific program has to be validated to ensure it interacts properly with the program. Using the feedback form as an example, an attacker may be able to manipulate it so that the web server can be used to send unsolicited mail.

NOTE

Matt's Formmail is one of the most popular scripts in use on the Internet. Older versions of the script contained a security hole similar to the one described. Attackers were able to exploit that hole to send unsolicited commercial mail to millions of people. The hole has been patched for more than a year, but there are still older versions of the script in use on thousands of websites.

The problem becomes even more insidious when attackers use the same type of attack to submit queries to databases on the server. An attacker can use this type of attack to find out usernames, phone numbers, and even credit card information. Restricting the type of information that can be submitted to a web server helps to reduce the chances that this type of attack will occur.

The third rule is that scripts should not rely on path information gleaned from the server. The Common Gateway Interface (CGI) specification has a variable called PATH, which can prepend the server-supplied path to any files or directories used in a script. So, if a script needs to access a file called sample.exe, the file can be called like this:

```
$PATH/sample.exe
```

Unfortunately, the PATH variable can be manipulated allowing an attacker to view the directory contents of the server. Rather than rely on information gathered from the PATH variable, programmers should hard code data paths directly into the scripts. Hard coding path information into a script prevents an attacker from manipulating the PATH variable to display files on the web server.

New security holes are constantly being discovered in web applications. It is important that web server administrators stay abreast of current security problems that are introduced and update software as quickly as possible.

Attackers are especially quick to take advantage of security holes in web server software, so quickly patching security holes is critical. Web server attacks are successful because most of the time they resemble a standard HTTP connection attempt. Rather than using malformed packets or spoofing addresses, an attacker makes a standard HTTP GET request, but is sending bad information to the server.

In August 2001 hundreds of thousands of web servers started receiving quests like this:

```
"GET/
default.ida?NNNNNNNNNNNNNNNNNNNNNNNNNNNNNNNNNNNNNNNNNNNNNNNNNNNNNNNNNNNNNNNN
NNNNNNNNNNNNNNNNNNNNNNNNNNNNNNNNNNNNNNNNNNNNNNNNNNNNNNNNNNNNNNNNNNNNNNNNNNNN
NNNNNNNNNNNNNNNNNNNNNNNNNNNNNNNNNNNNNNNNNNNNNNNNNNNNNNNNNNNNNNNNNNNNNNNNNNNN
NNNNNNNNNNNNNNNNNNNNNNNNNNNNNNNNN%u9090%u6858"
```

These requests were part of the Code Red worm. The Code Red worm took advantage of a security hole in Microsoft Index Server, which was susceptible to buffer overflows.[3] The security patch had been available for months, but most administrators had not patched their systems, leaving them vulnerable. The Code Red worm spread across several continents in a few hours. While the damage that was done by this worm was relatively mild, it could have been much worse.

The Code Red worm made administrators painfully aware of the inadequate steps that are often taken to secure web servers. The impact of Code Red would have been a lot less severe if companies that were not using Microsoft Index Server (installed by default with an installation of Internet Information Server) had disabled the service and deleted files related to Index Server.

Just as a good administrator would not dream of leaving unnecessary services running on a server, unused web services should be disabled. The most popular web servers, Apache, Microsoft Internet Information Server, and Sun iPlanet, bundle additional services that not all websites will use. It is important to review

---

3. This is the reason why scripts should never accept unchecked data.

configuration information when this software is installed to ensure there are no unnecessary web services running. Every unused web service presents a potential security hole, so leaving the service disabled will improve security, simply by not having it active.

Another common mistake made by web server administrators is to store customer information on the web server. No matter what precautions an administrator has taken it is still possible, if not likely, that the web server will be compromised. If this occurs, having a database filled with customer information is the worst thing that can happen. Customers are usually understanding about website defacements, but they are understandably less forgiving if an attacker gains access to confidential information.

To avoid this problem, website databases should be stored on a separate server. The web server can send database queries to the database server and pull the necessary information, on an as-needed basis. Queries between the web server and the database server should be encrypted, and the database username and password should also be secured.

The database server itself should be configured to not allow any logins using the public network address. All administration of the database server should be handled through the management network on the private network interface.

To provide an additional layer of protection, the database that is queried by the web server should be a scaled-down version of the real customer database. The web database can contain some customer contact information, but it should not contain all customer information. If possible, the database should not contain billing information. Unfortunately, it is sometimes necessary to make billing information available, especially for sites that are e-commerce oriented. In cases like this, the website database should only contain partial information, such as the last 4 numbers of a credit card. Now, even if an attacker is able to bypass the database server defenses, the information gained will be significantly less valuable than if all the billing information had been available.

Protecting customer information has to be a top priority for a web server administrator. Taking the proper steps to secure a database, and a database server, goes a long way to protect that information. It also ensures that customer's faith in an organization remains strong.

12.3.1 SSL Encryption

A common way to enhance the security of transactions conducted through a website is to use Secure Sockets Layer (SSL) encryption. Netscape developed SSL as a means of securing web-based transactions. The IETF has recently adopted most of the SSL specification to create a new protocol, designed to secure more than web-based transactions, called Transport Layer Security (TLS).

SSL uses public key cryptography developed by RSA Data Security, Inc., to secure transactions. Public key cryptography uses a public/private key pair to validate the information being sent between parties.

The default SSL port is 443 TCP; however, SSL can run over other ports, and many administrative applications now require SSL connections over different ports. Traditionally, to make an SSL connection to a web server to Port 443, a user simply typed in https://www.example.com; if the connection were to be made on a different port, the user would type https://www.example.com:[port number]. The effect is the same: The transactions between the user and the web server will be encrypted.

The process of setting up an SSL on a web server varies depending on the type of web server being used, but the backend functionality is the same across all web servers. The public/private key pair is generated on the web server. The private key is stored separately from the public key which is sent to a Certificate Authority (CA), such as VeriSign or Thawte. The CA verifies the identity of the organization that sent the key and issues an x.509v3 certificate. The x.509v3 certificate contains the organization's public key and is signed by the CA. The newly generated certificate is installed on the web server, and SSL sessions can begin.

NOTE

SSL sessions will actually run without a certificate generated by a CA. The web browser will generate an error window when a user visits an SSL-encrypted website that does not have a CA-signed certificate. The error will indicate that a trusted authority has not signed the certificate, and therefore the information is suspect. The data sent between the user and the server is still encrypted, but there is no third-party verification that the website is owned by the organization that claims to own it.

When a user attempts to connect to a web server using SSL, several things happen. The first is that the user initiates an SSL connection with the web server, and tells the web server the minimum SSL version it will accept (Version 3.0 is the current standard). The web server responds with a copy of the x.509v3 key. The web browser chooses a random symmetric key, encrypts it with the server's x.509v3 key, and sends it back to the web server. The web server decrypts the symmetric key using the server's private key.

The web server and the client use this symmetric key to encrypt traffic during the SSL session. The web server also assigns a unique ID to each encrypted session, called an SSL Session ID. The SSL Session ID is unencrypted and sent between the user and the server with each request.

SSL is a great tool for encrypting data between users and a web server. It should not be thought of as a tool for securing a web server. SSL does not assist with securing data once it is on a server. This is an important point: Many administrators feel that if they have SSL encryption their web server is automatically secure. That is not the case. SSL encryption should be used with other security measures as part of an overall web server security solution.

12.3.2 Load Balancing

So far in this section, the discussion has revolved around attackers attempting to deface a website, and attempting to get customer information. Those attacks are common, but another common attack faced by web server administrators is a DoS attack.

DoS attacks are different in that they often serve no other purpose than to see if the attacker can take a website offline. The attacker may have a grudge against an organization, or may have been frustrated in attempts to attack a server in other ways. Whatever the reason, a DoS attack against a web server is often difficult to defend against, especially if it is a DDoS attack.

A typical website consists of a single server, with a database server sitting behind it. Even if a DoS attack does not saturate an Internet connection, it is not difficult to generate enough requests to knock a server offline. Firewalls can stop many, but not all, DoS attacks, especially if the attacks appear to be a great number of legitimate requests—which they often are.

A common method used to protect a website against DoS, and other types of attacks, is to load balance the site across multiple servers. Load balancing has traditionally been used to distribute traffic across multiple servers as a means of improving performance and customer experience. As some websites increased in popularity, a single server was not enough to handle the number of requests received.

The solution was to set up multiple servers. At first these multi-server solutions were primitive. A company would create multiple records in their zone file pointing to the IP addresses of different servers, as shown in Figure 12.7.

From a security perspective, there are two problems with this approach. (1) It does not take into account availability. If a web server is unavailable, the DNS server will still direct people to it, because the DNS server does not have any way of knowing the server has failed. (2) DNS information is publicly available, so an attacker can find all of the servers associated with a website and attempt to break into sites.

Two other forms of load balancing have become popular for use with web servers: clustering and network load balancing. Clustering has been used with other types of servers for many years, but it has only recently become common-place for web servers. A cluster is a series of servers that act as a single server (Figure 12.8). The servers either communicate with each other or with a cluster controller to process requests as they are made. The cluster is assigned an IP address, and each individual server can learn that IP via ARP to requests for that IP address. The individual servers are also assigned unique IP addresses, which allow for server management and communication between the servers.

When a request to the web server is made, the clustered servers determine which is going to accept it based on a preprogrammed set of rules, known as metrics. Depending on the metrics used, a single server may handle all requests from one source IP address, or the requests may be distributed between the servers. If one of the servers fails, the other servers in the cluster pick up its requests and service goes uninterrupted.

Clusters add to the security of a web server not simply because they increase availability, but also because they make it more difficult to launch an attack against a server. Each time a request to the website is made a different server

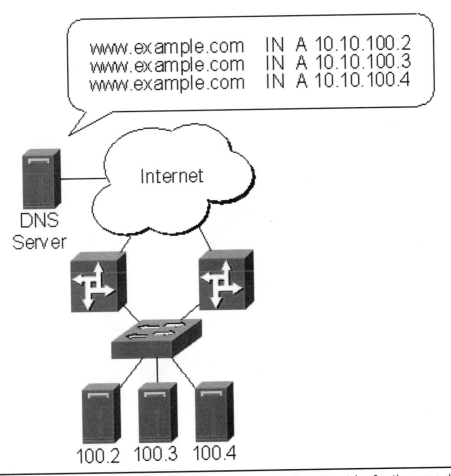

Figure 12.7   Increase availability by having multiple DNS entries for the same domain pointing to different servers

may respond to the request. An attacker engaged in a complicated break-in attempt will need to restart the process each time a request is made because there is no way to guess which server will respond. In addition, if a private network is used to maintain the servers, then there is not a public address to which an attacker can latch on in order to complete an attack. Even within a small cluster, this advantage can give an administrator additional time to catch the alarm, track down the attacker, and stop the attack before it is successful.

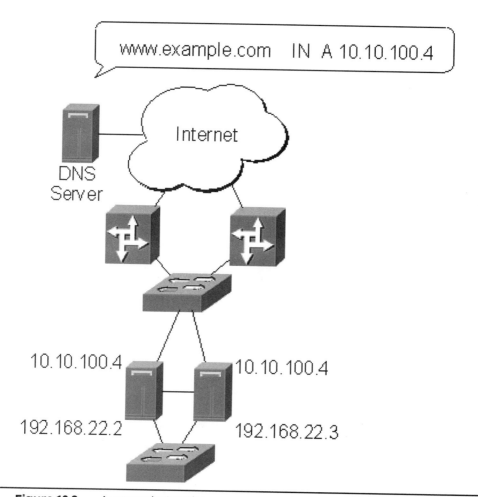

Figure 12.8   A server cluster. The servers answer to the same IP address on the public side but have unique, private IP addresses for management and intraserver communications.

One area in which clustering generally cannot assist is with DoS attacks. A well-executed DoS attack can still overpower several servers, rendering them unavailable to legitimate requests. For administrators concerned about DoS and DDoS attacks, network load balancing may be a better solution.

Network load balancing uses a switched device, such Cisco CSS11500, Nortel Network Alteon 184, Extreme Network SummitPx1, or F5 Network BIG-IP

5000, to direct traffic between multiple servers. The load balancer, or balancers, if deployed in pairs for redundancy, assumes the IP address of the website, as shown in Figure 12.9. Website requests reach the load balancer and are forwarded to the appropriate server, depending on the set metrics. Each server is configured with a private IP address that is used for management purposes.

If a server fails, it is taken out of rotation by the load balancer and an alert is generated. No traffic is lost as the load balancer simply redirects requests to another server. As with clustering, load balancing provides additional protection from attackers. Because there are multiple servers, each with a private IP address, an attacker may to have to continually restart an attack.

In addition, because most network load balancers are, essentially, switches, they are designed to handle large amounts of traffic. Many load balancers include DoS and DDoS detection utilities. These utilities can be used to drop bad requests before they reach the servers. The load balancer is able to pass legitimate traffic to the server and deny bad traffic without any performance

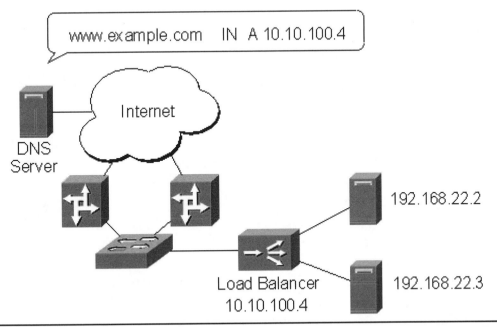

Figure 12.9   Network load balancing. A switched device sits on the network in front of the servers and distributes traffic between the devices. The load balancer assumes the IP address of the website, and the servers are privately addressed.

degradation. Load balancers are usually deployed in pairs, so if an attacker is able to launch enough traffic to overwhelm one, and it becomes unreachable, the second load balancer will take over and continue to forward traffic.

Keep in mind that these devices are able to process several gigabits of information at any one time, so a DoS attack is more likely to overwhelm an Internet connection than the load balancer itself. The ability of load balancers to stave off a DoS attack, even if the Internet connection has been overwhelmed, is actually beneficial. Many attackers count on DoS attacks crashing the web servers, leaving the servers more susceptible to other attacks. If the load balancers can prevent the site from being overwhelmed, the server will remain intact. The site may be unavailable while the DoS attack is going on, but the servers will remain secure.

Load balancers are certainly not a cure-all for web server security. If a server is not properly patched, or does not have the proper access restrictions, it will be susceptible to simple attacks, which will fall below the radar of the load balancer. A load balancer can be used in conjunction with a solid web server security policy to enhance the security of a web server.

12.4 Mail Server Security

There are two types of mail server security that need to be considered: the message transfer agent (MTA) and the user mailboxes. Most security resources are focused on the MTA, because that is the program responsible for routing mail to and from network users. It has also, traditionally, been one of the weakest security points on the network. Weak MTA security cannot only lead to attacks on a network, it can also result in mail from an organization being blacklisted. An organization that winds up on an MTA blacklist will be unable to send mail to sites that subscribe to the blacklist.

Before reading any further, conduct an experiment to gauge how secure your organization's MTA is. Visit the following website in your favorite browser: *www.abuse.net/relay.html*. Where it asks you to enter the address to test, put the address of your MTA (your outgoing mail server), and select test for relay.

The site performs a series of tests to determine how secure an MTA is against relaying. The results of your test should be similar to Figure 12.10. If not, there may be some serious mail server security work ahead.

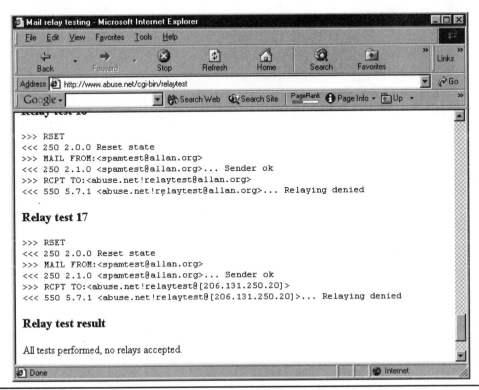

Figure 12.10   Results of the Network Abuse Clearinghouse mail relay test

This test, sponsored by the Network Abuse Clearinghouse, is one of many open relay testers on the Internet. The purpose of these tests is to help mail administrators determine the security of their mail relays.

The purpose of an MTA is to route mail traffic from one server to another, or from a server to the desired mailboxes. E-mail is, by far, the most used application on the Internet; more than 1 billion e-mails are exchanged everyday, and e-mail is generally considered crucial to large and small organizations.

Because e-mail is so ubiquitous, it is also a prime target for attackers. Until recently it was also an easy target. The most common method of attacking an MTA is to use it to send unsolicited bulk e-mail (UBE), commonly known as spam, to other organizations. As recently as a few years ago, it was not uncommon for an MTA to be left open, so anyone could send mail through the server.

As UBE has become more prevalent, organizations began closing their mail servers. Organizations that did not close their mail servers found that they were added to one or more of the many blacklists that have been created, and were unable to send mail to large portions of the Internet. Blacklists are generally maintained by a group of volunteers. The volunteers add IP addresses of machines that are either open relays or that allow UBE to be relayed. Other organizations subscribe to these lists and will not accept mail that originates from these mail servers,[4] effectively "black holing" the mail traffic.

NOTE

As with just about anything else on the Internet, these lists have stirred some controversy. Because the volunteers are not accountable to anyone, some lists have come under fire for blacklisting servers simply because of a grudge against the organization. Blacklists have also come under fire for failing to remove MTAs that have been changed to be compliant with the standards of the list owners. Most of these lists are run in a professional and responsible manner, but it is important to know that there is the potential for problems.

Fortunately, as awareness of the problems with open relays has increased, the security of the three most popular MTAs, Sendmail, Microsoft Exchange Server, and Lotus Domino Server, has increased as well. Out of the box, none of these products allows any relaying, so an administrator has to add the IP addresses or domains that should be allowed to relay.

One of the simplest and most effective ways to enhance the security of an MTA is to limit the range of IP addresses that can use it as a mail relay. An MTA cannot be closed off to all outside connections, because it has to be reachable by other servers that are sending legitimate mail to users on the network. But only users within the network of an organization should be able to send mail to remote mail servers using the MTA. Some administrators use the domain name as the determining factor, allowing users to relay mail through the mail server if the from address matches the organization's domain name. Unfor-

---

4. In other words, you do not want to get listed on one of these lists.

tunately, it is too easy to bypass this security measure by forging the originating address in the mail program.

Another method of MTA security being used by many administrators is called POP-before-relay. Before a user can connect to send mail, he or she must first connect to the POP mail server and authenticate against it. If authentication is successful, that user's IP address will be allowed to relay for a set period of time, usually 5–15 minutes. This method of security is especially common when an MTA has users on diverse networks, or using dynamically assigned IP addresses (such as a dial-up ISP connection).

The other side of the mail server security problem is the user mailboxes. When the MTA delivers mail into the user's mailboxes, there are two protocols that can be used to retrieve it: the POP or Internet Message Access Protocol (IMAP). Of the two protocols, POP is more widely deployed, though both have similar security problems.

One of the primary problems associated with POP and IMAP is that users have to have an account on the MTA in order to receive their mail. In every other security situation, the rule of thumb is to remove any unnecessary accounts, and to restrict the number of accounts created on the server. In this case every user on the network needs to have an account on the mail server. To solve this dilemma, most administrators create a group on the mail server that is reserved for mail users. The group should have no access privileges to the server, only the ability to check e-mail. If the mail group is tightly controlled, with very restricted access, then none of the users should be able to cause any damage to the server, especially if their password falls into the wrong hands.

A second problem, but one that is equally important, is that both POP and IMAP transactions are conducted in clear text. The username and password, as well as all data, are transmitted so that anyone on the network with a packet sniffer can read them. In general this is a problem because it means anyone can find another user's login and password and check their mail. The problem is even more pronounced in networks that have centralized the login process. A username and password that may be used in multiple locations on the network will be exposed when the user logs into the mail server, thus jeopardizing the security for the entire network.

A mail server administrator can increase mail security by forcing users to use a different method of mail authentication. One way to increase security is to switch mail authentication to Authenticated Post Office Protocol (APOP). APOP functions in the same manner as POP mail, but it encrypts the user's password using the MD5 one-way hash algorithm. APOP also requires a separate authentication database, so that even if a user's password is compromised, an attacker will not be able to gain access to the rest of the network.

A more secure solution for POP or IMAP sessions is to connect over a TLS session. TLS is a form of encryption, based on Netscape's SSL. SSL is commonly used to encrypt web sessions, but the underlying technology is being used to encrypt other types of traffic.

TLS-encrypted POP and IMAP sessions function in the same manner that HTTPS-based encryption does. A certificate is generated and submitted to a CA, then the certificate is installed on the mail server. The mail clients are configured to use TLS (or SSL, depending on the client) encryption when connecting to the mail server.

Using this method, not only is the password encrypted, but the entire session is encrypted as well. This provides the greatest level of security, but it has a downside: Continuously encrypting and decrypting POP or IMAP sessions can create an extreme load on the server. This load is compounded by the fact that many users set their clients to check for mail every minute. On networks with a large number of mail users, this type of encryption should probably be used in conjunction with an SSL-accelerator. SSL accelerators, from companies like Intel, Nortel, and Cisco, offload the encryption-decryption process from the server, therefore decreasing the load. Using an SSL-accelerator in conjunction with TLS authentication of POP or IMAP sessions will increase security without negatively impacting the server's performance.

12.4.1 Mail Scanning

Mail scanning is a common practice on enterprise networks. E-mail messages should be scanned for three things: viruses, UBE, and employee theft or violation of e-mail policy. As with any other security policy, when an e-mail security policy is implemented it should be clearly explained to network users. The explanation of the security policy should detail what is being scanned for, as well as why it is being implemented.

E-mail scanning is sometimes controversial because users think of their e-mail account as a private communication tool as opposed to a communication tool owned by the company. A detailed explanation, coupled with a gentle reminder that the mail server and its contents are property of the organization can help ease any tension a new policy may cause.

Prior to presenting the scanning policy to employees it should be reviewed by an organization's legal counsel. Privacy laws can vary from area to area. It is important that the policy be presented in such a way that an organization cannot be sued for scanning activities, or worse, sued because something was missed by the scanning.

Virus scanning is the most common form of mail server scanning and is something that should be implemented on every enterprise network. No matter how careful network users are when it comes to viruses, worms, and opening of attachments, users from remote networks may not show the same level of care. A virus or worm that is introduced into a network can cause tremendous damage before it is stopped.

Incoming and outgoing mail messages should all be scanned for viruses and worms. Many companies, like Trend Micro and Sophos, make virus scanners designed specifically for mail gateways. The products are fast and able to keep up with even a heavily loaded mail server.

Virus scanning on the mail server does not mean that virus scanning software should not be used on end user workstations. Instead, the two should be used in tandem, preferably running software from different vendors on the server and the workstations. Running two different virus detection software products decreases the chances that a new virus will slip through an organization's defenses.

Virus definitions on the mail server should be updated frequently, preferably daily. The mail server is the first line of defense against viruses and should have the most up-to-date information to prevent the viruses from spreading.

In addition to virus scanning, many companies have begun scanning mail messages for UBE. UBE has proliferated to such a point that some organizations have found that 20 percent or more of their incoming mail is UBE. There are many programs on the market that can help an organization eliminate UBE at the mail server. Messages are automatically deleted or filed away for review. These programs help shift the burden of deleting unwanted messages from employees to the server, where the process is automated.

Most UBE scanning programs will allow a mail administrator to mark the messages as UBE before delivering them to the end user mailbox. Before implementing a new UBE scanner, it is probably a good idea to do a test run for a couple of weeks in tagging mode to see if any false positives—messages tagged as UBE, but which are not—appear. If there are a lot of false positives, the server administrator will have to adjust the sensitivity level of the software.

In addition to scanning for UBE, the blacklists mentioned earlier are a common tool used by administrators to avoid being burdened by UBE. Before using one of these lists it is important to understand what the criteria are for getting listed, and the process for being removed from the list—information that should be publicly available. If the criteria seem excessive or harsh, do not subscribe to the list, especially if it might alienate existing customers.

The final, and often most controversial, form of scanning is content scanning of e-mail. Content scanning is used to ensure that no information that is not approved by an organization is transmitted through that organization's e-mail server. This can include scanning for inappropriate language, jokes, images, sound files, and video files. Content scanning can also be used to examine files to make sure that confidential information is not being sent to the wrong people, or at all.

Products from MessageLabs, Sandstorm, and Sophos will scan incoming and outgoing messages and flag those with the key words or phrases that need to be monitored. The messages can either be rerouted to an administrator's mailbox or a report can be generated and presented to the security administrator.

Once again, this type of monitoring should be done in consultation with the legal department to ensure that the organization is not doing anything that could run afoul of the law.

12.5 Outsourcing

Mail servers and web servers are unique in that they are intended to be public. People from all over the world have to be able to reach an organization's web and mail servers to find out information and communicate. The uniqueness of these servers requires special security consideration, and the security monitoring and maintenance takes up an inordinate amount of time, compared to other servers.

Many organizations may choose to outsource the management of mail and web services to an ISP or Application Service Provider (ASP). Outsourcing mail and web service needs has several advantages, the primary one being that it can increase the security of the corporate network. Web server attacks are the most common type of external network attack. If the web server is removed to a remote location, even if it is successfully compromised, the rest of the network will most likely remain intact. In addition, outsourcing allows security administrators to tighten network security and further restrict the type of access allowed into the network, increasing overall network security.

Managed hosting and mail providers also usually have staff onsite 24x7 monitoring for network anomalies and looking for security breaches. Non-technical organizations may not have the staff, or the resources, to monitor systems around the clock in this manner.

Some companies specialize in secure web and mail server hosting. These companies generally use secured versions of operating systems and provide very restrictive access to servers.

Setting up these services can be outsourced as well. A Managed Service Provider (MSP) will help an organization create secure web and mail solutions, either at the customer site or in a remote data center. These MSPs build the web infrastructure and handle the day-to-day maintenance of the servers. Some will also handle any security monitoring needs for an organization.

An organization that does not have a lot of experience with mail and web server maintenance should consider the possibility of outsourcing. The monthly costs involved are minimal compared to the costs of hiring competent staff, and certainly are nothing compared to the potential damage that can be caused if a web server is compromised.

12.6 Summary

Server security is important because servers are the last line of defense against an attacker. While router and firewall security breaches are on the rise, servers are still the number-one target of attackers, and all servers should be configured to be as secure as possible.

The best way to ensure server security is to limit who has access to the server, limit which interface the server can be accessed on, and enforce a strong password policy. If these steps are combined with regular software patch updates, most servers will be relatively secure.

Public servers, such as web and mail servers, are a different story and these servers have special security considerations. These servers have to allow access to anyone, but they can be configured to restrict direct access, except through the required ports, and they can be made to be more secure.

Web and mail server services can also be outsourced to one of many companies that provide this type of service. If an organization does not have the in-house expertise to manage these servers in a secure manner, outsourcing may be a viable option.

Because servers may provide an attacker access to proprietary company data, it is important to take server security very seriously and monitor the server farm closely for break-ins and attempted break-ins. The sooner an attack is stopped, the less damage the attacker will do.

13

DNS Security

DNS is complex, and can be difficult to understand. This complexity is compounded by often conflicting advice on how DNS should be managed. Most of this advice is accurate, depending on your needs, but it is important to understand that not all advice applies equally to all situations.

As with any other part of the network, there are several aspects of DNS security that need to be addressed:

- The domain name
- The authoritative DNS server
- Individual zone files
- The caching DNS server

Before understanding the idea behind DNS security strategies, it is important to know a little of the history of DNS. When the Internet was still a project, called ARPANET, run by DARPA, administrators realized they needed an easy way for machines to communicate with each other. To resolve this problem a file called hosts.txt was created and stored on a server run by the InterNIC. The purpose of the hosts.txt file was to map a host name to an address allowing servers connected to the DARPA network to talk to each other. Administrators would download the hosts.txt file from the InterNIC machines every night and have the latest information.

NOTE

The hosts.txt file obviously did not scale well, but it became an ingrained part of most operating systems. Chances are if you do a search for the file hosts.txt on your machine, you will find a remnant of that file.

In the 1980s ARPANET adopted TCP as the official protocol, and in 1983 Jon Postel released RFC 880, containing a proposed plan for developing DNS. Paul Mockapetris also introduced RFCs 882 and 883 outlining a domain name infrastructure. The ISI, a department of the University of Southern California was tapped in RFC 990 to manage the root name servers and SRI International was tapped to manage the first top-level domains (TLDs), which included: .arpa, .com, .edu, .org, .mil, and .gov.

NOTE

The first .com domain ever registered was symbolics.com on March 15, 1985.

In 1992 the Defense Information Systems Agency (DISA) transferred control of the .com, .org, .edu, .gov, and the .net domains to the National Science Foundation (NSF). In 1993 the NSF outsourced control of these domains to Network Solutions, a division of SAIC. Network Solutions began charging for domain names in 1995. When the contract between the NSF and Network Solutions expired in 1998, a new organization was formed. The Internet Corporation for Assigned Names and Numbers (ICANN) was created to open up the registration for TLDs. ICANN also coordinates the generic top-level domain (gTLD) and the country code top-level domain (ccTLD) system, and is responsible for ensuring the root name servers function properly.

The DNS architecture is often compared to a tree. While that analogy is not too far off it does not go far enough. To get a better idea of how DNS works think of the ugliest tree on the face of the earth. The tree has hundreds of limbs that grow off the trunk, each spreading out in a different direction. The branches are often ensnarled, and each limb appears to have a different type of leaf. Some branches have maple leaves, while others have oak leaves, still others look like they belong to weeping willows. Every sort of leaf, flower, or fruit imaginable hangs off this tree. If you have no trouble picturing this tree, then DNS should be a snap.

The DNS tree starts with the root domain, which is ".". All other domains stem from there, so the gTLD .com, is really .com. The same applies to .edu, .net, and so on. From the TLDs spring domain names, such as example.com, and a fully qualified domain name (FQDN), www.example.com for example, stems from the domain names.

Information about domain names is stored on domain name servers. There are different name servers assigned for each branch of a domain name. The root domains are hosted on the root name servers. There are currently 13 root name servers spread throughout the world; their names, IP addresses, and location are mapped out in Table 13.1.

Table 13.1   The Root Name Servers

FQDN	IP ADDRESS	LOCATION	OWNER
A.ROOT-SERVERS.NET	198.41.0.4	Herndon, VA	Network Solutions
B.ROOT-SERVERS.NET	128.9.0.107	Marina del Rey, CA	USC, ISI
C.ROOT-SERVERS.NET	192.33.4.12	Herndon, VA	PSINet (Cogent Communications)
D.ROOT-SERVERS.NET	128.8.10.90	College Park, MD	University of Maryland
E.ROOT-SERVERS.NET	192.203.230.10	Mountain View, CA	NASA
F.ROOT-SERVERS.NET	192.5.5.241	Palo Alto, CA	ISC
G.ROOT-SERVERS.NET	192.112.36.4	Vienna, VA	DISA
H.ROOT-SERVERS.NET	128.63.2.53	Aberdeen, MD	Army Research Laboratory

Table 13.1   The Root Name Servers *(Continued)*

FQDN	IP ADDRESS	LOCATION	OWNER
I.ROOT-SERVERS.NET	192.36.148.17	Stockholm, Sweden	NORDUnet
J.ROOT-SERVERS.NET	198.41.0.10	Herndon, VA	Network Solutions
K.ROOT-SERVERS.NET	193.0.14.129	London, England	RIPE
L.ROOT-SERVERS.NET	198.32.64.12	Marina del Rey, CA	ICANN
M.ROOT-SERVERS.NET	202.12.27.33	Tokyo, Japan	WIDE

The root name servers maintain information about all the ICANN-approved gTLDs and ccTLDs. The information they have is collected from a master database maintained by the authority for the particular TLD. For example, the .com gTLD is maintained by VeriSign Global Registry Services (GRS). VeriSign GRS has a database of information that has to be retrieved by the root name servers periodically, so that information about the .com gTLD is available to everyone. The root name servers receive similar periodic updates from the authoritative registry servers for all the ICANN-approved TLDs.

The ICANN-approved label is important, because there is nothing preventing anyone else from starting a registry that competes with the ICANN-approved registry. In fact, every couple of years a new one, New.net is the current example, seems to surface. These competing registries generally allow individuals, or companies, to register domains with different TLDs, such as .tech, or .kids. The problem with a registry service not associated with ICANN is that the vast majority of the people on the Internet will not be able to access the domain names, because most people query the root name servers for information. These domains are not ICANN-approved, so they are not part of the data that is stored on the root name servers. A name server administrator can adjust their name servers to query the servers maintained by the alternate registry, but most won't.

How does the whole process work? When a user wants to visit a domain name, for example, types *www.example.com* into a web browser, the request is first sent to a caching name server. The caching name server has a list of the root name servers, usually in a file called named.root, root.hints, or db.cache, with information similar to what is in Table 13.1. The caching name server queries one of the root name servers for information about the domain example.com. The root name server answers the caching name servers with information about example.com; specifically, it tells the caching name server what the authoritative name servers for example.com are.

Authoritative name servers are generally either run by an ISP or are located within a company premises, and they provide information about a domain name. Each domain should have at least two authoritative name servers, in two different locations. The two authoritative name servers will have the same information about a domain name. The information is stored in a zone file.

The caching name server, having gotten the authoritative name servers from the root name servers, sends a query to the authoritative name server for information about *www.example.com*. Assuming the authoritative name servers are configured correctly, the IP address for *www.example.com* will be sent to the caching name server, which passes it to the user who made the original query. This process is illustrated in Figures 13.1 and 13.2.

The distributed, tree-like, nature of DNS is its greatest asset. Information is stored in a redundant manner: There are 13 root name servers, with identical

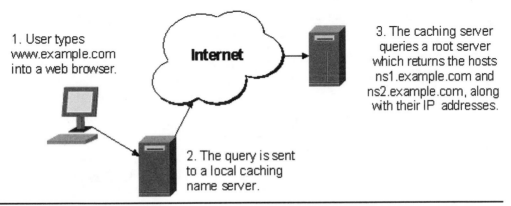

Figure 13.1   The first part of the DNS process. a network user queries a caching name server, which queries a root name server.

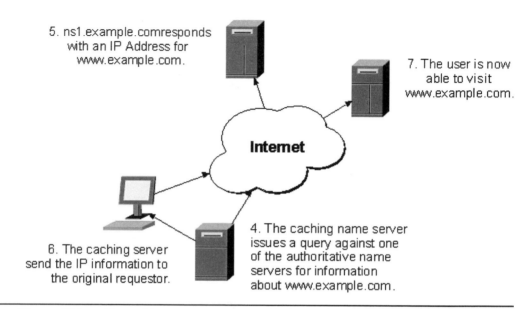

5. ns1.example.comresponds with an IP Address for www.example.com.

7. The user is now able to visit www.example.com.

6. The caching server send the IP information to the original requestor.

4. The caching name server issues a query against one of the authoritative name servers for information about www.example.com.

Figure 13.2   The caching name server uses the host information from the root name servers to query ns1.example.com, which returns an IP address for *www.example.com*. This address is passed onto the original user, which queries the name server.

information; there are at least two authoritative name servers for each domain, and most companies have at least two caching name servers. This type of data replication provides a robust infrastructure, giving DNS a high level of availability. For the most part, even if multiple servers in the DNS process fail, a user will still be able to reach the intended destination.

It is extremely important to remember that distribution is crucial to the security of DNS. It is essential that authoritative name servers reside on two different networks, preferably in two different geographic locations (i.e., not the same office). This is known as the two-network rule. Many companies have fallen victim to DNS attacks because their DNS servers were sitting on the same network segment. If an attacker cannot exploit a security hole within the DNS server, then he or she only needs to launch a DoS attack against that network segment. It is significantly more difficult to launch a DoS attack against DNS servers in different locations, especially if one of those servers is located within your ISP's data center.

In addition to following the two-network rule, many DNS experts recommend running different operating systems on each server. The strategy is the same as the two-network rule: If an attacker is able to exploit a security weakness in one DNS server, the same weakness may not exist on the second server.

The distributed nature of DNS is also its greatest liability. With so many servers involved in the DNS process, there are many potential areas for security breaches:

- How does the caching name server know that the root name server has the right information?
- If it does get the right information, how does the caching name server know that the information from the authoritative name servers is accurate?
- How does the user know that the information coming from the caching DNS server is the right information?

These liabilities, part of the challenge of securing DNS, exist in part because DNS, as a protocol, has been around for so long. DNS is 20 years old and was not originally designed with security in mind. Obviously, things have changed, and there are ways to secure DNS, but not all of these methods are in widespread use. Because DNS is crucial to the infrastructure of the Internet, it is important to ensure that all aspects of your DNS process are secure.

13.1 Securing Your Domain Name

When ICANN opened the registration process so multiple registrars were allowed to register domains, two things happened: Prices for domain names dropped and the number of new domains registered took off.

Millions of new domains are registered every month. As of this writing, there are 150 ICANN-accredited registrars, and countless resellers. All of these options mean that you have to be as concerned with the security of your registrar as you do with the security of your web host.

When ICANN created the rules for becoming a registrar, security was not included as a consideration, so there is no minimal level of information protection that a registrar has to provide. In fact it was not until March 2002 that a security committee was appointed by ICANN. While the committee will undoubtedly set minimum security standards that registrars must follow, it may take years before registrars are forced to comply.

Given the importance of a company's domain name, this is a scary thought. Knowing that there is no minimum security required by registrars is a red flag that a set of security questions needs to be posed to any prospective registrar. This is especially true if your company maintains a lot of domain names.

The primary question a company should ask of their registrar is how the registrar handles domain name updates. Each .com, .net, and .org domain name has five pieces of information that can be updated by the domain owner:

1. Company information
2. Administrative contact
3. Billing contact
4. Technical contact
5. Name server information

All registrars have to supply this information to the gTLD database for a domain to be activated. When Network Solutions controlled all domains, the contacts were three different accounts—as long as three unique contacts were listed. Some registrars still follow that model, but others have opted for a different approach: A single account is created, even though three separate contacts may exist.

A single account for a domain can create several problems. Generally one person maintains this account. If that person leaves the company, especially under less-than-pleasant circumstances, this person may or may not share that account information. If the circumstances are extremely unpleasant, that person may decide to make changes to the domain prior to departure.

If this does happen, most registrars have alternate ways of updating information, but those methods can take significantly longer, and the domain will be unavailable while the information is being changed.

Many companies opt to give multiple users access to the account provided by the registrar. Unfortunately, most registrars use a web-based interface to manage domain names, so there is no way to track which user logged in and made changes. There is also no fail-safe way to prevent a disgruntled employee from making changes to the domain before quitting or being asked to leave.

The best way to avoid problems associated with a single account is to avoid a single account. Some registrars specialize in working with enterprise organizations and understand the unique requirements of a midsize to large company. Consider using a registrar—such as Network Solutions, Domain Bank, or Alldomains.com—that has special corporate programs. These programs may be more expensive, but the cost is nothing compared to the amount of money that can be lost by having a domain disabled, or worse, redirected to another location.

Another security precaution is to store current domain name information in a file. This will make it easier to get the information restored, should a problem arise.

Most UNIX systems have a program called whois, which allows users to look up domain information. There are also Windows and MacOS whois clients available for download. The output of a whois query will look something like this:

```
whois example.com
[whois.crsnic.net]

Whois Server Version 1.3

Domain names in the .com, .net, and .org domains can now be
registered with many different competing registrars. Go to http://
www.internic.net for detailed information.

 Domain Name: EXAMPLE.COM
 Registrar: NETWORK SOLUTIONS, INC.
 Whois Server: whois.networksolutions.com
 Referral URL: http://www.networksolutions.com
 Name Server: A.IANA-SERVERS.NET
 Name Server: B.IANA-SERVERS.NET
 Updated Date: 07-jan-2002
```

The registrar for this domain is Network Solutions. Registrars have their own whois server, which can be queried for more information:

```
whois -h whois.networksolutions.com example.com
[whois.networksolutions.com]

Registrant:
Internet Assigned Numbers Authority (EXAMPLE-DOM)
 4676 Admiralty Way, Suite 330
 Marina del Rey, CA 90292
 US

 Domain Name: EXAMPLE.COM

 Administrative Contact, Technical Contact, Billing Contact:
   Internet Assigned Numbers Authority (IANA) iana@IANA.ORG
   4676 Admiralty Way, Suite 330
   Marina del Rey, CA 90292
   US
```

```
310-823-9358
Fax- 310-823-8649

Record last updated on 07-Jan-2002.
Record expires on 15-Aug-2010.
Record created on 14-Aug-1995.
Database last updated on 20-Apr-2002 14:07:00 EDT.

Domain servers in listed order:

A.IANA-SERVERS.NET    192.0.34.43
B.IANA-SERVERS.NET    193.0.0.236
```

The administrative, technical, and billing contact are all the same, so there is only one contact listing. This is another common mistake made by companies: not using three separate contacts. For something as important as a domain name, a company should not have a single contact. Whenever possible have three different contacts, and make sure those people are aware that they are the contacts for the domain. Also, make sure the people who are contacts are aware of the update procedures for the domain.

The three contacts are important not just for security reasons, but also for domain availability. If a company has a single domain contact, and that person leaves, even if it is on good terms, there is a good chance no one will know when the domain is up for renewal (most registrars send e-mail notification for domains that are about to expire). One of the most common forms of DNS failure is simply an expired domain. This is especially true now that registrars are allowing companies to register domains for up to 10 years. It may not occur to anyone to check the expiration date until e-mail and everything else stop working.

To this point, the focus has been on internal security breaches related to domains. The focus on internal security issues is because most security incidents concerning the domain name occur internally. While external security incidents related to domain names are less frequent—attackers tend to hit DNS servers rather than the domain name itself—they are not unheard of, and proper precautions should be taken.

If your registrar uses a web-based interface, make sure any changes are made over an SSL-encrypted connection. As with other services, make sure the password you choose for your account, or accounts, is secure. In addition to being secure, the password should be changed frequently.

Keep in mind that most companies will not use their registrar password very often. Most companies can go for years without making changes to their domain name (this is not the same as DNS changes, which happen more frequently). Regular password changes help keep a company protected in the event that a registrar's database is compromised.

If possible, request a method for domain name updates that is more secure than an SSL connection. An encrypted e-mail message, or at least one that is signed, would be preferable, although most registrars will not support methods other than web access for making domain changes. In that case, find out what security precautions are taken to protect both the web servers and the database. If a satisfactory answer cannot be given, transfer registrars.

Today a domain name is a crucial part of any company's business. Considering how important the domain name is, the cost, often less than $30 a year, to maintain it is insignificant. Unfortunately, because the cost is so low, some registrars do not take adequate security precautions. As with any other vendor a company has a relationship with, a registrar has to be able to show that it has adequately secured its data.

13.2 A Secure BIND Installation

The discussion of DNS has largely focused on theoretical information to this point. It is time to shift to more practical aspects of DNS security; in particular, the focus will be on securing a BIND installation.

BIND is the software that allows DNS to function for most of the Internet; in fact, BIND servers handle more than 90 percent of all DNS queries on the Internet. BIND is incredibly robust. Many of the root name servers use BIND, and they are answering more than 200 million queries a day.

BIND was first developed in 1983 at the University of California-Berkeley as a way to handle DNS queries. Over the years the ownership of BIND has moved from organization to organization. Currently, the Internet Software Consortium maintains BIND. Like the DNS protocol itself, BIND was not originally designed with security in mind, and over the years BIND security exploits have given system administrators a fair share of headaches. Between 1998 and 2001,

BugTraq reported 14 exploits found in various versions of BIND,[1] compared to five exploits found in Sendmail during the same time period.

BIND exploits often have a significant business impact because they can cause e-mail and websites to become unavailable, or, worse, directed somewhere else at the whim of an attacker.

BIND vulnerabilities first came into the public light in 1997 when Eugene Kashpureff, who operated a now-defunct alternative registry called AlterNIC, used a common BIND exploit to direct traffic away from the Network Solutions website and to the AlterNIC website. Mr. Kashpureff used a well-known exploit that would allow additional information to be sent to a caching name server when a request was made. More about this exploit will be explained shortly.

Two steps can be taken to immediately increase the security of a BIND installation:

1. Upgrade to the latest version.
2. Separate caching and authoritative functions.

The current version of BIND is Version 9.2.x; no known security holes have been exploited to date for this version of BIND. That does not mean they don't exist, but it does mean that upgrading to BIND Version 9.2 is one of the best ways to secure your BIND installation. It is also a good idea to subscribe to the ISC mailing list bind-announce, a low volume list that sends out announcements about new versions of BIND, security fixes, and patches. This allows administrators to stay current about the latest BIND information.

In addition to having the latest version of BIND, it is a good idea to separate caching from authoritative functions whenever possible. BIND is designed to handle both services. Because the two perform such different functions, there are usually different security policies associated with each function. By separating them it is easier to apply more stringent security restrictions to the servers.

Not only is it a good idea to separate the services, but also it is critical to ensure that BIND is not running on any machines that are not acting as DNS servers. Because BIND is an open-source software project, it is often distributed by default with operating systems, including Solaris and most versions of Linux.

---

1. As of this writing no bugs had been reported for 2002.

Whenever an audit is performed on a server, BIND should be one of the packages that is watched for and removed.

The separation of caching services gives an administrator a couple of benefits. First, it makes the firewall rule very easy: Block all traffic on Port 53 (the DNS port), but allow UDP and TCP traffic from any source IP address on any port destined for the authoritative server on Port 53.

Typical DNS traffic uses UDP to send and receive queries, but if a zone file is larger than 512 KB (the largest allowed UDP packet), a DNS server will return the information in one or more TCP packets.

Second, the separation allows administrators to apply different security policies to the different name servers. Machines from all over the world query an authoritative name server. On the other hand, a caching name server should only be queried by local users on your network—or possibly remote offices if they are connected to the network. Either way, an administrator should have control over who accesses a caching name server, and can limit to whom the caching name server will issue responses.

NOTE

In addition to standard server security precautions, it is usually a good idea to install software-based firewalls, such as IPFilter, on a DNS server.

13.2.1 BIND Security

Before different types of BIND servers can be secured, a better understanding of how to secure a BIND installation is needed. BIND can be unwieldy to manage without a basic understanding of how the program works.

When BIND is first started it has to bind itself to Port 53. On most systems a program cannot bind itself to a port unless the system administrator runs it. This was one of the biggest security holes within BIND. Having the BIND daemon owned by the administrative user meant that it was susceptible to root exploits. A root exploit is carried out when an attacker is able to successfully gain administrative access to a system through a program that is owned by the administrative user.

Current versions of BIND do not have this problem. BIND is still started by the administrative user, but ownership of the BIND daemon is transferred to an nonprivileged user, in most cases a user created specifically for the purpose of running BIND. The conventional name for the BIND user is `named` because named is the program that actually handled DNS queries. : The process status command is great for determining the owner of a process, in this case the owner of named:

```
[root@ns1 root]# ps -aux | grep named
named 4764 0.0 0.8 12276 4260 ? S 18:38 0:00 named -u named
named 4765 0.0 0.8 12276 4260 ? S 18:38 0:00 named -u named
named 4766 0.0 0.8 12276 4260 ? S 18:38 0:00 named -u named
named 4767 0.0 0.8 12276 4260 ? R 18:38 0:00 named -u named
named 4768 0.0 0.8 12276 4260 ? S 18:38 0:00 named -u named
```

In addition to running BIND as a nonprivileged user, many people recommend running BIND in a chrooted environment, on UNIX servers. Chroot creates a sandbox that can help limit the damage an attacker can cause should an application be exploited. A sandbox is a restricted shell that is used to limit the access a user has to a system, by essentially making that directory the root directory and keeping the user trapped.

As with any other security measure, it is important not to rely too heavily on chroot to protect a server. While it is a powerful tool, there are ways out of a chroot environment. That's why it is better to run BIND as an unprivileged user in a chrooted environment, rather than running BIND as the administrative user.

Running BIND in a chrooted environment is simply a matter of starting it with the –t flag:

```
[root@ns1 root]# /usr/sbin/named -u named -t /var/named/
```

This command will start BIND as root, but have it run as the user `named`. It also creates a chrooted environment with /var/named/ as the root directory. The only caveat to using this type of security is that the value of some of the variables in the named.conf file will need to be changed so that they are within this new root directory.

13.2.1.1 Named.conf

The heart of any BIND installation is the named.conf file. Usually located in the /etc directory on a UNIX system, and dns\etc\ on a Windows system, this file is what allows an administrator to change the security and configuration settings of the DNS server. The owner of the named process should own the named.conf file. Permissions should be set so that only the named process owner has read access; other system users should have no access to the file (chmod 600 on a UNIX server). The named.conf file has several sections, and looks like this:

```
options {
    directory "/var/named";
    // query-source address * port 53;
};

zone "." IN {
    type hint;
    file "named.ca";
};

zone "example.com" {
    type master;
    file "example.com.hosts";
    };

zone "example2.com" {
    type master;
    file "example2.com.hosts";
    };
```

This is a simple version of the named.conf file. The first section, labeled options, defines information that will be universal to all of the zone files. The next section is a list of the actual zones that the name server has information about. The server is acting as an authoritative and caching name server. The first zone in the list ".", with the type hints, indicates that this server can be queried for information about domain names not located on the server.

If this were a caching-only name server this would be the only entry in the named.conf file. The next two zone entries, example.com and example2.com, are domains for which the name server thinks it is master. The actual zone is stored in the file listed in the file entry (i.e., example.com.hosts and example2.com.hosts).

The named.conf file allows an administrator to add directives, called statements, to modify the configuration of a zone file. A complete explanation of the various statements is beyond the scope of this book. For more information refer to the BIND documentation available online.

By default BIND logs all queries to syslog (generally /var/log/messages). Using the logging statement an administrator can direct logs to a separate file and monitor the BIND logs individually. This may not be an ideal solution for all companies. If syslog information is being sent to a separate server and monitored by third-party software, as is often the case with large companies, separate BIND logging may not provide any benefit.

However, the `logging` statement does allow an administrator to split logs depending on the channel, severity, or category. This is particularly useful if one person, or a group, is dedicated to managing the DNS infrastructure. It is possible to use the logging directive to send warning, and more severe, messages to the syslog daemon, while notice, and less severe, messages are send to a separate log file. A basic `logging` statement will look like this:

```
logging {
channel default_syslog {
 syslog daemon;
    severity info;
};
channel default_debug {
 file "named.debug";

};
};
```

This `logging` statement sends errors that are informational, and above, to the syslog daemon. All debug errors are sent to a file called named.debug. It is a relatively simple configuration, and will not meet the needs of a complex DNS solution. However, it makes a good starting point from which to grow.

Another commonly used practice to secure a name server is to hide the version information. Ordinarily, an attacker can use the dig command (installed by default with BIND) to determine the version of BIND a remote name server is running:

```
[root@ns1 root]# dig @ns1.example.com version.bind chaos txt

;; QUESTION SECTION:
;version.bind.          CH    TXT

;; ANSWER SECTION:
version.bind.     0   CH    TXT   "9.1.3"

;; Query time: 2 msec
;; SERVER: 192.168.0.40#53(ns1.example.com)
;; WHEN: Sun Apr 21 18:31:06 2002
;; MSG SIZE rcvd: 48
```

Now an attacker can look for exploits to which Version 9.1.3 of BIND is susceptible and act accordingly. While version.bind is a BIND convention, it has been incorporated into other DNS servers, so this command is a common way of finding exploitable systems. You can change the information that is output by making the following adjustment under the options statement:

```
version "DNS, we aint got no stinkin DNS";
```

Now, if the same command is issued, the following will appear:

```
[root@ns1 root]# dig @ns1.example.com version.bind chaos txt

;; QUESTION SECTION:
;version.bind.        CH    TXT

;; ANSWER SECTION:
version.bind.   0   CH   TXT   "DNS, we aint got no stinkin DNS"

;; Query time: 2 msec
;; SERVER: 192.168.0.40#53(ns1.example.com)
;; WHEN: Sun Apr 21 18:38:33 2002
;; MSG SIZE rcvd: 74
```

As you can see this prints out the message "DNS, we aint got no stinkin DNS," instead of the version of BIND. The merits of this form of security are somewhat debatable. The wrong message may simply serve as an enticement for an attacker to try to break into your system. By changing the version information you are attempting to understand the psyche of an attacker, and that may or may not be a good idea. Some administrators prefer not to change the version, but simply leave it blank so that no information is provided to a potential attacker.

Other named.conf security considerations will be discussed in the next section.

13.3 Limit Access to Domain Information

Generally there are two goals when trying to secure a DNS server: Limit information access to authorized users and limit the information authorized users can access. Of course, how DNS information is secured depends on the type of server that is being secured.

Regardless of whether you are trying to secure a caching or authoritative name server, a tool that can help this process is an ACL. ACLs are a statement within the named.conf file. An ACL can be applied universally, or to specific domains, depending on the administrator's needs.

The process of using ACLs to protect routers was outlined in Chapter 4. Securing BIND using ACLs is very similar, with the difference being that with BIND there is no need for an implied allow statement at the end of an ACL. BIND assumes that anything that is not implicitly denied is allowed. A common DNS security practice is to blackhole all requests that originate from RFC 1918 addresses:

```
acl badaddresses { 10.0.0.0/8; 172.16.0.0/12; \ 192.168.0.0/16; };
```

In the `options` statement, include the following line:

```
options {
..
   blackhole { badaddresses; };
..
};
```

Placing the ACL in the `options` statement blackholes all requests to the name server from addresses in the RFC 1918 space. An ACL can also be applied to only a specific domain (for example, if separating caching and authoritative name servers is not an option). An ACL can be created specifically for local addresses and bound to the caching zone entry. In fact, BIND has a built-in ACL for local address called localnets. The localnets ACL consists of any address in one of the netblocks bound to the name server interface. For example, if the name server has an address of 10.10.0.10 with a netmask of 255.255.255.0, then addresses 10.10.0.1 through 10.10.0.254 would be able to connect to a localnets ACL.

BIND has three other native ACLS:

1. Any allows all hosts to connect.

2. None denies all hosts.

3. Localhost allows any IP that is bound to an interface on the name server.

There may not be a need to apply ACLs to the name server if they duplicate what is already attached to the router. On the other hand, redundant security is rarely a bad thing.

13.3.1 A Caching Name Server

Many of the security precautions discussed in this chapter can be applied to a caching-only name server. In particular, very stringent ACLs should be applied to this device. For example, using the localnets ACL described in the previous section, the `options` statement should probably look like similar to this:

```
options {
directory "/var/named";
 // query-source address * port 53;
allow-query { localnets; };
};
```

Add in the hints zone and a zone file for the localhost address:

```
zone "." IN {
   type hint;
   file "named.ca";
};

zone "0.0.127.in-addr.arpa" {
   type master;
   file "127.0.0.in-addr.arpa";
};
```

More verbose logging can be added to improve security, if desired, but if syslog monitoring is in place, that may not be necessary. As long as standard server security precautions are taken (limited access, strong password policy, etc.), a simple caching name server configuration can be fairly secure.

13.3.2 An Authoritative DNS Server

An authoritative DNS server can be much more difficult to secure because, like a web server, it has to allow access from anywhere. The best strategy with an authoritative DNS server is to block access to rogue addresses, at the firewall or router level, and to restrict the information that the authoritative DNS server will provide.

Once again, using ACLs can help secure an authoritative name server. A common tool used by attackers to map your network is to perform a zone transfer:

```
[root@ns1 root]# dig @ns1.example.com example.com axfr

; <<>> DiG 9.1.3 <<>> @ns1.example.com example.com axfr
;; global options: printcmd
example.com.       38400 IN    SOA  ns1.example.com. dns.example.com.
99
5551903 10800 3600 432000 38400
example.com.       38400 IN    A    192.168.0.20
example.com.       38400 IN    MX 10 mail.example.com.
example.com.       38400 IN    MX 50 mail.uu.net.
```

```
example.com.       38400 IN    NS    ns1.example.com.
example.com.       38400 IN    NS    auth50.ns.uu.net.
anoncvs.example.com.  38400 IN   A    192.168.0.20
cpanel.example.com.   38400 IN   A    198.93.70.124
cpanel2.example.com.  38400 IN   A    198.93.70.125
dcw.example.com.      38400 IN   A    192.168.0.20
exuunet.example.com.  38400 IN   A    192.168.0.20
ftp.example.com.      38400 IN   A    192.168.0.20
jrun.example.com.     38400 IN   A    192.168.0.9
mail.example.com.     38400 IN   A    192.168.0.20
test.example.com.     38400 IN   A    192.168.0.40
www.example.com.      38400 IN   A    192.168.0.20
example.com.       38400 IN    SOA  ns1.example.com. dns.example.com.
99
5551903 10800 3600 432000 38400
;; Query time: 5 msec
;; SERVER: 192.168.0.19#53(ns1.example.com)
;; WHEN: Mon Apr 22 17:58:54 2002
;; XFR size: 18 records
```

Using the supplied information, an attacker has a pretty good idea about the netblocks used on the example.com network, and also has an idea of what services are being run on which machines. This information can be used to build a network map and launch attacks against a particular server.

You can stop unauthorized machines from making zone transfers in this manner using the allow-transfer tag. Some machines, a secondary name server for example, have to be able to perform full zone transfers, others do not; a caching name server only needs to pull information for the host name that is being queried. The allow-transfer tag can be applied on a per-domain basis, or it can be applied to all domains. If you have multiple domains, with multiple secondary servers, you may need to apply this information on a per-domain basis.

In the previous example, the secondary name server is auth50.ns.uu.net, or 198.6.1.161. An entry can be made in the zone entry for example.com allowing this IP to perform transfers:

```
zone "example.com" {
   type master;
   file "example.com.hosts";
   allow-transfer { 198.6.1.161; };
   };
```

Now, when the attacker tries to perform a full zone transfer, there is an error:

```
[root@test root]# dig @ns1.example.com example.com axfr

; <<>> DiG 9.1.3 <<>> @ns1.example.com example.com axfr
;; global options: printcmd
; Transfer failed.
```

However, normal caching server behavior is not affected:

```
root@test root]# dig @ns1.example.com www.example.com A

;; QUESTION SECTION:
;www.example.com.      IN    A

;; ANSWER SECTION:
www.example.com. 38400 IN   A   192.168.0.20

;; AUTHORITY SECTION:
example.com.    38400 IN    NS    ns1.example.com.
example.com.    38400 IN    NS    auth50.ns.uu.net.
```

On the slave server the zone entry can be configured to not allow any transfers:

```
zone "example.com" {
    type slave;
    masters { 192.168.0.19; };
    file "example.com.slave";
    allow-transfer { none; };
};
```

To further enhance security, an administrator can restrict transfers from the master name server to slave name servers that supply a correct key. Combining key security with the allow-transfer limitations provides additional security and ensures that domains will not be transferred to spoofed IP addresses—assuming the spoofed IP address does not also have the key.

Messages secured using encrypted keys are called transaction signatures (TSIG), outlined in RFC 2845. BIND has supported TSIG messages since Version 8.2. Messages are secured using an MD5 algorithm. The master and the slave server both need to have the same secret key. When the slave name server requests information from the master server, it sends the secret key. The master verifies that it is the correct key and sends the information. Most experts recommend at least a 128-bit key, though there are no minimum requirements. BIND 9 supports 64-bit through 512-bit keys.

Versions of BIND that support TSIG messages include a tool for creating the secret key. The tool, called dnssec-keygen, is first used to create the keys:

```
[root@test root]# dnssec-keygen -a HMAC-MD5 -b 512 -n \
HOST auth-ns1.example.com
```

The standard convention is to name the keys after the secondary and primary name servers, in this case auth-ns1.example.com. The –b tag tells BIND that the key should be 512-bits. The dnssec-keygen command creates two files, the .key and the .private file. Both files contain the newly generated key; the key file should be copied into the BIND root directory /var/named/. The key will look something like this:

```
EhCCOHJHYYbcoJWIsN7Sh7tfeA8rBCi7KhesBbm/d \
+uEZwIQA2awWdV7 tY8jVprr1OO3fkXbSjY73yBO73lpwA==
```

The key has to be defined on the master name server, in the named.conf file:

```
key auth-ns1. {
 algorithm hmac-md5;
 secret " EhCCOHJHYYbcoJWIsN7Sh7tfeA8rBCi7KhesBbm/d \
+uEZwIQA2awWdV7 tY8jVprr1OO3fkXbSjY73yBO73lpwA";
};
```

The key name needs to be included in the zone file entry:

```
zone "example.com" {
type master;
file "example.com.hosts";
allow-transfer { key auth-ns1.; };
};
```

The same key entry needs to be made in the named.conf file on the slave server:

```
key auth-ns1. {
 algorithm hmac-md5;
  secret " EhCCOHJHYYbcoJWIsN7Sh7tfeA8rBCi7KhesBbm/d \
+uEZwIQA2awWdV7 tY8jVprr1OO3fkXbSjY73yBO73lpwA";
};
```

BIND has to be told that all messages to the master server should be signed:

```
server 192.168.0.19 {
keys { auth-ns1.; };
};
```

Then create the slave zone file as before:

```
zone "example.com" {
    type slave;
    masters { 192.168.0.19; };
    file "example.com.slave";
    allow-transfer { none; };
};
```

The master and slave authoritative DNS servers have now been secured so that the master only allows zone transfers to the IP address of the slave, and it requires that the requests include the encrypted key. The slave name server will not allow any transfers.

Assuming standard security precautions have been followed on both the master and slave name servers, DNS transactions between the two should now be secure.

13.4 DNS Outsourcing

Managing DNS security can be a headache, especially for large organizations. For companies that do not have the staff to manage and support large zone files, outsourcing may be a better alternative.

Some companies, like UltraDNS, Nominum, and easyDNS, offer managed DNS, while other companies, such as Men & Mice, will set up DNS service in-house. The services can range from having the company's team manage and support some, or all, aspects of an organization's in-house DNS services to a fully managed off-site DNS service.

There are some obvious advantages to this type of service. Outsourcing DNS frees up in-house network administrators so they do not have to worry about the day-to-day maintenance of DNS servers, and an organization can quickly have a scalable DNS solution that is redundant and secure.

DNS outsourcing has been around for a long time. Most organizations that do not have the expertise to manage their own DNS let their ISP, or even their registrar, manage their zone files. While these solutions are adequate for smaller companies, midsize and larger companies should consider a dedicated out-sourced DNS provider. Many ISPs and registrars are not equipped to handle hundreds of thousands of request per day to a single domain. ISPs and registrars are not always equipped to handle frequent updates to zone files as well. If your organization makes several DNS changes each week, or even each day, a DNS outsourcing provider may be the best solution.

As with other outsourcing providers, managed DNS providers should be quizzed thoroughly about their security precautions and the types of guarantees they provide.[2]

Managed DNS providers not only provide authoritative DNS services, they can also provide outsourced caching DNS. Again, this may be useful for companies that do not want to manage caching DNS servers in-house. However, for a large organization, switching caching DNS from an internal server to an external server can cause significant traffic changes. The impact of those traffic changes should be carefully weighed against the benefits of outsourcing caching DNS.

13.5 djbdns

BIND can be very secure, with the proper precautions. Unfortunately, as BIND has grown, the number of supported features has grown as well. Consequently, most implementations of BIND ship with very few security precautions in place. If a DNS administrator is not familiar with the steps required to secure a DNS server, BIND can be an easy target for an attacker.

One solution is to use an alternative to BIND. The most commonly used alternative is djbdns. Named for its creator, Dan Bernstein, djbdns is a minimal DNS server. It was designed to be small and secure.

Djbdns improves security in several ways. Most of these security enhancements can also be done with BIND, but they are not enabled by default. One of the primary security enhancements administrators get with djbdns is that by default it runs in its own chrooted jail. This separates djbdns from the rest of the operating system and prevents the djbdns user from being able to access files in other parts of the system. Djbdns also separates caching functions from authoritative functions. If a server is only acting as an authoritative name server, it will not be able to perform any recursive queries. Djbdns also uses various security enhancements to secure zone transfers.

NOTE

There are many additional security enhancements to djbdns. For more information about djbdns and its security enhancements, consult the djbdns website: *cr.yp.to/djbdns/*

---

2. You are welcome to send them a copy of this book to verify they follow all procedures listed in this chapter.

There are some downsides to djbdns. The primary concern is that it does not handle zone transfers in the same manner other DNS servers do. This means that while it is possible to set up a BIND server and Windows DNS server as primary and secondary servers, it is not as easy to set up a BIND server and djbdns server as primary and secondary servers.

13.6 Summary

DNS is a complex area, with a lot of potential for security breaches. It is also an essential service that organizations have to run, if they are going to communicate with the rest of the Internet.

While securing DNS can be complex, it really boils down to five basic principles:

1. Always run the latest version of BIND.
2. Each DNS server should run on a separate platform, in a different network.
3. Separate authoritative and caching functions.
4. Restrict access to caching name servers.
5. Limit the information provided by authoritative name servers.

Depending on how comfortable an organization is with DNS management, it may consider running an alternative to BIND. While BIND is undoubtedly the leader in terms of domains served and available support, many other DNS daemons exist.

These daemons are often smaller and boast much better security than BIND. Programs such as djbdns have gained a lot of fame because of their inherent security. Be careful though; because the following for these programs is small and the development team is also small, they tend to come and go. Dents and MaraDNS are two other alternatives to BIND that have faded away in recent years. Building a large DNS infrastructure around these programs may not be advisable.

14

Workstation Security

Workstations are the most common source of internal attacks on a corporate network. The obvious reason is there are more workstations on a network than any other type of device. A less obvious, but related, reason is users are generally not as concerned about security, nor are they sure what constitutes good network security practices.

Attacks originate from, or through, workstations because of lax file permissions, bad passwords, older software, installation of insecure software, and every administrator's favorite: opening viruses or worms sent via e-mail.

Because workstations are so prevalent in the network, it is crucial that workstation security policies be enforced and communicated to the users. The trick when communicating workstation security policies is to do it in plain language that even non-technical users can understand. Often, workstation security policies are developed and written by technical staff. There is nothing inherently wrong with this, but non-technical staff should review the policies and ensure they are readable. This is not to say that technical staff members are incapable of communicating clearly, but there is a difference between communicating with other technical staff and end users. Documentation provided to users may need to reflect this, although ideally, it should not because much of the responsibility for workstation security administration should be removed from the hands of the end users.

In this respect, there are really two aspects to workstation security:

1. The steps taken by security and administrative staff to control the people who have workstation access, and what the people who have access can do

2. The security steps that have to be followed by the workstation users

Again, the ideal situation is to eliminate as many of the security risks as possible at the administrative level and provide simpler, common sense guidelines to the workstation users.

This balance can be difficult to maintain, especially with users who are more technically advanced and determined to treat a corporate machine as if it were their own. Once again, this illustrates the importance of buy-in from senior management when implementing security policies. If the support for these policies is in place, it will make it much easier to enforce. Violation of these policies should have real consequences.[1] While playing the latest elf bowling game sent by a friend may seem harmless to Jack in accounting, the virus hidden in the software that takes out the entire network and takes three server administrators two days to clean up is not.[2]

14.1 General Workstation Security Guidelines

The single most important, and sometimes controversial, aspect of workstation security is choosing the right operating system or systems. It is okay to run multiple operating systems, as long as the staff exists to properly support them, especially in a large organization. However, the operating systems have to be able to facilitate administrative security, and should ideally allow administrators to use one or two network protocols for communication across the network.

The less traffic there is on the network, the better. It is significantly more difficult to sift through network data looking for patterns when there is a lot of network noise. Because there are more workstations on the network than any other device, most network traffic originates from the workstations.

Limiting the number of unique operating systems deployed on the network can help reduce network traffic, especially if the number of protocols those

---

1. No, public floggings are not allowed.
2. Yes, public flogging is really not allowed.

machines are speaking is limited. It is important to understand that it is not always possible to limit everyone in an organization to a single operating system. Some operating systems are simply better than others at performing certain tasks, and the needs of employees have to be taken into consideration. Your engineering staff may need access to Unix workstations, while marketing may need access to Macintosh systems, and sales and billing may prefer Windows systems. Again, as long as the support staff exists to support these operating systems, running three different types is not a detriment to security. However, within each operating system, a single version should be used.

For Windows users this generally means running Windows 2000, or possibly Windows XP Professional—although Windows XP Professional is still relatively new and may contain serious security holes that have not been uncovered. Windows 98, Windows XP, or Windows ME should not be run in a secure networked corporate environment. The lack of proper authentication capabilities can hinder efforts at security protection.

As with server security, Unix workstations are often a much more hotly debated topic. All modern implementations of Unix have the tools available to properly secure them, but some Unix-based systems are more secure out of the box than others. The two most commonly used Unix-based workstations in the United States are Sun Solaris and Red Hat Linux; this mirrors the server market. Traditionally, Sun Solaris was the only option that server administrators would consider running on an enterprise network. As the security track record for Red Hat has improved, and the number of enterprise applications available for Linux has increased, Linux, especially Red Hat, has become more prevalent in the enterprise environment.

Some organizations have also opted to run one of the many BSD variants, such as FreeBSD and OpenBSD, on workstations that require a Unix operating system. The BSD variants have a reputation for tight security and stability that makes them very popular among technical staff. The downside is that not many applications have been ported to BSD, so it may not fit the business needs of an organization.

Until recently security has not been a primary focus for Macintosh users or systems. As the Macintosh operating system has increased in market share over the last few years, Apple computers have started appearing in corporate environments where they have never been before. Older versions of the Macintosh operating system did not have the native security requirements to run in an enterprise network. There are third-party applications that will allow an administrator to remotely manage network logins, but that means managing another application, and the expense may not be justified if there are only a few Macintosh users.

The latest version of the Macintosh operating system, Mac OS X, changes that. Built on the BSD kernel, but with a Macintosh interface, Mac OS X provides the same level of security that BSD does, including remote login management, while still maintaining the Macintosh interface. As with Windows XP Professional, Mac OS X is still relatively new, and security holes are constantly being discovered. If Apple properly addresses security problems, Mac OS X may become a viable operating system for enterprise networks.

14.1.1 Version Control

The primary reason for wanting to limit the number of operating systems allowed on a network is version control. When dealing with a program as large and complicated as an operating system, security holes will undoubtedly be found. If there are 10 different operating systems in use on a network, it becomes infinitely more difficult to maintain all of the patches and bug fixes for the different operating systems.

Version control is not only a component of operating system security, it is also important for all approved applications installed on the network. There should be one approved version of an application for each operating system, and all workstations that are running that application should have the application installed.

Software security updates are a part of life for administrators; the idea is to make it as easy as possible to perform the updates. This starts by having a base image installed on all workstations using a tool such as Symantec Ghost or a Kickstart server for Solaris or Red Hat Linux. If hardware configuration is generally not done in-house, many hardware vendors will allow companies to send them a workstation image. The image is used whenever a new system is ordered, so the new workstation is a replica of existing workstations.

For a Ghost or Kickstart image to work, workstations have to be configured with the same hardware. Again, this is generally not a problem. Most hardware vendors will support a standard configuration for a company and keep that information on file. This process can also be aided by ordering workstations, as opposed to standard business machines, from manufacturers. Systems labeled as workstations by hardware vendors tend to be more expensive, but they also use uniform parts from one year to the next. The last thing an administrator wants is to have to keep drivers on hand for 10 different types of LAN cards, in case there is a problem with one of them.

With some vendors, such as Sun and Apple, hardware consistency is not usually a problem. Both companies manufacture their own hardware as well as creating the operating system. When a company buys a specific model from Apple or Sun, the hardware configuration remains pretty stable from one year to the next.

After the operating system and hardware platforms have been selected, the next step is to select what software will be installed by default on each system. Generally this includes a productivity suite (e.g., Microsoft Office), calendaring software and groupware (e.g., Notes/Domino), a mail program (e.g., Eudora, Outlook, or Notes), and antivirus software (e.g., Norton Anti-Virus or McAfee VirusScan). Again, it is important to standardize on certain versions of these programs and create the image from those versions.

Starting from a small number of base systems in this manner makes version control much simpler. As new patches for operating systems, drivers, or applications are released, they can be stored on a server within the network and thoroughly tested by the operations staff to ensure the patches do not cause additional problems.

Most network operating systems allow administrators to schedule tasks, so the workstations on the network can often be configured to automatically check the server on which the patches reside, and download and install the necessary patches. Depending on the size of the network, it is usually a good idea to stagger the scheduled task so all the machines on the network are not trying to access the patch server at once.

14.1.2 Desktops vs. Laptops

A common problem facing administrators is the decision to use desktops or laptops. Desktops are often easier to manage, because they don't move. When an administrator needs to access it, the desktop is there. Laptops, on the other hand, are more popular with users, especially users who are on the road a lot or do a lot of work from home.

As laptops become more powerful they are slowly displacing desktops in the corporate environment. Employees want to telecommute, and they want to be able to work from home without having to install special software on their home machine.

While the benefits of laptops are obvious, they can be an administrative and security nightmare. Employees who use the laptops both at work and at home tend to view the laptops as "theirs" and treat them as such. This can mean installing software, or operating systems, that are not approved and may not be licensed by the company. A user who does not like Windows 2000 may decide to load Windows XP on the laptop. Not only will this prevent the laptop from performing automatic updates, leaving it open to possible security holes, it may make the organization liable for having unlicensed software.

Laptops are also harder to back up. If the laptop is not plugged into the network when the backup is scheduled, it may not be done. File servers are, therefore, much more important to laptop users, and they should be manually copying files to the file server whenever possible.

The only remedy for this problem is good communication on the part of the security and operations staff. The importance of leaving the laptop intact has to be explained to all users when they are issued a laptop. Many organizations resolve this problem by issuing desktops to users automatically. If the user requests a laptop, the request has to be approved by the manager, and the employee has to read and sign a security document that explains the security issues surrounding a laptop.

Some companies require new laptop users to attend a security seminar, which details many of the security problems associated with using a laptop. Depending on the size of an organization, this may be a little excessive. On the other hand, if laptop training is already part of a new-employee orientation then it should be easy enough to add a section about laptop security.

14.1.3 Physical Security

Physical security involves access to the computer. There are two areas of concern when it comes to physical security:

1. Someone stealing a workstation
2. An unauthorized person gaining access to the network through a workstation

Laptops are especially prone to the first problem. A user leaves the laptop sitting in a docking station overnight, and it is gone the next morning. But, the security of desktop systems should not be discounted. A random, or spontaneous, thief will generally not walk off with a workstation, but someone who is committing corporate espionage will.

All desktop machines should be anchored to a desk or, when possible, something more secure. Again, this will not dissuade someone who intends to get a particular desktop, but it makes the desktop machines less attractive to random thieves.

Security can be increased for both workstations and laptops by ensuring that files are stored on the file server, and not on the local hard drive. This makes backups easier, and it means that if someone does steal a workstation, there will be very few useful documents on it.

Monitoring other aspects of physical security can also enhance workstation security. Aside from the standard measures taken to secure an organization's physical premises, senior level staff should lock their office door when they are not in the office. This makes it more difficult for even a determined thief to steal a machine.

Laptops that are not being taken home should be locked away overnight, either in a filing cabinet or in a secure storage area. The harder they are to get at, the less likely they will be to be stolen.

The second area of physical security—unauthorized users gaining access to the network through a workstation—is most often accomplished because users don't lock their workstations. All network operating systems allow users to lock the workstation when they are away. The machine does not have to be shut down and the user does not have to logout. The lock simply prevents anyone from using it while the user is away from the workstation.

Workstation locks should be common practice when someone goes to a meeting, steps out to lunch, goes to get a cup of coffee, or even goes to the lavatory. Anytime a user does not have a direct view of his or her workstation, it should be locked. After all, there is no point in taking extensive network security measures if an attacker can just sit down at an unused workstation and have instant access to the network.

Many operating systems also allow a workstation to go into lock mode automatically if it sits idle for a certain period of time (five minutes is generally a sufficient time). The lock mode takes into account the fact that a user may be reading a document online, or writing notes based on a document, but does not provide an attacker with a large window of opportunity. The very paranoid may want to set this timer to two minutes.

14.2 Virus and Worm Scanning

How much virus and worm scanning is enough? After all, a good security administrator is running virus scans on the mail server to catch any incoming, or outgoing, worms. Virus scanners are being run on all of the file servers, the web server, and possibly even on the firewall. Is virus scanning on the workstations necessary?

Of course it is. As has been repeatedly stated, security works best when applied in a layered approach. The more areas in which security checks are performed, the more secure the network.

Virus scanning has become a fundamental part of the security process. There are too many viruses[3] and worms on the Internet today not to perform virus scans at multiple layers, and not to have multiple levels of protection. Even if mail and files are protected at the server level, without workstation virus protection, there is nothing to prevent a user from introducing a virus through a floppy, CD-ROM, or website download.

Some security experts recommend running products from different vendors at different layers of the network. For example, a company can run Sophos Mail-Monitor to protect e-mail on the mail server, and McAfee VirusScan to protect workstations. This does improve the level of protection slightly: One program may catch a virus that is missed by the other. On the other hand, it also means monitoring at least two sets of virus updates, and storing at least two sets of signatures. The decision whether or not to use two or more software vendors for virus protection is dependent largely on how problematic viruses and worms have traditionally been in a given network.

If proper precautions have been taken and security patches are applied regularly to all workstations, a single vendor solution may be enough. If, on the other hand, viruses and worms have been a problem in the past, and they still occa-

---

3. Some people are unsure whether the plural of virus is viruses or virii. According to the alt.comp.virus FAQ, both are acceptable.

sionally slip through the virus protection that is in place, a multivendor solution may be in order.

As with software updates, new virus definitions should be downloaded to a local server from the vendor's website. The workstations should then be programmed to download the new definitions from that server. New virus definitions should be downloaded at least weekly. (Daily is probably too frequently, unless there is a sudden surge in virus activity around the Internet. Biweekly is too infrequently, as many worms can spread across most of the Internet in a shorter span of time.) Of course, if the virus vendor has a mailing list that informs users of new viruses that pose a serious threat, server administrators should subscribe to the list and make adjustments to the download policy as needed.

To further assist in virus and worm protection, programs that are particularly susceptible to viruses and worms (e-mail programs being a prime example) should run in the most secure or restrictive mode. This type of restriction may cause users to complain; however, as long as programmers are going to make worms that take advantage of weaknesses in common programs, it is a necessary step in the process of securing a network.

14.3 Administrative Access

The administrative account, usually known as administrator on Windows systems and root on Unix systems, is the account that has full access to any program or file on the system. The administrative user can also make global changes to the system configuration and add and delete other system accounts. In short, the administrative user has a lot of power.

As has already been established, when a user logs into their workstation, that user is really authenticating against a remote server. Generally there is also a local account for the user created on the workstation. This allows the user to log in, even when not connected to the network. There is a profile associated with each user on a network. There may be multiple users who have the same profile, and these users are generally part of one group.

An administrator has the ability to limit the type of access available to both users and groups. For example, the user Bob may have access to certain file servers and the ability to install some types of software on his machine. Conversely, an administrator may choose to limit the group Accounting so its members only have access to the accounting file server, and members of the Accounting group cannot install any files on their machine.

Obviously, managing security access by group is a lot easier than managing it by individual user, and this is the route most administrators choose. Assigning certain rights and privileges to a group allows an administrator to control traffic flow on the network, and can help prevent unauthorized access to network devices.

This can also create a nightmare for the desktop support group. When users can no longer install their own applications, they will have to be installed by desktop support, which may or may not have the manpower to handle these requests.

It is very important to control the types of applications that are installed on workstations. The easiest way to do this is to not allow anything to be installed; only users with administrative access will be allowed to install applications. This is not always the best answer though. Some users will need to be able to regularly install software for testing purposes, and several calls a day to the support desk can be frustrating, especially during times of heavy testing.

One solution is to give some users administrative access to their workstations. As with the laptops, a user has to fill out a form asking for authorization, and it has to be approved by a manager. The user would also have to be aware of the possible security implications of installing non-approved software. While this will not prevent security breaches from occurring through the installation of bad software, it will reduce the number of problems that occur because of bad software installations.

A second, and more expensive, solution is to create a lab environment where users can test and install software. The users would have full administrative access to the machines within the lab. The lab would have to be carefully managed, and secured, so that not all users have access. The lab would also have to be separate from the network, so workstations within the lab would be unable to launch an attack on the rest of the network.

A third solution is to give users limited ability to install software. Generally administrators accomplish this by limiting the directories that can be written to, preventing any software that overwrites system files from being installed. While this offers an additional level of security, it is most definitely possible to install software that can be used to launch attacks on a network. If some level of control is going to be allowed for users to install software, a list of approved applications should be communicated to users.

Two areas that are especially of concern to network administrators are instant messaging and file-swapping services. Instant messaging services such as AOL Instant Messenger or Microsoft Messenger are used to share short messages with other users on the Internet. They have become a popular communication tool in recent years and provide a great way for users to quickly share information. The problem is that all messages are routed across the Internet to a third-party server, and then forwarded to their intended recipient, even if that recipient is on the same network. The messages communicated between the two parties are unencrypted, adding to the insecurity of these services.

Rather than relying on public messaging services, a better solution is to use one of the private messaging services, like Lotus Sametime or Odigo. They will allow employees to communicate with each other, without administrators having to worry about sensitive company information leaving the network. Putting a corporate messaging system in place is not enough; employees must also use the system. This may mean disabling access to other messaging services. If other instant messaging services are commonplace within the organization, there may be many complaints if they are disabled.

Once again, it is a matter of weighing the security benefits of disabling the services against the needs of the users and corporate policy. Consider this: How much productivity is being lost by users with five messaging windows open simultaneously, especially if none of the people they are chatting with are employees?

File-swapping software has come under a lot of fire because of the nature of the software: It exists so users can download and upload material that is usually copyrighted. More recently some of these services have come under attack because of applications that are bundled with the swapping software. These applications may be used to monitor user movement, help in CPU-sharing systems, or other types of applications that involve using workstation resources and company bandwidth for purposes other than those intended.

Most organizations have set up rules specifically disallowing file-swapping services and blocking access to them at the firewall. They use system and network resources to provide users access to material that may be illegal or contain hidden viruses. These services may also make a company culpable in the event that one of its users is sued for copyright violation. While the political issues surrounding these file-swapping services are murky, and there is validity to both arguments, they should probably be avoided within the corporate network.

The solution most often opted for by companies is to allow users to install some programs, but not be given full access to their machine. This allows users to install some applications that may be useful for work, but not full-blown applications that may not be on the approved application list. In conjunction with this policy, administrators will make a list of the type of software that is not permitted, under any circumstances, on workstations owned by the organization.

Allowing users some freedom to install applications means that fewer desktop support personnel are necessary. At the same time informing users what they should not install, and blocking access to the ports used by known programs in violation of this policy, will help maintain the security of the network.

14.4 Remote Login

Users should never need remote access to their machines from outside the network. In addition, it is very doubtful that users would need remote access to their machines from within the network.

To that end, all remote access software should be disabled on workstations; this includes products like PCAnywhere, VNC, SSH, and Terminal Server. Understand that does not mean these software packages should not be installed on corporate workstations; there are very valid business reasons for using most of them. Instead, these products should not be used to allow remote access into the workstation—even from within the network.

Firewall rules will stop remote users from trying to access workstations but that does not stop them from using these tools within the network. In order to stop this, a security auditing system should be put in place. This will be discussed in detail in Chapter 16, but it boils down to using a network scanner to scan workstations looking for ports that should be closed, but are open. Security audits, performed on a regular basis, can help spot security holes before they cause problems.

It is not necessary, or advisable, to disable remote access to workstations completely. Administrative personnel often need access to workstations to investigate a problem or install new software. Most network operating systems have built-in facilities to manage these types of tasks, and they should be used.

As with anything else, before using a remote login service to administer machines, make sure that all of the security risks are analyzed. If an attacker can sniff the administrative password to a workstation when a desktop support person logs in remotely, consider a different method of remote access. Whatever type of remote access system is chosen by administrators, it is important that all messages between the administrator and the workstations are properly encrypted.

14.5 Summary

Workstations often present the biggest challenge to security administrators. Not only are there more workstations than any other network device, but many users are uneducated, or not concerned, about security issues. While it is relatively easy to block outside access to workstations within the network, it is a lot more difficult to prevent an attack from within, whether or not that attack is intentional.

As with other parts of the network, the best path to workstation security is multipronged. Limit the access users have to the network and their ability to make configuration changes to the machine. Virus software should be run on every workstation as well and should be updated with new virus definitions on at least a weekly basis.

By clamping down tight on workstation security, a lot of potential security problems can be averted before they happen.

15

Managing Network Security

To this point the primary focus has been on best practices for securing a network. The rest of this book will focus on how to monitor and enforce the security policy that is in place. This is another area where organizations often fall short. After gathering the requirements, putting together a strong security policy, and locking down the network, employees and administrators will allow security practices to lapse. New equipment is not properly secured and the importance of the organization's security policy is not properly stressed to new employees.

Loosening of network security occurs because administrators and managers allow it. The help desk is understaffed so employees are allowed to install their own software. A manager allows an employee to bring a wireless access point, or even a computer, from home and plug it into the network. There are numerous ways in which insecure devices are introduced into a network, but they all boil down to the same thing: Most employees (and some administrators) are not as concerned about security as they should be.

Ideally, an administrator should never have to worry about how security conscious employees are. The network should be locked down so tight that an employee should be able to set up an IRC server and use it to attack IRC servers over the world without administrators having to worry about the security implications. But the truth is that employee action, and inaction, has a tremendous impact on network security. In order to run a truly secure organization, security policies need to be continually enforced, and the network has to be constantly monitored for security weaknesses.

15.1 Enforcing Security Policies

After a security policy has been put in place and a network has been secured a good deal of time should be spent ensuring the security policy is enforced throughout the organization. Obviously, this means that senior management has to express full support of the security policy. It also means that security education of employees should be an ongoing task. Education can be accomplished through security seminars, e-mail newsletters, or other forms of communication. The point is that users should be reminded, at regular intervals, about the importance of security within the network.

Such reminders, or detailed explanations about certain policies, will help keep network security on the mind of all employees. This is not to suggest that reminders need to be daily, or weekly; once a month is a good interval. These updates do not have to cover all aspects of network security; instead, they can focus on one area and give details about the potential security problems with that area. For example, a monthly e-mail security newsletter could be sent to all employees. Each newsletter can focus on a different topic that directly affects users. Topics discussed might include e-mail security, virus scanning, web server security, and so on.

E-mail newsletters are especially effective when changing or introducing a new security policy. Keeping users informed about why a policy is being implemented or changed will cut down on the number of complaints that the help desk has to field. Security policy cannot be implemented based on popular opinion, but security policies are more likely to be adhered to if users, and management, understand the reasoning behind the policies.

In addition to communicating security policies to users, security administrators should work with management and the human resources department to develop a set of repercussions for violating security policies.

Different violations should have different repercussions, depending on the severity of the breach of security. But each policy should clearly state the punishment, or stepped punishment, for violating it. Some violations, such as plugging nonstandard networking equipment into a network, may result in a verbal warning. Other violations, such as sniffing traffic on the network, should result in immediate termination.

Management and human resources will ultimately have to determine how violations of security should be handled, but security administrators will need to explain the severity of violating each policy, so an intelligent decision can be made.

NOTE

Most likely working with employees who have violated security policies will not be completely new territory for human resources. Many companies have created policies against passing offensive jokes or images via e-mail. These policies may include termination for people who violate them.

After policies have been communicated, and procedures for violations developed, the next step is enforcement. Once again, this requires support from both management and human resources.

A violation may first be noticed by either a manager or a coworker. A policy should be put in place so anyone who notices a security violation can report it and have it quickly investigated. *Quickly* being the operative term. If reports of security violations are responded to 24 or 48 hours after they are reported, users will get the impression that security is not a high priority and will not bother to report future incidents.

If a violation is reported, there should be clear procedures in place to escalate the incident. It should be investigated, and if the incident turns out to indeed be a violation of security policy, the procedures in place should be followed. Oftentimes the manager of the offender should be notified, as well as the human resources department.

15.1.1 Personnel Management

Proper personnel management is important, but network management is equally important. If a serious violation is reported, the user's account should be suspended immediately, and the switch port to which they are connected should also be disabled. This is why a centralized authentication system makes sense in an enterprise network environment. Removing a user from the network only requires a two-step process, as opposed to removing multiple accounts from different machines—increasing the margin for error.

Assuming proper server logging is in place, there should be no additional accounts created on servers for the internal attacker to use to gain access to the server remotely. If there is concern that a rogue account exists, a thorough audit of servers the attacker had access to should be performed, especially if the employee is ultimately dismissed. Shared accounts, such as router or switch usernames and passwords, should also have their passwords changed.

These same steps should be followed if an employee leaves the company for whatever reason. Again, it is important to work with management and the human resources so that security administrators are notified when an employee leaves the company. The employee's network account, or accounts, should be deleted and their network port disabled. Shared passwords should also be changed.

In addition, when an employee leaves the company, his or her workstation should be audited to ensure there is no company information on it. After the audit, the workstation should be formatted and a fresh install of the operation system completed before it is assigned to a new user. If there are any programs or documents in violation of the security policy found on the machine, a record should be kept of the information.

If a security violation is first noticed by the security staff through one of the monitoring tools in place, extensive documentation of the violation should be completed. This process is discussed further in Chapters 16 and 17. The employee's account should be disabled, and the network port disabled, then either the employee's manager or the human resources should be notified—unless other escalation procedures are specified.

Not all violations of an organization's security policy will, or should, result in termination. However, the security staff should always err on the side of caution. In addition to protecting the network, a very strong response demonstrates an organization's commitment to security and will help users realize that they should take security seriously as well.

15.2 Understanding Network Security Risks

If a new security policy is being enabled within an organization, it is not only the end users who will need to be trained; network and system administrators will have to be trained as well. Because administrators are a vital component of strong network security, they should be trained to incorporate security as part of their daily routine.

NOTE

End users can be forgiven for ignorance about matters of security, but administrators cannot. To that end, it is important that all systems administrators understand the philosophy behind the company security policy, and what constitutes good security practices.

Security should be a basic tenet of every equipment or software evaluation that is performed. Software upgrades should be subjected to security testing, in addition to the regular testing, and the security impact of network changes should be evaluated alongside performance and redundancy considerations.

Some basic considerations that should be part of an evaluation of any device being added to an enterprise network include:

- Methods of access and administration: Is there a secure way to connect to the device for administrative purposes? If there are multiple ways, can insecure methods be disabled?
- Default accounts: What default accounts are on the device? Those should be recorded and changed, or deleted.
- System monitoring: What methods are available to monitor the health of the device, and any anomalous behavior? Are those methods secure?
- Logging: What logging facilities are in place? Will they work with the existing monitoring system?
- Redundancy: What type of redundancy is available for this device and is redundancy important for this device?

- Vendor reputation: What reputation does the vendor have for security and responding to security incidents? Security incidents are a fact of life for all vendors; how they react is important.
- Device security history: Look through online security databases. What types of security incidents have been reported for this device? Have there been multiple security holes?

There are undoubtedly other security needs that are organization specific, and this list is not intended to be comprehensive. Instead it is a starting point to help each organization build a list that meets its needs.

Just answering these questions is not enough. A thorough, methodical security evaluation should be performed on all new equipment being considered for deployment on the network. In other words, try to hack the box.

In a lab environment that mimics the corporate network, try to use the same tools an attacker would to break into the device. Ideally, the device being tested should be submitted to a security evaluation for a week. That should give administrators plenty of time to launch password attacks and DoS attacks, sniff traffic, and try the other attacks covered in Chapter 3.

It is important that the tests be methodical. Again, this is a lab environment and should be treated as such. A standard security test plan should be in place. The security test plan should describe how the attacks work, what the purpose of each attack is, and what information can be gained from a successful attack. Not all attacks will be appropriate for all devices, so several security test plans should be in place for each type of network device that will be tested.

The results of each attack should also be recorded. If a password-cracking attempt is successful after three days of trying, that should be noted. Bear in mind, if an attack is successful, that does not mean that the device should be removed from consideration for network deployment—it is simply a data point.

After the security audit has been completed for a network device, there are several options. If this is an evaluation of multiple products, the results should be shown to the individual vendors. The vendors will undoubtedly have best-practice configurations that are recommended for security; if these were not followed for the first test, a second test should be performed using them.[1]

---

1. Of course, asking for this information up front can save a lot of time.

If the second test, using the vendor's recommended best practices for security, has similar results or results that are only marginally better, the device should be removed from consideration for deployment. Oftentimes, a test like this may uncover security holes of which the vendor was not aware. If that is the case, the security audit will help the vendor fix bugs in the code, making an overall better product.

This type of security should be applied not just to network devices and software, but network protocols as well. An organization considering deploying routing protocols such as Intelligent Scheduling and Information System (IS-IS) or Multiprotocol Label Switching (MPLS) will want to perform similar security audits on these protocols to determine what the security weaknesses are.

The difference is that when a new protocol is being deployed it is generally done on existing equipment, rather than on new equipment. For that reason it is even more important that an organization be willing to work with vendors to patch any security holes that are found.

Protocol security evaluation is often a confusing topic. How does an administrator determine if there are security holes in a specific protocol, rather than in a network device, or software? The answer remains mostly the same. Many of the same guidelines can easily be applied to a protocol. When it comes time to perform a security audit on the protocol, the tests should be based on known security holes in similar protocols. If an organization is auditing a new routing protocol, then tests used to evaluate a BGP or OSPF implementation can often be used.

What is important is an understanding of the protocol, and what it is trying to accomplish. If a protocol is supposed to be designed to allow a user to securely connect to a server, an evaluation should be designed to test whether or not a username and password can be sniffed or decrypted. In short, administrators have to think like an attacker would. If someone were attempting to find out information about the network, how would that person attempt to exploit the protocol?

15.2.1 Ongoing Security Evaluations

Evaluations, whether of hardware, software, or protocols, should not just be conducted prior to deployment. A routine should be established to conduct security evaluations of existing network infrastructure on a regular basis.

A security evaluation is separate from the network monitoring that happens on a daily basis. Security evaluations generally occur in two forms:

1. Simulating a real attack
2. Testing equipment in the lab

The first test should be an assault on the network in a manner that simulates a real attack. Attempt to access servers, shutdown routers, or gain access with an unauthorized machine.

Simulated attacks should be conducted with no warning, giving the administrative or security staff a chance to respond in their usual manner. If the simulated attack is successful, it should be quickly noticed and dealt with.

If the attack were successful, the compromised device should be re-evaluated to determine its weaknesses and how best to correct them. The same type of evaluation should be applied to security staff if they fail to notice the attack.

Failure on the part of the security staff to stop an attack in progress should be taken very seriously. Determine why the attack was not noticed, and what steps can be taken to make sure the problem does not recur. These steps may involve additional training or improved monitoring processes. If repeated simulated attacks go unnoticed, steps also may involve the termination of employees who fail to notice the attacks.

The second type of ongoing security evaluation goes on in the lab. Network devices should be re-evaluated on a regular basis to determine if there are new security holes that can be exploited. This type of evaluation is more than checking security databases, which should also be done on a regular basis. Instead, the goal of this evaluation is to test the equipment in the lab, using the latest security tools available. New tools for testing network security, or to exploit weaknesses, are being developed all the time. Some of these tools will be useful to incorporate as part of a standard security evaluation. Devices already on the network will not have been subject to evaluation by those tools, which may be able to detect new security holes.

To make sure that all network equipment is subject to assault by the latest tools, schedule re-evaluations at regular intervals for each device or program in use on the network. The tests do not have to be run every month, but there should not be more than a six-month interval between tests.

Secure evaluation and re-evaluation of network equipment can help ensure that an organization's network is running at peak security performance, especially when combined with periodic attack simulations.

15.3 Avoiding Common Mistakes

Despite the best efforts of security administrators, there are still many common network security mistakes made. This is a top-10 list[2] of security mistakes commonly found on networks. Some are configuration mistakes while others are process mistakes. This list is by no means exclusive, but it is a good way to perform a quick evaluation of the security level of a network.

15.3.1 Bad Passwords

The number-one mistake found in a network environment is bad passwords. Bad passwords can be the result of a password policy that is too restrictive, or nonexistent. A password policy may be in place, but not enforced, rendering it useless.

In addition, this includes default passwords that are not changed. All default accounts on all network devices should be renamed, if possible, and the default password should be changed. If the account is not needed, it should be deleted, or the service should be disabled.

Even more grievous than default passwords are systems that are secured with no password. If a device does not require a password or some other form of security key to logon, it should not be part of an enterprise network.

NOTE

It bears repeating that a common source of "no password" network devices is the back door that administrators will often install on the network. Some terminal servers ship with no password set, allowing anyone who connects access into the network.

---

2. Despite our best efforts, we could not get David Letterman to run this list.

15.3.2 Failure to Create a Security Policy

One of the biggest mistakes made by corporations is the failure to create a solid, effective, and realistic security policy. Users and administrators are not going to know how to handle security issues unless it is communicated to them.

A security policy should be well documented and take into consideration not just security needs, but the needs of the business and the needs of the network users. If a policy is so restrictive that it prevents users from being able to do their jobs effectively, they will begin to find ways around it, and it will become useless.

Ineffective security policies also do not examine the entire network and can leave gaping holes easily exploited by attackers. Involve administrators and managers from all areas when devising a security policy and keep them informed of updates to that policy.

Keep users informed about security policies and explain to them the necessities for security restrictions in language that is clear and easy to understand. The more effective the communication of the policy is, the more likely network users will be to adhere to it.

15.3.3 Insecure Access to Devices

Too many devices in use on the network allow administrators to access them via Telnet, FTP, or some other form of access that is not encrypted. This is a mistake on the part of vendors and should not be perpetuated through an enterprise network.

All devices on the network, especially devices from the firewall out, should be accessed only through encrypted connections. If an encrypted connection is not available, demand one from the vendor, or switch to a new vendor.

NOTE

Remember, the vast majority of attacks occur in-house. Someone with a network sniffer can gather a lot of information about network topology very quickly. Don't further assist them by allowing them to gather password information as well.

15.3.4 Over-reliance on a Firewall

Firewalls are great. They can provide a lot of network protection, and can greatly increase the security of the network. However, firewalls should not be the only means of securing a network.

Too often, administrators rely on the firewall to completely protect a network, and a firewall is simply not able to do that. A firewall used in conjunction with solid security practices in other areas gives a network several layers of security and provides much better protection.

Over-reliance on a firewall can have especially disastrous results if the firewall rule set is not properly managed. It is not uncommon to start off with a firewall configuration that is especially restrictive and then add in rule sets as the need arises. If these changes are not carefully managed and filtered, an organization can wind up with a firewall that has so many holes that it is, essentially, useless.

15.3.5 Back Door Access

Administrators will often make secondary accounts, add a secondary network interface, or find some other way to give themselves a backup method of accessing a server or the network. There is nothing wrong with this as long as the method is properly documented and proper security precautions are taken.

Most of the time these access methods are neither documented nor properly tested for security holes. These access methods are put in place for convenience, but they may be creating huge security holes within the network.

After all, if back door access allows administrators to bypass security precautions, those same methods will allow an attacker to bypass the same security precautions.

15.3.6 Backups

Backups themselves are not a mistake, but many administrators do not take proper security precautions, and do not back up the correct information. This is especially true when it comes to networking equipment. Router and switch configurations are not backed up when they are initially deployed, or when changes are made. Firewall configurations are also frequently not backed up, or if they are, changes to the rule set are not backed up.

Backups should be done daily on servers and other machines considered critical to the network infrastructure. Router, firewall, and switch configurations should be backed up every time a change is made. In a dynamic network where changes are made frequently to these devices, backups should be performed every day, just as they are on the servers.

The part of backups where administrators are often very lapse is testing. Backups should be tested randomly to ensure that data is actually being backed up. There are two ways to do this:

1. Examine the log files for failures. If a backup failure is reported, the backup should be immediately rerun.

2. Spot restore. Attempt to restore files randomly—to a test workstation to ensure the backups are working. It is possible that a backup server will report everything was successful, when the file is actually corrupted. Even worse, the medium (the tape or disk) can become corrupted, ruining all the data stored on it.

The worst time to find out there are problems with a backup system is when there has been a critical failure, and a restore is the only fix.

15.3.7 Not Updating Antivirus Software

Antivirus definitions have to be updated often. Virus definitions should be updated weekly, at a minimum—more often if there appears to be a lot of virus activity. That may seem extreme, but remember when the Melissa virus was initially released it spread across three continents in less than 24 hours.

Consider running virus software from two separate vendors on your network as an added layer of security. One vendor should be used for mail and groupware servers where virus scanning is critical to prevent files from entering, or being propagated, through the network. A second vendor should be used for workstations, to catch any viruses introduced at the access level, and possibly catch any missed by the software on the servers.

15.3.8 Failure to Follow Through

After a security policy has been implemented, you must follow through. Security policies put in place should be adhered to and maintained by administrators, managers, and other network users.

If a user violates a security policy, appropriate action should be taken, and the human resources department should be willing to follow through with any punishment. If network users do not take security policies seriously they will become impossible to enforce, and render any network security ineffective at best.

There is a tendency among companies to get very excited about network security, and be very gung ho to implement tough security policies after a security incident has occurred. The excitement dies down several weeks later, and users relapse, returning to their old behavior patterns. This does not make for effective security, and should be discouraged.

15.3.9 Failing to Update Systems

Administrators are busy people with a lot of work that always seems to be piled up. There is never enough time to get caught up, and some things are forced to wait. Software patches are a prime example of something that is often put on the back burner, because a lot of testing may have to be done before the patch can be implemented.

That type of thinking cannot exist in a security-aware organization. Patches, especially patches that have security implications, should be tested and installed as soon as possible. After a security hole is made known, there will be attackers looking for systems to exploit. If an organization has not patched its system, that organization will be a likely target.

A time should be set aside each day to look for new security patches that apply to network devices within the network. A list of all potential security holes should be compiled and ranked in order of importance. After the list has been created, someone should devote one day a week to testing the patches, so they can be applied to the necessary systems.

Of course, if a patch is considered critical for good network security then it should take priority over other day-to-day tasks and be tested and installed immediately.

NOTE

In June 2002, a security hole was found in the Apache web server, leaving more than 60 million web users vulnerable to a theoretical attack. Within 48 hours, a worm was released that changed the theoretical attack to a very real possibility. Fortunately, the worm turned out to be a dud, and never spread. The Apache Software Foundation responded with a fix before the worm was released, but administrators who were not quick to update could have been at serious risk.

15.3.10 Unqualified Personnel

Effective security administration requires a lot of training. Not only does a security administrator need to understand security issues in great detail, he or she also has to have an extensive knowledge of different types of systems.

Security administrators frequently work with routers, servers, switches, firewalls, monitoring devices, intrusion detection systems, and many more devices. Because of this it is often hard to find qualified security personnel.

There is a temptation to use unqualified employees—or employees who only understand some of the technologies—and hope for the best. This is never a good idea. There is nothing wrong with having a new employee who is not familiar with all of the systems work with experienced employees to learn more, but the entire security staff should not consist of partially trained employees.

15.4 Summary

Managing network security is the unglamorous part of a secure network. The day-to-day enforcement of the security policy and monitoring of information for data can be monotonous. However, it is an essential part of network security and should be taken just as seriously as setting up the security policy and dealing with a security incident.

Part of the way security administrators can avoid falling back into bad practices that could leave security holes on the network is to keep the top-10 security mistakes in mind. Administrators should watch their actions throughout the day to make sure they are not slipping into bad security habits.

16

Monitoring

Accepting the fact that a network will be attacked is an important step for network administrators. Attacks will be launched against almost all networks eventually, and some will be successful. A good monitoring infrastructure can help detect attacks as they occur and often stop them before there is a problem.

Monitoring and logging are often used interchangeably. The truth is they serve very different purposes. Monitoring systems are in place to track and fix problems as they occur. Logging provides administrators with historical data about the network, while monitoring provides an instant snapshot of the network.

Network monitoring should be performed 24x7. Even if the administrative staff is not onsite 24x7, notifications should be sent to pagers—or cell phones—as incidents occur. To create accountability, one or more of the administrative staff should be on-call at all times to deal with potential security breaches.

This bears repeating yet again: The quicker a security incident can be detected, the quicker it can be contained and removed. An effective monitoring system is the best way to ensure that network changes are quickly caught and dealt with in a time-sensitive manner.

In order for a monitoring program to be effective it has to have two characteristics: It has to be secure and intelligent. An attacker should have a difficult time gaining access to the monitoring servers and preventing alerts from being generated. If alerts are not properly managed, it will be difficult for the monitoring staff to get to the heart of a problem. Intelligent monitoring means that alerts are generated only when there is a good chance that a problem exists. Rather than generating hundreds of useless alerts each day the monitoring system should only notify administrators when there is a real potential for a problem. Although, ultimately, the administrators will have to determine whether a problem is real or a false alarm. No software program can monitor a network device better than a human administrator.

Secure, intelligent monitoring starts with the positioning of the monitoring servers. An enterprise organization should have at least two monitoring servers, one located within the network, and another located outside of the network (Figure 16.1. If an organization has multiple locations one of the monitoring servers can be located in a remote location; otherwise, the remote server can be co-located with a hosting provider.

There are two reasons for using multiple monitoring servers located on diverse networks. The first is for redundancy. If the primary server fails, the secondary server is still monitoring and continues to maintain information about the network. The second reason is that servers on diverse networks can provide network administrators with different information about the networks being monitored, providing a more complete picture.

The server within the network should be located within the firewall DMZ and be connected to the management network. The monitoring server will need to be able to monitor both the primary and the management IP addresses of the network devices, which means it will have a complete network topology. Hence, it is critical that the machine be protected from attackers. As with DNS and logging servers, a layer of security, over and above the steps taken as part of standard server security precautions, should be used when provisioning a monitoring server. On a Unix server this usually involves using Netfilter, or their equivalent.

The remote server, or servers, will only monitor the public IP addresses and should be allowed through the firewall to monitor any server or network device within the network. As indicated, the remote monitoring server should be on a separate network. This will help administrators determine how devices are performing both internally and externally. Remote monitoring can also give administrators advance warning of WAN connectivity problems.

There are many applications designed to monitor different aspects of the network. In general, it is best to limit the number of different applications in use for monitoring. Programs like OpenView and Netcool can meet the monitoring

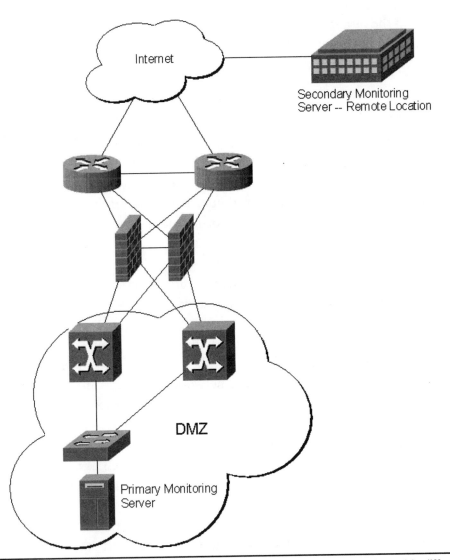

Figure 16.1   Multiple monitoring servers increase redundancy and provide different views of the network

needs of just about any organization and are sufficiently customizable to be tailored to the particular needs of a network. Running multiple monitoring applications on a network can cause more confusion for administrators trying to sort through all the different error messages. Each additional application also poses a potential security risk and is another program that administrators have to track for security holes and bug fixes.

16.1 What to Monitor

The first quandary when building a monitoring policy is to determine what needs to be monitored. There is often a rush to monitor as much of the infrastructure as possible, but that is rarely a good idea. Instead, it is better to focus on network devices that will impact more than one user if they fail. That leaves a large part of the network open to monitoring, but it does not bog administrators down with unnecessary monitoring messages.

The goal of a monitoring infrastructure should be to monitor all devices that provide service to multiple users on the network. In addition to the devices that are monitored, it is important to determine what services need to be monitored on each device, and how to overcome problems when they occur.

The escalation process involves determining which group is responsible for which devices. While monitoring should be centralized, in most organizations different groups will handle different network devices. If an organization has separate systems, network, and security groups, then ownership of devices will need to be assigned, and the escalation process will have to be worked out within each of those groups. Most intelligent monitoring software allows for multiple escalations, and most with remote access capabilities, such as OpenView, allow different views to be created, depending on the needs of an organization.

For example, if routers and switches are the responsibility of the network group, then that group can create a view of just those devices. The networking group will be able to monitor those devices throughout the day, and escalation procedures specific to the networking group will be assigned to those devices.

Outside of the escalation process, different devices have different monitoring needs. While all network devices need to be checked to determine whether or not they are available, some devices require more detailed monitoring.

16.1.1 Servers

Servers often require the most extensive monitoring, because there are so many possibilities for failure. In addition to general availability and bandwidth usage, server monitoring also requires examination of the hard drive for partitions that are nearly full, and for bad sectors.

CPU and RAM utilization needs to be closely watched on a server to ensure that neither reaches critical levels. High CPU and RAM usage is often a sign that a server has been compromised and is being used to launch attacks against other networks. At the very least, it indicates that an application is using significant resources and should be investigated.

Servers should be monitored for unauthorized ports as well. If a port that should not be available on a server suddenly opens up, that could be a sign of an attack. At the very least it may indicate that an application recently installed on the server is opening unnecessary ports and poses a potential security risk.

Individual applications should be monitored as well. This is different than monitoring the overall health of the server. Rather than focus on the server, monitoring the health of an application means testing to ensure it responds with proper information. As an example, many monitoring applications will alert server administrators when the content of a website changes. If someone has bypassed security measures and gained unauthorized access to the web server, the monitoring application will catch it quickly and notify the appropriate party. Databases should be queried as part of the monitoring system to ensure that the database returns valid information. The more forensic the network monitoring is, the sooner problems will be caught. Servers are the most common target; they need the greatest levels of monitoring.

16.1.2 Routers and Switches

Routers and switches need to be monitored for availability, RAM and CPU usage and for bandwidth usage. Routers and switches are especially sensitive to bandwidth spikes after a network device has been compromised. If unusual traffic patterns occur suddenly on a switch or a router, it can be a sign that a security breach has occurred. It also may indicate that unauthorized applications, such as file-swapping software, have been installed. Keeping a close eye on shifts in bandwidth usage for routers and switches can help administrators track down problems much more efficiently.

Routers and switches should also be monitored for unauthorized port access. If an attacker connects to a port that is supposed to be unused on a switch, it should show up in monitoring. Equally important is if a disabled interface is activated on a router. Again, administrators should know when new interfaces are brought up and quickly investigate unknown access to these devices.

NOTE

Each network device has unique monitoring needs. It is important to check with the vendor to find out what those needs are and what monitoring facilities exist within the device. It is also important to check with the vendor to ensure the device's monitoring facilities are compatible with the monitoring applications in place on the network.

16.1.3 Security Monitoring

In addition to monitoring for the availability of network devices and applications, it is necessary to perform regular security monitoring. Security monitoring can include performing port scans on network devices looking for unauthorized applications or open ports that should not be open. It also includes testing for password security, launching common attacks against network devices, and load testing of servers and routers.

While all these tests should be performed in a lab, it is also necessary to perform regular security monitoring on the live network to ensure that all systems are operating at peak efficiency, and with the proper security measures in place. Some of these tests can be performed with an IDS, while other tests require special software.

The goal of these tests is to look for vulnerabilities that an attacker would look for and correct them before an attacker can find them. When these tests are performed, it is important to act fast and fix any holes that are found. As with any other type of monitoring, the more proactive administrators can be when it comes to finding and fixing security holes, the harder it will be for an attacker to find a way into the network.

16.2 SNMP

SNMP is, by far, the most popular method of monitoring network devices. The reasons for SNMP's popularity are threefold: modularity, scalability, and adaptability. A SNMP monitoring system (Figure 16.2) can be developed to gather as

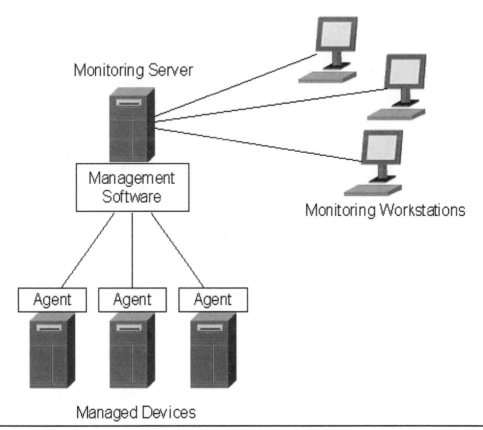

Monitoring Server

Management
Software

Monitoring Workstations

Agent   Agent   Agent

Managed Devices

Figure 16.2   A typical SNMP monitoring network. The monitoring server receives information from and polls the managed devices. Workstations responsible for monitoring pull information from the monitoring server

much information about a network as possible, or it can be used to gather only selected information.

SNMP works for high-traffic devices and networks just as well as it works for low- and medium-traffic devices and networks. The SNMP framework has been ported to just about every device that can be used on a network.

SNMP is an UDP-based protocol (Port 161) that is used to exchange management information between devices on a network. The devices can be part of the same network or on disparate networks. SNMP relies on three different components: the managed devices, agents residing on those devices, and the network management system or systems (NMS).

As Figure 16.2 illustrates, the software agents reside on the network devices and communicate information about the devices to the management software, usually referred to as the manager. Workstations pull monitoring information from the monitoring server, or servers, and can generate alerts about the network devices.

The agents and the monitoring server communicate using a series of different commands. The four commands used by the manager to communicate with the agents are:

1. GetRequest
2. GetNextRequest
3. GetResponse
4. SetRequest

The agents can also send information directly to the manager using the Trap command.

Different vendors often have different names for these command types. For example, Cisco uses the following SNMP commands to communicate with its network devices: read, write, trap, and traversal. This underscores the importance of ensuring that a network device is compatible with the monitoring software being used on the network, or that the monitoring software is modular enough to allow new devices to be added to it.

SNMP uses protocol data units (PDUs), usually packets, to communicate between the manager and the agents. The manager will send a GetRequest or SetRequest to the agent. The agent responds with a GetResponse PDU which contains the results of the request. The GetRequest command asks for certain objects and their values. These objects can be current CPU temperature, amount of hard drive space available, amount of bandwidth, or anything else that can be managed through SNMP. SetRequest, on the other hand, provides a value to which the remote agent should be set.

GetNextRequest is used to traverse a series of agents on a managed device to extract information from all agents. This command is commonly used when the manager does not know exactly what it should be looking for, so it requests everything.

The `Trap` command is a PDU that originates from the agent. It is the only command that originates from the agent, and it is used to communicate unusual events, such as sudden spikes in traffic, CPU usage, or a network failure, that have occurred on the remote device. A trap can even be configured when a hard drive reaches a certain capacity. When a trap is sent from the agent to the manager it is usually a sign there is a problem, or a pending problem.

Agents collect information about the network device using a Management Information Base (MIB). An MIB is a set of information, organized hierarchically, about a managed device. This hierarchical organization is also known as an MIB tree (Figure 16.3). Each MIB is made up of objects, and is categorized by object identifiers. An object is specific information about a device, and the object identifiers are the variables that are the possible values for those objects.

Figure 16.3 is a partial view of the MIB tree of a router. This information can be automatically collected by most monitoring devices that support SNMP. In this case, WhatsUp Gold, from IPSwitch, built the entire MIB tree

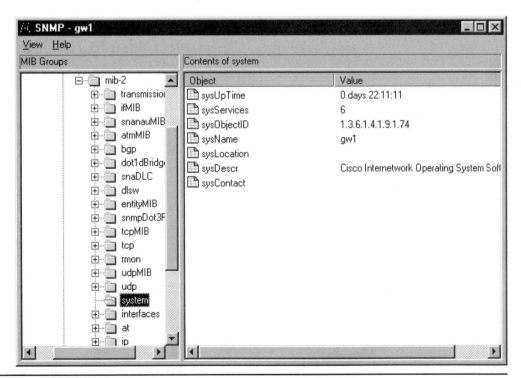

Figure 16.3   A partial view of the SNMP MIB tree for a Cisco router

automatically. An MIB tree is similar to a directory structure, with each part of the MIB tree branching off to smaller parts. Again, using Figure 16.3 as the basis for discussion, this SNMP view contains a mib-2 group, under that is a system group, and within the system group are the objects.

Each of the objects has an assigned value that is communicated from the agent to the monitoring server. For example, the object sysUpTime has a value of "0 days 22:11:11". While this information is useful, it is not really necessary.

Figure 16.4 contains slightly more useful information. It is a partial view of the information available from one of the interfaces on the same router. The interface is located within the ifTable group, and contains a different set of objects, all of which represent information normally available using the command line interface (CLI). Information for which objects are available includes the interface type, speed, errors, number of packets, and the Maximum Transmission Unit (MTU) speed. Some of these objects, such as the MTU, can be changed remotely, while others are set to read-only.

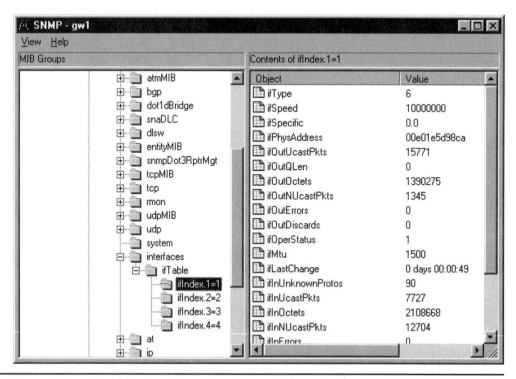

Figure 16.4   The interface information from a Cisco router

The MIB tree-like interface allows network administrators to drill deeper into a problem when it is necessary. If an administrator logs into a router and notices that it is extremely slow, he or she can examine individual objects closer to see what may be causing the problem. Figure 16.5 shows an extended view of ifInOctets. There is a sudden spike in the number of octets directed at that interface, which may account for the poor performance of the router. The next step would be to determine why the sudden spike occurred.

Obviously, different devices will have different MIB trees, even when the same manufacturer makes them. However, all devices made by the same manufacturer should have the same top, or root, MIB entry. These root MIBs are registered through the ISO. For example, all Extreme Network devices are part of the root MIB: iso.org.dod.internet.private.enterprises.extremenetworks. Different group MIBs are assigned based on the purpose of the device. Switches have

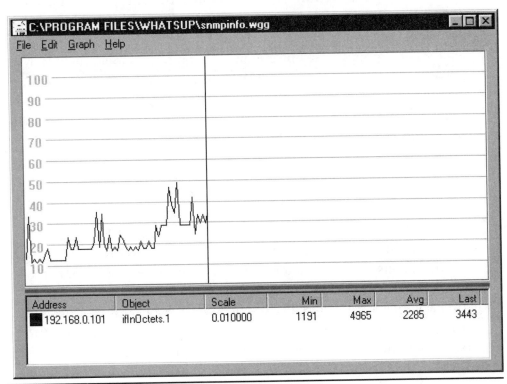

Figure 16.5   Drilling deeper into the MIB objects allows an administrator to gain a deeper view of problems on the network

different group needs than routers, and both have different needs than a firewall, or IDS.

Fortunately, SNMP is versatile enough to monitor any type of network device, and can be easily adapted to fit any type of network device and meet the needs of network administrators. Most monitoring programs will allow administrators to track as much or as little information as desired. Full-blown SNMP monitoring of every device on the network may not be advisable, so it is usually a good idea to select just those objects and groups that are critical to network stability and monitor them. This allows the administrative staff to catch emergencies faster, without having to sift through reams of irrelevant data.

NOTE

The MIB tree for a network device is simply a list of the groups and objects within the MIB, stored in a plain text file. For some devices this list can be dozens of pages long. To make it easier for administrators to filter out unnecessary groups and objects, many monitoring tools include MIB viewers, which will import the MIB tree and allow an administrator to examine the information within the MIB. Companies like SolarWinds and MG-Soft also make applications that are stand-alone MIB browsers, which are very handy tools to have around.

16.2.1 SNMP Security

SNMP is a great tool for monitoring and managing networks. This is evidenced by the fact that SNMP is so widely deployed. While SNMP has proven to be a reliable and stable product, it has not proven to be very secure. In fact, considering the amount of information that can be polled using SNMP, the level of security contained within it is atrocious.

The original version of SNMP, SNMP Version 1.0, only included community strings as a means of securing communications. Community strings are, essentially, passwords used to determine whether a device has read or read and write access to the network device. These passwords were not encrypted and were sent in clear text from the manager to the agents on the network device.

NOTE

The most common passwords used for SNMP are public and private, for read, and read and write access respectively. Attackers know this and will often try to poll a network looking for network devices that have SNMP enabled with these default passwords. For this reason it is crucial that SNMP be disabled on all devices that are not actively being polled for SNMP information.

SNMP Version 2.0 added several enhancements over SNMP 1.0. SNMP 2.0 was designed to be relatively backward compatible with SNMP 1.0, although some enhancements made complete backwards compatibility impossible.

The creators of SNMP Version 2.0 realized the importance of security, and tried to implement it with mixed success. There were actually several versions of SNMP 2.0 released; the two that are most important to security are SNMP Version 2c and SNMP Version 2u. SNMP 2c basically abandoned the security features included in the original SNMP 2.0 specification and reverted to the community string model used in SNMP 1.0.

SNMP 2u took a different approach, and introduced a user-based security model to SNMP. SNMP 2u is documented in RFC 1910 and defines a method of access control for SNMP-based systems. The goal of SNMP 2u was to provide a way to authenticate users and prevent unauthorized access of information. SNMP 2u was never widely adopted, but many of the enhancements in SNMP Version 3.0 are based on SNMP 2u.

NOTE

SNMP is a very common attack target because it is ubiquitous. SNMP attacks can allow root compromises, crash operating systems, and be used to launch other types of DoS attacks. For that reason, many security experts recommend strong filters be placed on networks that rely on SNMP for monitoring.

16.2.2 SNMP 3.0

In 1998 the IETF released a series of RFCs that defined several security enhancements to SNMP. These security enhancements, known collectively as SNMP 3.0, were not developed to create a new version of SNMP. Rather, they enhance the existing versions of SNMP by creating several different types of security. The RFCs that outlined the SNMP 3.0 architecture are RFC 2271 through RFC 2275.

There are three areas of security on which SNMP 3.0 focuses: authentication, privacy, and access control. As with SNMP 2u, SNMP 3.0 PDUs can use authentication to ensure the validity of the information. On top of authentication, SNMP 3.0 supports DES encryption between managers and agents. Finally, agents can be configured to only allow certain managers, or groups of managers, to have access to information. Similar to authentication, access control limits the type of information provided to different groups—unlike authentication, access control is handled at the group level, not the user level.

The security enhancements in SNMP 3.0 are made possible by the use of a principal. The principal is a user, or set of users, that resides on the manager and issues SNMP requests to the agents. When the principal issues a request to the agent, a negotiation takes place. The principal and the agent determine what security features will be used, and the agent uses the information provided by the principal to determine how much information will be shared. When the principal sends an SNMP request to an agent it includes a field in the PDU called msgSecurityModel. The msgSecurityModel will be set to 1, 2, or 3 depending on which version of SNMP is being used. The receiver should then use the same security model to process the message.

Authentication is the most commonly used form of security with SNMP 3.0. Defined in RFC 2274, authentication of SNMP messages has two aspects: the actual authentication and the timeliness of the message. Authentication between the manager and the agent is handled through a shared-key process. The authentication is handled using a Keyed-Hash Message Authentication Code (HMAC). The key will need to be provided to the manager and the agent, prior to the first authentication.

In addition to authentication, SNMP 3.0 checks for the message time. Previous versions of SNMP 3.0 were susceptible to replay attacks. To avoid this problem, when an agent or manager receives a message it verifies the time of that message to ensure it is within the system's acceptable parameters.

To maintain the time synchronization between devices, each SNMP-enabled device has two values, `snmpEngineBoots` and `snmpEngine-Time`. The values contain the number of system boots since SNMP was installed and the number of seconds since the last boot. Every time an SNMP PDU is transmitted these values are transmitted as well, allowing other SNMP devices to maintain a database with this information for all SNMP devices with which they communicate.

When an SNMP manager or agent receives a PDU from a device it checks the information in the msgAuthoritativeEngineBoots and msgAuthoritativeEngineTime fields. If that information is within 150 seconds of the information the device has stored in its local database, the PDU is considered valid and is accepted.

While authentication is useful, sending data in clear text is still a problem, especially if an organization is monitoring across a WAN. To resolve that problem SNMP 3.0 allows network administrators to use DES encryption to secure messages between devices. Keep in mind that any time encryption is used it can increase CPU usage significantly. While the security gains certainly make encryption worthwhile, its use should be monitored closely.

Encryption is used in conjunction with authentication to increase the level of privacy and security. The manager and the agent use the cipher block chaining (CBC) mode of DES to encrypt the data. The encryption is accomplished by creating an initialization value using a number found in the msgPrivacyParameters field of the PDU.

The View-based Access Control Model (VACM) is the SNMP version of an access control system, and is defined in RFC 2275. VACM is used to provide varying levels of control to managers, or groups of managers. VACM works by creating a table on each agent with different groups; the groups correspond with managers who can request data—and what type of data can be requested—from that agent. VACM rules can be applied to an entire MIB, groups of objects within an MIB, or a single object within the MIB.

There are several levels of security available using VACM rules. The most basic occurs when a request is made for an MIB object—the agent checks the tables to determine whether the manager making the request is authorized to access the content. If not, the agent returns an error. The error returned is `noSuchContext`, rather than a not allowed error. This slows down a potential attacker who is trying common MIBs to determine what type of device it is.

In VACM architecture SNMP requests from managers will include two additional fields: securityModel and securityName. Both fields need to be propagated; the agent will examine the vacmSecurityToGroup table to determine if there is a match for both fields. If not, the agent returns a `noGroupName` error.

There is also a vacmAccessTable that needs to be checked. The agent examines the groupName, securityModel, contextName, and securityLevel sent by the manager against entries in that table. If a match is found, then requests can be processed up to the defined securityLevel for the requested content. In other words, if a manager wished to write information to the agent, he or she not only has to be allowed to access the MIB object, he or she has to have write permissions. This gives administrators a very granular level of control for each MIB and MIB object on a device.

VACM can enhance the security of network devices by granting different groups very specific levels of control. Unfortunately, there is not a method available—at this time—to apply VACM rules across multiple devices. This means each rule has to be defined on every device to which it applies. This can be a tedious task, especially in large networks. The tradeoff for the amount of planning and configuration time involved is that VACM allows administrators to create multiple device views without having to rely on software such as Open-View or Netcool to do it.

16.2.3 SNMP Recommendations

All SNMP requests should be using some form of SNMP 3.0 security, preferably a combination of the HMAC algorithm and DES encryption. However, not all devices support SNMP 3.0 security measures at this time. If a vendor does not support these enhanced security measures, they should be encouraged to do so.

If SNMP 3.0 is not an option at this point, there are still a few other options:

- Change the default passwords. This won't stop an attacker who has access to the LAN and therefore may be able to sniff the information, but it will make things more difficult for attackers outside the network.

- Disable write capabilities to all network devices. An attacker who is able to gain write access to these devices can cause a lot of damage in a very short time. Disabling write capabilities will slow the attacker down considerably.
- Filter SNMP requests at the firewall level. SNMP should not be monitored remotely, only from within the network (ICMP, HTTP, and other requests can be monitored remotely). If requests are filtered at the firewall, an attacker will not be able to use the SNMP tool to map out a network and plan an attack.

16.3 Centralizing the Monitoring Process

To maximize the effectiveness of a monitoring infrastructure, everything should be centralized within a few servers. This means using software that is modular enough to allow for different types of monitoring. Some of the most common programs used for this type of centralized monitoring include HP OpenView, Netcool, Big Brother, WhatsUp Gold, and Nagios.

Most of these programs allow administrators to plug in only the monitoring tools needed, and to develop their own modules to accommodate special needs. Limiting the monitoring tool to only the functionality required increases security and prevents administrators from being deluged with too much information.

Monitoring should never be done directly from the monitoring server. Instead the people responsible for the monitoring should use remote agents to communicate with the monitoring server. There are a couple of ways this can be done. The monitoring server can send alerts to the syslog server, which will then generates an e-mail alert to a ticketing system. Rather than overburden the syslog server, monitoring information can often be accessed through a console, or a web browser.

If console or browser access to the monitoring server will be used, ensure all information is transmitted securely between the monitoring station and the server.

The monitoring servers themselves should be secured. It has already been mentioned that the monitoring server should use an internal firewall, such as Netfilter, as well as standard external security precautions. In addition to these steps, the monitoring server should be located on the management network, so it is removed from general public access. The workstations accessing the server will need to be part of that network as well.

Security of the monitoring server is critical, as it contains information about the entire network. An attacker who gains access to one of the monitoring servers will have a much easier time determining where attack efforts should be directed.

16.4 Summary

Monitoring is a critical component of any enterprise network. Extensive monitoring of a network helps to ensure the performance and availability of all network devices. Monitoring can also alert administrators to possible attacks before they escalate out of control. The quicker an attack can be stopped, the less damage can be done.

Monitoring can be used by attackers to map out a network and launch attacks on that network. Proper security measures are critical for a network's monitoring infrastructure. This means not only securing the server, but also securing the protocols being used for monitoring.

One of the biggest monitoring security holes is SNMP. Because SNMP data is transmitted in clear text, it is easy for an attacker to sniff out SNMP information and use it to launch network attacks. The newest version of SNMP, SNMPv3, contains several security measures that should be implemented whenever possible. These security measures include authentication, data encryption, and access control.

17

Logging

Logging and monitoring are so closely tied together that they often overlap in the minds of network administrators. There is an important distinction that has to be made between these two aspects of network security: Monitoring provides a picture of the present situation. Logging provides historical data. The historical data may only be a few minutes old, but it is still not necessarily a representation of the current network state.

Logging tracks changes in the state of a network device and requests made to the network device. Logs are incredibly useful for tracking down information about attacks. Attackers know this, and a skilled attacker will edit log files to hide the fact he or she has accessed the system. Editing log files is preferred to actually deleting them. Deleted log files are usually an immediate warning to administrators that a problem exists on the server. The longer an attacker can successfully hide the existence of a break-in the more information about the network that can be gathered.

The log structure for most applications is the same. It is based on either the Unix-centric syslog structure or on the Windows Event Logging structure. Most networking devices opt for the Unix syslog structure, because syslog has been designed to allow for remote logging. Because attackers are aware of how the two logging structures work, it is fairly easy to modify log files.

Using syslog as an example, if an attacker were to gain access to a server, there would be a record of that access. The record of the access would be written to a file called messages, generally located in the /var/adm/ or the /var/log/ directory. The messages will look like this:

```
May 27 12:09:53 test sshd[1825]: Accepted password for \
root from 192.168.0.2 port 1903
May 27 12:09:53 test sshd(pam_unix)[1825]: session opened \
for user root by (uid=0)
```

It is a trivial matter for an attacker to change or erase those lines to mask the fact that someone logged into the server at that time. Any changes to the server, which would normally be logged, can also be deleted as necessary, while still allowing the expected logs to be collected. The Unix logging structure will be discussed in detail in the Syslog section.

Windows NT and 2000-based systems have a similar logging system, called Windows Event Logging. The same type of information is collected, though in a slightly different format. Notifications are parsed into one of three groups: System, Application, and Security. While different types of messages are included in each Event Viewer, the format is the same (Figure 17.1):

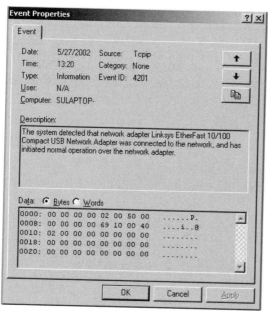

Figure 17.1   A system notification in Windows 2000. It contains the date, time, type of event, the user, and the name of the computer on which the event occurred

NOTE

By default Windows NT and 2000 do not log user authentications to the server. This should be changed on all servers to ensure that logins can be properly tracked.

Windows assigns an Event ID to each logged system activity. The Event ID serves as a means to quickly gauge what type of event occurred; it also makes it easier to sort events according to their potential to indicate a security breach. Microsoft has maintained the same Event ID classification between Windows NT, 2000, and XP—though new events are added with each progressive version of the operating system. To find out the most up-to-date information about an Event ID, and its meaning, consult the Microsoft website. Table 17.1 lists the logon events under Windows NT, 2000, and XP.

Table 17.1   Windows Logon Events

EVENT ID	DESCRIPTION
528	Successful Logon
529	Logon Failure: Reason: Unknown user name or bad password
530	Logon Failure: Reason: Account logon time restriction violation
531	Logon Failure: Reason: Account currently disabled
532	Logon Failure: Reason: The specified user account has expired
533	Logon Failure: Reason: User not allowed to logon at this computer
534	Logon Failure: Reason: The user has not been granted the requested logon type at this machine
535	Logon Failure: Reason: The specified account's password has expired
536	Logon Failure: Reason: The NetLogon component is not active
537	Logon Failure: Reason: An unexpected error occurred during logon
538	User Logoff

Table 17.1   Windows Logon Events *(Continued)*

Event ID	Description
539	Logon Failure: Reason: Account locked out
540	Successful Network Logon

These events are common to Windows NT, 2000, and XP

A standardized logging infrastructure, like those on Unix and Windows servers, makes it easier to maintain a secure network. All applications can write logging data in the same format, to the same log files, and it becomes easier to centrally monitor the logs for all applications on the server. A similar logging infrastructure also makes it easier to centralize the logging infrastructure and to develop third-party applications to assist with the process of watching log files.

Log files are also useful for gathering information about pending attacks. Prior to a break-in attempt an attacker will usually initiate a port scan against the network, looking for vulnerabilities. Because port scans are so commonplace most administrators ignore them. However, repeated port scans from the same address, or netblock, could be an indication that a network is being targeted.

Centralizing application logging to a few directories, or a single server on the network, is necessary because, even within small networks, so much information is generated within the log files that it can be difficult to isolate patterns. It can be difficult to take appropriate proactive steps to stop an attack. As with monitoring, there are many tools on the market that help sift through log files and pull out the important information, but they are not always perfect. Many administrators opt to write their own programs that parse through log files and generate alerts, although these are more customized to individual network needs. They are, again, far from perfect.

There are aspects of logging that are of equal concern to security administrators: protecting the log files and retrieving the necessary information from the log files. If the information collected by various devices on the network cannot be aggregated and examined for patterns or trends, then logging is useless. In addition, if an administrator cannot be sure that logs have not been tampered with, there is no point in keeping log files.

17.1 Protecting Against Log-Altering Attacks

Log file security starts by protecting the files from being altered. Because log files are stored as plain text files it is very easy for an attacker who has gained access to a system to edit the log files and cover his or her tracks.

There are multiple methods to secure log files. These methods can be used alone, or in conjunction with others. The more log file security methods used, the more secure the logging infrastructure of the network will be.

Whenever possible, the logs from all network devices should be directed to a separate server. Most network devices, including routers, switches, firewalls, and servers, have the capability to do this. Storing log files on a secured remote server that is only accessed across a management network can be a primary step in securing the logging infrastructure. This will be discussed later in this chapter.

In cases where log files cannot be directed to a dedicated logging server, steps should be taken to secure the log files created on the server. This means protecting not only the log files but configuration files as well. If an attacker is prevented from accessing the log files, but can change the configuration that generates those files, a lot of damage can be done.

Only the administrative user for the system should be able to read and write to log files and make changes to the configuration information for those files. This means that no other groups should have any sort of access to the files. Even applications that are run by a nonprivileged user should be configured so that only the administrative user has access to the log files generated by the applications.

Of course, protection against nonadministrative users accessing the log files is pointless if an attacker is able to gain administrative access to the network device. To that end, the log files need to be protected against those who have gained unauthorized administrative access. The most common way to do this is to encrypt the log files.

Log file encryption is not supported in many applications, and there are some problems associated with encrypting log files. Most notably, encryption requires a lot of CPU usage, which can be a serious hindrance to a busy server. For example a busy website, with a lot of CGI and database calls, will create a heavy load on a web server. Adding the burden of encrypting log files in real time has the potential to slow a server to a crawl. This can be especially apparent while other CPU-intensive applications are running.

That is not to say that an administrator should not encrypt log files, but it is important to weigh the security needs against the available system resources of the network device. If a server is already heavily loaded an attacker might be able to force it offline by launching a DoS attack against it, forcing even heavier CPU usage because the device will have to encrypt all of the requests.

Products like Syslog-ng from BalaBit IT, Ltd., and Core Wisdom from Core Security Technologies can be used to encrypt log files on Unix servers, and ELM Log Manager from TNT Software for Windows servers. It is also possible to write custom applications to encrypt log files. The syslog daemon is open source, so the code is freely available, and Microsoft makes an API available for the Event Manager, which other programs can tie into.

NOTE

When encrypting log files never leave the encryption key on the server. A common mistake administrators make is to store the key in a file on the server, making it relatively simple for an attacker to find the key and use it to alter the log files.

Another way administrators protect against log-altering attacks is to write the log files to a write once, read many (WORM) device. A WORM device can be a CD-W, tape, or any type of storage media that support one-time only writing. Some SAN devices can be configured to support WORM mode, and some operating systems, BSD, for example, can support this mode as well.

When a storage device is in WORM mode, information can be appended to the log files, but the files themselves cannot be overwritten. As the name implies, the data contained within the files can be read repeatedly. It can even be extracted into a database or some other monitoring tool. But, once written into the file, the data cannot be overwritten, affording server administrators an additional level of protection.

Aside from being in WORM mode, the storage media should be either a separate partition, or at least the log files should be on a separate partition. If there is an attack designed to overload the logging system, the separate partition will limit the amount of damage an attack can do.

In extreme cases a printer can be used as a logging device. Log information is sent to the printer, then printed. This is not advised, as printed data is much more difficult to sort through to find patterns. Busy servers also generate a large amount of log files, and storing that amount of paper would quickly become difficult—especially if an attacker intentionally floods the log files.

When log files cannot be propagated to a remote server, it is generally considered best practice to write the files to some form of WORM-enabled media. In addition, log files should have very restrictive permissions, only granting the administrative user the ability to read them. In most cases, this provides enough security. In extreme cases, encryption can be used, but again, weigh the use of encryption carefully against the performance of the network device.

17.2 Syslog Servers

The syslog Protocol was originally designed for the BSD operating system that has since been incorporated into other operating systems. The syslog specification is outlined in RFC 3164. The syslog protocol has two uses: to collect logging information from applications on a server and to collect logging information from other devices on the network.

A syslog server is an excellent tool for collecting information from routers and switches. Because these devices do not have a lot of storage space, sending logging information to another device gives network administrators a chance to maintain a historical perspective on network events, and can help track changes in the network.

A syslog server also helps to increase network security. If devices are configured to send logging information to another server, it is more difficult for an attacker to modify those log files to cover a security breach. Of course, this is assuming that proper security precautions have been taken to secure the logging server.

Syslog has grown in popularity because it has a relatively simple format that is adaptable to any network device, and it is fairly liberal in the type of data it will accept. All syslog messages should be sent over UDP Port 514, and must be less than 1,024 bytes. Syslog also has extensive configuration options, allowing the creation of different files for different logging purposes. Syslog can even be configured so that some messages are sent to a remote logging server, while others are stored on the local server.

A syslog message is divided into three parts: PRI, HEADER, and MSG. PRI indicates the priority of the message, the HEADER contains the time and the hostname of the message, and the MSG is the actual message being transmitted by the remote host. Each of the fields must be separated from the other fields, so they can be easily parsed by a human reviewing the log file, or an application that is scanning the log file. None of the three parts are mandatory.

A typical syslog message will look like this:

```
May 28 19:29:06 test sshd(pam_unix)[3257]: session opened \ for user
root by (uid=0)
```

Or, a message from a remote device:

```
 May 28 19:49:32 192.168.0.101 14: 00:13:38: \
%SYS-5-CONFIG_I: Configured from console by allan on console
```

In these examples a priority code is not used. If the priority code were used, it would be enclosed within "< >" at the beginning of the message, prior to the date. The priority code is the combination of two numbers, the facility that is generating the message, and the severity. Each facility is assigned a number, as shown in Table 17.2. That number is multiplied by eight and the numerical value of the severity, outlined in Table 17.3, is added to it.

Table 17.2   Numerical Value of Facility Messages

NUMERICAL VALUE	FACILITY
0	Kernel
1	User
2	Mail
3	System
4	Security, Authorization, Audit
5	Syslog Daemon
6	Printer
7	News

Table 17.2   Numerical Value of Facility Messages *(Continued)*

NUMERICAL VALUE	FACILITY
8	UUCP
9	Clock
10	Security, Authorization, Audit
11	FTP
12	NTP
13	Log Audit
14	Log Alert
15	Cron
16–23	Local Use 0–7

There is some duplication because different operating systems assign different facility values to some functions.

Table 17.3   Numerical Value of Severity Messages

NUMERICAL VALUE	SEVERITY
0	Emergency
1	Alert
2	Critical
3	Error
4	Warning
5	Notice
6	Information
7	Debug

Based on the two charts, a message generated by the kernel with a severity of Emergency would have a priority of <0>. A message generated by the FTP daemon with a severity label of Critical would have a priority of <90>. The priority field should have no more than 5 characters in it (191 would be the maximum numerical value) including the "< >."

The HEADER field of a syslog packet will have the date and the time that the message is logged; in other words, it contains the date and time of the local system, not the system sending the message. The format of the HEADER field is very specific, in that it should be sent as:

```
Mmm dd hh:mm:ss hostname
```

Mmm represents the three-letter abbreviated form of the month, with the first letter capitalized (e.g., Jan, Mar, Sep, etc.). The date is separated by a single space and is represented by a two-digit number. In cases where the date is a single-digit number, an additional space should be added between the month and date columns. A zero should not be used as filler for single-digit numbers. The hour, minute, and second field are separated from the date by a space, and listed in 24-hour military time.

The hostname can be the canonical hostname of the remote device—without the associated domain name, the IPv4 dotted decimal address, or the IPv6 address. A space should follow the hostname field as well.

The message field contains the bulk of the information in which an administrator will be interested. It has the name of the application that created the message as well as the message itself. The message contains two fields, the TAG field, a 32-character or less field that has the application name, and the CONTENT field. The content field contains the actual message. There is no limit to the size of the field (other than the constraints of the 1,024 byte packet), and the message can be in any format.

Although there is no limit on the type of information that can be sent in the CONTENT field, most vendors standardize the format of the messages, making it easier to monitor the log files. This information should be published on each vendor's website or in its manuals. It is important to understand how each vendor writes its syslog messages so it will be easier to pull the necessary information from a logging server.

17.2.1 Syslog Configuration

There are a lot of different options when using syslog to create a logging server, making it sometimes difficult to decide how a server should be configured. Many administrators start by logging everything, from all network devices. After spending a week doing nothing but reviewing information on the logging server, administrators usually change this policy.

The goal of any centralized logging system is to gather the information needed, without overloading administrators with information. The easiest way to do this is to use the syslog configuration file to sort the logged information into separate log files.

The syslog configuration file is usually syslog.conf, located in the /etc directory on most Unix servers. The format of the syslog configuration file is relatively simple:

```
facility.severityhostname or file
```

Because syslog configuration allows an administrator to send different messages to different locations, it is easier for an administrator to isolate messages that may be critical to system security. The better job administrators do of determining how messages will be logged, the easier it will be to isolate messages and the faster a potential attack will be caught.

As a general rule all devices that use the syslog server should receive all messages that are at a severity level of informational and above. (Of course emergency messages should be sent to all users logged onto the affected system as well.) Debugging messages are only used when there is a system problem and can be activated as needed on the local device. If a network administrator designates the server 10.10.100.130 as the syslog server, then the following entry is all that is needed in the syslog.conf file of the remote servers:

```
# If there is an emergency, display it to console
*.emerg *

# Otherwise, everything, including emergency messages,
# but mail messages should go to the Syslog server.
*.info;mail.none  @10.10.100.130
```

The syslog server will have a more complex configuration file. In order to make the monitoring process easier on the administrative staff, it is best to divide up the messages. Messages of differing importance can be sent to different files, or even to different servers. A sample syslog server configuration file might look like this:

```
# Different Facilities are logged to different files
kern.*   /var/log/kernel
mail.*   /var/log/maillog
local7.* /var/log/boot

# Emergency messages should be sent to a separate file so
# they can be dealt with immediately

*.emerg/var/log/emergency

# Authentication messages are obviously important, as are
# instances of users using the su command, these should
# be logged to secure files.
auth,authpriv.warn;user.*  /var/log/secure
auth,authpriv.=notice   /var/log/sulog

# Other messages are sent to the system log file
*.info;mail,news,lpr,authpriv,auth.none /var/log/messages
```

NOTE

Syslog will not automatically create the log files. If a new entry is added to the syslog configuration file, the file has to be created before information will be logged to it. The file creation is usually accomplished using the `touch filename` *command.*

This type of setup is great for network devices that are true to the Unix-based syslog system, but different vendors have their own lists of facilities, and those facilities do not always follow the Unix standard. Tables 17.4 and 17.5 list the Juniper and Cisco, respectively, facility information for log messages.

Network administrators must understand the facility information that is being sent to the syslog server, so the proper files can be generated. Even if a catch-all file, such as /var/log/messages, is used, sorting through that file looking for critical messages is a waste of CPU and manpower. It makes much more sense to isolate important messages from different network devices into easily manageable files.

Table 17.4   Juniper Syslog Facilities

FACILITY NAME	DESCRIPTION
Any	All facilities
Authorizations	Login attempts
Change-log	Configuration changes
Cron	Cron daemon
Daemon	Daemons not specified by other facilities
Interactive commands	Commands issued in a terminal or console
Kernel	Kernel messages
User	Any user process

Table 17.5   Cisco Syslog Facilities

FACILITY NAME	DESCRIPTION
Auth or security	Login attempts
Bootp	Bootp daemon
Daemon	Daemons not specified by other facilities
Named	DNS messages
Gated	Gateway messages
Kern	Kernel messages
Mail	Mail daemon
NTP	Network Time Protocol messages
Local0–local7	User-defined messages

So, if a network administrator wants to log all bootp messages from Cisco devices into a separate file, a line like this would need to be added:

```
# Log all bootp messages to a separate file
bootp.info /var/log/bootp
```

The configuration process for different devices is also different than the configuration process for Unix systems. Most routers and switches will allow network administrators to configure syslog entries through the command line interface. However, the manner in which this is accomplished varies from router to router. Juniper routers have a syslog command at the [edit system] hierarchy. Assuming the name of the Juniper router was GW1, and the syslog server was 10.10.100.130, the configuration would look something like this:

```
syslog {
  host 10.10.100.130 {
    * info;
    log-prefix gw1;
  }
```

The asterisk represents all facilities; alternatively, a line could be created for each facility that is to be logged.

The Cisco method, using the IOS command line, is a little different. The syslog configuration information is referred to as "logging" in the global configuration section, as shown in Figure 17.2. As with other syslog configurations, the Cisco logging facility allows network administrators to set the IP address of the syslog server and create different logging rules for different facilities, as well as different types of access (e.g., terminal versus console access).

Different hosts can also be specified for different types of logging. Cisco's IOS will also allow administrators to determine from which interface the syslog messages should be generated. This feature is particularly useful for syslog servers that use IPTables or some other firewall facility to limit traffic allowed to the server.

17.2.2 Windows and Syslog

The internal logging facility on Microsoft servers is not compatible with syslog. Generally, administrators either use the Microsoft Windows logging facility to create a centralized logging system, or they use a third-party, Windows-based syslog facility.

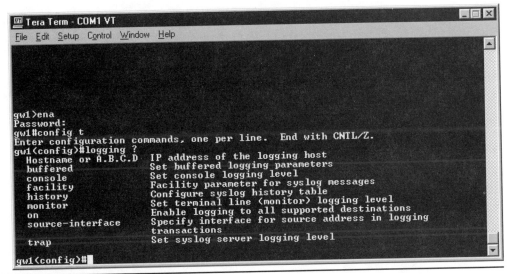

Figure 17.2   The Cisco logging facility. Cisco's version of syslog

Truthfully, trying to manage two, or more, logging systems is a pain, and can create unnecessary confusion. Many administrators in a mixed-network environment are opting to meld them into a single syslog system, even when multiple syslog servers are used. It is still more efficient to manage multiple syslog servers than it is to manage different logging facilities.

A commonly used Microsoft Windows syslog system is Winsyslog, shown in Figure 17.3. Developed by Adiscon, Winsyslog takes standard Microsoft Windows event messages and converts them into syslog format. These messages can then be sent to a remote machine, just like other syslog messages, making log management relatively simple.

17.3 Sifting Through Logged Data

Now that the logging information has been secured, centralized, and sorted into separate files, the next step is to determine how to isolate important information. A trap that some administrators fall into is relying too heavily on monitoring information to determine when there is a problem and using logging data only after an incident has occurred. Monitoring information is important, but it doesn't always tell when there is a problem. Logged data can help bring to light

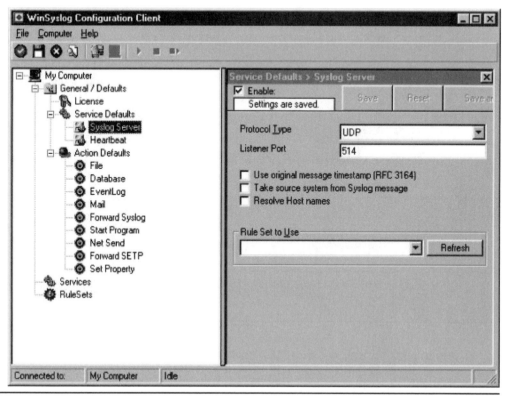

Figure 17.3   Winsyslog converts Microsoft Windows error messages into syslog messages

emerging patterns on the network, which indicate there may be a potential security breach.

As has already been mentioned, the problem is that so much logging data is generated by network devices that relying on a human to pick out patterns may be difficult. Fortunately, there are several programs—both open source and commercial—available that aide in the monitoring of log files.

17.3.1 LogSentry

One of the most common tools used to monitor log files is Psionic Technologies LogSentry. Like syslog itself, the strength of LogSentry lies in the fact that it is extremely customizable and can be configured to match the needs of most organizations.

LogSentry runs as a cron job on a Unix syslog server (LogSentry is not designed to work on Windows servers). Every hour, or more frequently if desired, it searches through the log files on the server looking for possible attacks. LogSentry will determine if there is a problem in one of two ways: by the severity of the log entry and by searching for certain patterns that are indicative of attacks.

If suspicious activity is identified then notification is sent to the address listed in the configuration file. The default contact is root; however, that can be changed. In fact most settings can be changed in the LogSentry configuration file. By default this file is called logcheck.sh and is located, after installation, in the /usr/local/etc directory.

In the configuration file the address to which alerts should be addressed can be changed. The files that should be searched can be changed, and the types of alerts that should cause alarm can be changed. This gives administrators a great deal of control over what alerts are generated, and can be a useful tool for fine-tuning the alert process so fewer false alarms are generated.

NOTE

As with monitoring, getting the syslog checking process down takes time. Initially the administrative staff will undoubtedly be flooded with alerts, but as the checking process is refined, the alerts should begin to more accurately reflect the state of the network.

In addition to the information within the check.sh file, there are four other files that aid in the log file checking process:

1. HACKING_FILE
2. VIOLATIONS_FILE
3. VIOLATIONS_IGNORE_FILE
4. IGNORE_FILE

The HACKING_FILE is a plain text file that contains known words or phrases often associated with attacks. The words and phrases in this file should generate very few false positives, and are usually a sign of an attack, or potential attack. LogSentry includes a default HACKING_FILE, logcheck.hacking, which comes with the following entries:

```
"wiz"
"WIZ"
"debug"
"DEBUG"
ATTACK
nested
VRFY bbs
VRFY decode
VRFY uudecode
VRFY lp
VRFY demo
VRFY guest
VRFY root
VRFY uucp
VRFY oracle
VRFY sybase
VRFY games
vrfy bbs
vrfy decode
vrfy uudecode
vrfy lp
vrfy demo
vrfy guest
vrfy root
vrfy uucp
vrfy oracle
vrfy sybase
vrfy games
expn decode
expn uudecode
expn wheel
expn root
EXPN decode
EXPN uudecode
EXPN wheel
EXPN root
LOGIN root REFUSED
rlogind.*: Connection from .* on illegal port
rshd.*: Connection from .* on illegal port
sendmail.*: user .* attempted to run daemon
uucico.*: refused connect from .*
tftpd.*: refused connect from .*
login.*: .*LOGIN FAILURE.* FROM .*root
login.*: .*LOGIN FAILURE.* FROM .*guest
login.*: .*LOGIN FAILURE.* FROM .*bin
```

```
login.*:  .*LOGIN FAILURE.* FROM .*uucp
login.*:  .*LOGIN FAILURE.* FROM .*adm
login.*:  .*LOGIN FAILURE.* FROM .*bbs
login.*:  .*LOGIN FAILURE.* FROM .*games
login.*:  .*LOGIN FAILURE.* FROM .*sync
login.*:  .*LOGIN FAILURE.* FROM .*oracle
login.*:  .*LOGIN FAILURE.* FROM .*sybase
kernel: Oversized packet received from
attackalert
```

As new attacks are recorded within a network, or on any of the security sites, pattern matches can be added to this file.

The VIOLATIONS_FILE consists of words or phrases, similar to the HACKING_FILE, that indicate someone may be attempting to violate the network security policies. These words or phrases can be things like an attempted root login, restarting a network device, someone attempting to use the superuser (su) command, and more. A sample file is also included, as a way to help administrators develop their own file.

The VIOLATIONS_IGNORE_FILE is used for log messages that contain words that are in the VIOLATIONS_FILE, but can be ignored in some situations. These are usually more complete sentences, and they override the messages in the VIOLATIONS_FILE. An example of this might be a case where an administrator does not necessarily care about denied messages generated by BIND. The keyword denied is included in the VIOLATIONS_FILE, but an entry could be added in the VIOLATIONS_IGNORE_FILE similar to this:

```
named*: client *: update denied
```

NOTE

The asterisks indicate a wildcard in this entry. Use wildcards judiciously in the VIOLATIONS_IGNORE_FILE. If they are too liberally applied, they can result in a potential security problem slipping through.

The IGNORE_FILE consists of everyday log messages, which are expected and should not be treated as security violations. LogSentry includes a log list of log file messages: cron, FTP, Sendmail, and NTP, which can be ignored in the reporting process and would simply create more information for an administrative staff to sort through. Clearing these entries out makes it easier to determine which messages are possible security threats, and which are not.

Because LogSentry relies on mail to deliver messages, it can be used in conjunction with a ticketing system, such as Remedy. It also means that administrators should hardly ever need to access the syslog server directly. Alert messages will be sent to a remote mailbox or a ticketing system and processed from there.

17.3.2 IPSentry

IPSentry is a Windows-based monitoring application. While its primary purpose is to perform ICMP, SNMP, and other types of remote monitoring services, it also has a built-in syslog server that can be used to receive remote messages from other network devices.

There are two ways to view the monitored data created by IPSentry. The first, and most common, method is through a console located directly on the server, as shown in Figure 17.4. The console runs in the background on a Windows server and shows monitoring information, as well as syslog messages, as they appear. The problem with this method is that it is inherently insecure. Having to allow continual access directly to the monitoring server can open potential security holes, leaving the monitoring server vulnerable.

The second method, which is a way to increase the level of security, is to opt to use the web interface to view logged data, so no direct access to the server is required. This is more secure, but because IPSentry does not allow for HTTPS access to the remote server, it could create additional security problems. To maximize security, HTTP connections should be made over the management network.

Syslog configuration within IPSentry is relatively simple. Select a device that is currently being monitored, and choose the Syslog tab from the options. A screen similar to Figure 17.5 will be presented; simply fill in the appropriate fields.

IPSentry allows an administrator to fill in the facility as well as the priority for each device being monitored. Unlike LogSentry, IPSentry relies strictly on the priority information to determine whether or not an alert should be generated. If a problem is generated through syslog, a notice will be sent to the monitoring screen, which forwards it to the web interface.

There are other tools available for both Unix and Windows systems that can be used to monitor syslog events. Keep in mind, when choosing a program, the

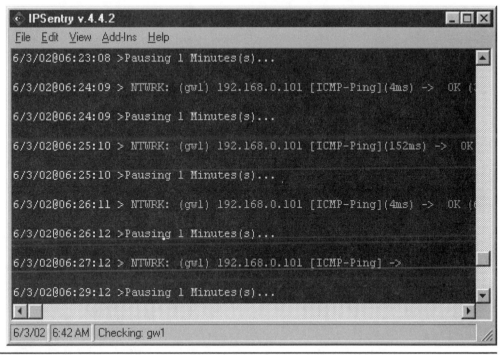

Figure 17.4   The IPSentry monitoring screen. It can be used to monitor on several different ports, as well as to monitor syslog entries.

goal of a syslog monitoring system is to communicate information to the appropriate administrators in as secure a method as possible.

The more secure the syslog server is, and the more secure the methods to communicate information are, the more reliable the information from the server will be. In the event of a security breach, secure logs are going to be important.

NOTE

Another commonly used application to monitor syslog files is SWATCH, short for the Simple Watcher. SWATCH, written by Todd Atkins and available for download from *www.oit.ucsb.edu/~eta/swatch/*, works in a manner similar to LogSentry, except log anomalies are reported as soon as they happen.

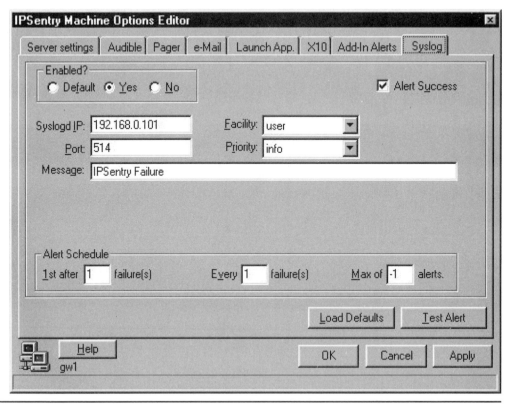

Figure 17.5   The IPSentry syslog screen

17.4 Summary

Syslogs are useful because they can provide administrators with analysis of a break-in. They can also help track down how an attacker managed to successfully break into a system. For these reasons, it is imperative that syslogs be secured.

At a minimum all syslogs should be stored on a separate partition and only readable by the administrative user of the server. Additional security steps that can be taken include writing the log files to a WORM device and encrypting the log files.

The best security enhancement for log files is to not store them directly on the network device. Most network devices have a facility called syslog, which will help direct the files to a separate location. The syslog server should be locked down using the usual methods and have an extra layer of protection in the form of a software-based firewall, such as IPTables. Syslog entries should also be written to a WORM device whenever possible.

To make the life of administrators easier, there are tools, such as LogSentry and IPSentry, that can sift through syslog messages and generate alerts to administrative staff when suspicious activity is noted.

18

Responding to an Attack

Despite all security systems in place, and regardless of the precautions taken, the fact is that most networks will be attacked. There are simply too many people who launch attacks against networks and too many security holes to be able to say with any assurance that a network is not vulnerable to attacks. In fact, it is extremely foolish to think that a network is invulnerable.

When an attack does occur, an organization should have four goals:

1. Detect the problem.
2. Isolate the problem.
3. Stop the problem.
4. Report the problem.

A fifth goal, which is not always possible, should be to prosecute the person who caused the problem. Too many organizations end the process after the problem has been stopped. It is important to let appropriate organizations know, and to prosecute when possible. Too often an attacker is not properly prosecuted because an organization is worried about the bad press, or losing face with customers. A tough stance against attackers is necessary to send the message that launching an attack against a network is not acceptable behavior, just as entering the offices of a company and stealing information is not acceptable. This message can only be sent if organizations are willing to prosecute when they can.[1]

---

1. Many attacks are launched from countries where the law enforcement agencies are uncooperative with law enforcement agencies from other countries. In those cases, prosecution is not an option.

The key word when creating a plan to meet each one of these goals is *speed*. The faster an attacker is detected, isolated, stopped, and reported, the less damage will be done to the network. Not only that, but, if an organization acts quickly, it is less likely that an attacker will be able to cover his or her tracks, making it easier to document the attack.

A well-documented response procedure will be part of a good security plan. Every employee of an organization should know who is responsible for dealing with an attack, and how an organization responds to attacks. Response is particularly important, because an attack has to be contained as soon as possible. That means that a security incident should be escalated properly, and not handed off to the wrong person or group. An efficient and organized response makes it easier to meet the response goals.

18.1 Create a Response Chain of Command

The first step in responding to an attack is to develop a clear chain of command, and ensure that it is distributed to everyone. A well-thought-out chain of command will serve two purposes: It will help get security incidents resolved faster, because the right people will be notified, and it prevents the security department from being overrun with unrelated requests.

There are usually three groups involved in creating and supporting the response chain of command: network administrators, server administrators, and security administrators. Each of these groups should have different responsibilities, and be responsible for different security incidents. The idea is to have the group most closely associated with a problem act as the first level of response. That group should be able to make the quickest and most accurate assessment as to whether or not a network anomaly is harmless or a possible security incident.

Some organizations collapse the duties of network, system, and security administration into one group. In cases like this, different people within that group should have a primary responsibility for security escalations.

At least two people within an organization should be ultimately responsible for handling all security incidents. Ideally, the primary responsibility for managing security incidents should rest with the chief security officer (CSO), with secondary responsibility resting with the manager of the security administration group. If there is no CSO or security administration group, the responsibilities can be assigned to the manager of the network and system administrators groups.

Redundancy in personnel is just as important as redundancy in systems. If the primary contact is unavailable, a secondary contact—who is aware of the procedures for dealing with an attack—should always be available and listed as part of the chain of command.

A central point of contact, at the senior management level, is very important because decisions that affect the company network and connectivity will often have to be made on the spot, and it is important to have someone who can speak for the company.

The chain of command for security incidents should vary depending on the type of attack. Each group is responsible for managing its own areas of responsibility, but the same procedures should be followed organization-wide. For the rest of this section, assume an organization that has a separate group to manage workstations/servers, network devices, and security devices. The security administration group manages the firewalls and IDS; the network administrators manage other network devices. The primary point of contact is the CSO.

Each group is responsible for maintaining and monitoring its own systems. The groups are not staffed 24x7, but there is extensive monitoring in place on the network, and personnel are notified if a suspicious incident occurs after hours.

Figure 18.1 shows one way in which this organization could manage its security escalation. Each group is responsible for certain devices on the network. If a device within the realm of its responsibility is attacked, the group is responsible for proper escalation of the incident. Notice there is a crossover between the network administrators and the security administrators with regard to DoS attacks. DoS attacks may be noticed at the router level first, or they may be noticed at the firewall, or even by the IDS. Whichever group notices it first, it should be reported to the other group, and escalated appropriately.

The second thing that should be added to this escalation chart is a response time for each incident. Some attacks, like a root compromise, are more serious than other types. The more serious the threat, the swifter the response needs to be. This is where the escalation becomes important, because a response needs to be formulated in minutes, not hours, in order to stop an attack and be able to gather evidence against an attacker.

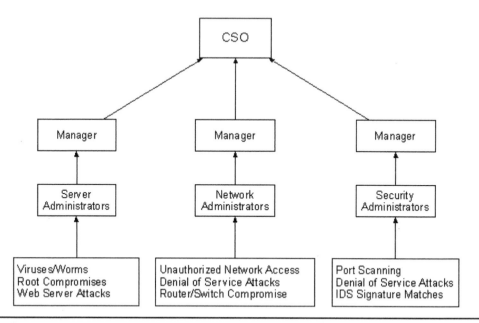

Figure 18.1   A sample escalation chart for security incidents

For each incident, a response time needs to be assigned. If the appropriate party does not respond within the allotted time, the incident should be escalated to the next level, and so on through the list of contacts.

Response times do not have to be assigned individually. They can be grouped depending on the severity of the incident and what needs to be done in response to the incident. One idea is to create three priority levels:

1. Priority 1 with a response time of 10 minutes or less
2. Priority 2 with a response time of 30 minutes or less
3. Priority 3 with a response time of 1 hour or less

Figure 18.2 outlines a sample escalation process. In this case a root compromise is in progress when a server administrator notices it. The server administrator has to escalate to the server manager. If the attack happens during the day, this is no problem, but if it happens at night the escalation point may not be on premises.

In cases where the contact is not on premises he or she should be paged or called. As soon as the first attempt to contact the escalation point is made, the timer should start. While waiting for the escalation contact to call in, it is a good idea to begin taking notes and documenting what is happening. If the initial escalation point does not call in within the allotted time, then the server administrator should attempt to reach the backup. The backup will have less time to call in, because this is such an important issue. Again, if the backup does not respond within the allotted time the next escalation point should be tried (in this case the CSO). If an incident is escalated through the entire chain of command with no response, the process should start all over again.

Obviously, for this escalation process to be effective (see Figure 18.2), current contact information should be made available for all employees in the escalation chain. Ideally, all employees who are part of the escalation should have pagers or cell phones issued by the company. This information should not only be current, but also listed on paper, with regular updates also handed out in paper form. If an attacker does manage to compromise the database server, it is possible that he or she will find these escalation procedures, and delete them, or delete pertinent information such as phone numbers.

The escalation point does not have to be on site. The person simply has to be able to authorize the administrator to take a server offline, and may have to be responsible for contacting other parties involved in the incident, as well as contacting authorities.

In some cases, the infected boxes should be taken offline immediately. For example, if a new worm is found on a workstation, but it has not had a chance to spread, the workstation can be disconnected from the network.

NOTE

Notice the phrasing above—"disconnected from the network," not "powered down." A virus or worm may contain commands to erase a hard drive, or destroy the boot sector of a disk, so an infected machine should never be turned off until the virus/worm has been removed or a server administrator inspects it.

Each type of incident should be broken down with a separate escalation process. The escalation process should include the steps to be taken before a call is made, what should be done while waiting for a response, and the escalation path, in case there is no immediate response.

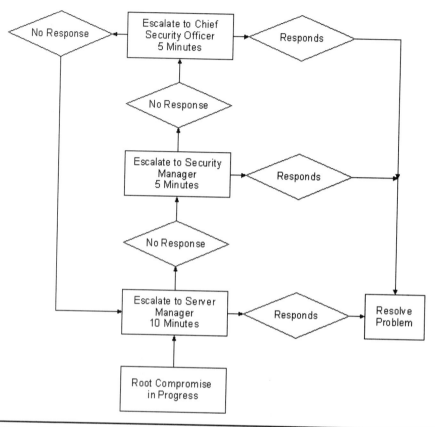

Figure 18.2 A sample escalation process. A root compromise occurs, the security administrators notice it in progress and escalate to the server administration manager. If response occurs within the allotted time, the problem is resolved; otherwise, it continues to escalate.

Again, it is important to remember that only the escalation contacts should make the call as to whether a server, or other network device, should be taken off the network. Only the top escalation point, in this example the CSO, should make the decision to take the entire network offline.

18.2 Take Notes and Gather Evidence

The note-taking process should begin as soon as a problem is noticed. Because computer files can be altered, or deleted, by an attacker, the notes should be written on paper. The preferred method for this is a shared logbook reserved for security incidents.

It may not always be possible to use a shared logbook, especially in cases where technical staff is not onsite 24x7. A central logbook should still be maintained, and notes taken during a security incident should be transcribed to the logbook. This centralizes the process, making it easier to track down information in the future.

Logging of information is important because it demonstrates that the proper security procedures were followed. Logging is also important in the event authorities have to be contacted. Because the importance of a security incident is not always known until after the investigation is well under way, starting the logging process when the investigation opens helps to ensure there will be sufficient evidence for authorities.

There are four things that need to be included in all log records of a security incident:

1. The time and date of the attack and follow-up actions
2. The total amount of time spent working on the attack
3. Names of those contacted during the investigation
4. The systems and programs affected

The first item to be recorded in the log is the time and date that the attack was first noticed, as well as the time and date of any subsequent actions. Subsequent actions include phone calls, responses from the phone calls, escalations, actions taken, and so forth. All steps taken to resolve the security incident should have the time and date marked down, along with a brief description of the action.

Recording the total amount of time spent working on the attack is especially important if it is escalated through multiple levels, or has an ownership change (e.g., the night shift takes over the incident from the day shift). The amount of time each employee spent working on it, as well as the total amount of time organization-wide that was spent dealing with the attack, should be recorded.

Anyone contacted in the process of the investigation should be noted. This can be either phone or e-mail contacts, and it should include people from outside the organization who initiate contact. For example, if another administrator e-mails an organization to inform them a DoS attack is being launched from their servers, that should be noted.

Finally, record the names of systems that have been infected, as well as any applications that have been compromised by the attack. If the attack spans multiple network devices, record the network segment that was impacted. Of course, if the entire network is affected, through either a worm or a DDoS attack, then note that the entire network is affected, and also try to pinpoint what the original target was.

In addition to taking copious notes, it is important to gather log information as soon as possible. An experienced attacker will attempt to alter the log files to cover his or her tracks. If logging is properly handled, this will be extremely difficult to do; however, nothing should be taken for granted. The log files implicating the attacker should be removed from the syslog server and stored on a floppy or CD-writable disk as soon as possible. Again, the log files may be necessary as evidence if the attacker is caught and prosecution is an option.

The more information noted during an attack, the easier it is to create a postmortem and to contact authorities with the information gathered during the attack. More information also makes it easier to track down the attacker.

18.3 Contain and Investigate the Problem

An attack should be contained as soon as possible, especially an attack that affects other networks. Depending on the severity and nature of the attack this may happen right away, or at the behest of the escalation contact.

Containing an attack should always involve removing a system from the network. It is important to do this quickly, before an attacker has a chance to cover his or her tracks. Taking a system off the network has business continuity implications as well, which is why it has to be authorized by an escalation contact. This is especially true in cases where either a large part of the network or the whole network has to be taken offline.

Worms are a prime example of a case where an entire network might have to be taken offline—to have the worm removed, and prevent it from spreading to other networks. Of course, if the network is taken offline, it is much more difficult to access the software needed to correct the problem (software patches, virus updates, etc.). Any patches needed should be downloaded prior to taking the network offline, and it is probably a good idea to keep a dial-up account with a local ISP, just for such emergencies.

As mentioned previously, when containing a problem, remove the device from the network, but do not power down the system. In most cases, simply disabling the port on the switch is enough. However, if the problem occurs at one of the edge routers, or worse, the firewall, it will be necessary to disconnect the network from the Internet until the attack can be isolated and the system restored.

Powering down a system can actually hinder the troubleshooting process. Many attackers, especially when dealing with viruses and worms, will include software that attempts to format a hard drive or destroy the boot sector of a machine in an attempt to cover the tracks of the attacker. After the system has been powered down, a console connection should be made to the system and any damage should be assessed in that manner.

On Unix systems, while consoled into the server, it is a good idea to grab any information from the history file, as well as any locally stored logs. If it is a Windows-based system, saving information in the event viewer can be useful, as well as any local log files. Of course, any information stored on the affected machine, or machines, should be viewed as suspect until it can be compared with the data on the remote log server.

18.4 Remove the Problem

After a problem has been contained, thoroughly investigated, and all evidence has been gathered, the next step is to remove the problem. Removing the problem means that full system restore has to be completed. A good attacker will often create multiple back doors into a system, allowing the attacker easy access back into the device, and possibly the network.

Because it is almost impossible to find all of these back doors created by an attacker, it is important to completely restore the system that was affected. If an accurate estimate can be made of the time and date the attacker penetrated the system, then the system can be restored from a backup prior to that date. If an accurate time cannot be estimated, then a full operating system restore should be completed, and the data restored from backup should be carefully monitored. In fact, if an administrator is unsure of the data integrity, it might not be a bad idea to place the server on an isolated network segment and monitor it closely. If an attacker has buried a method of back door access on the device, it should respond to unusual ports, or even attempt to contact the attacker.

Before any data restoration is done, a system has to be cleaned. If it is a server, the hard drives should be fully formatted. If it is a network device, such as a router or switch, it should be reset to factory defaults before restoring the configuration file.

If the attack occurred as a result of a vulnerability in a particular application, patches for that application should be downloaded and installed on all systems that run the application—or the application should be temporarily disabled while the code is reviewed.

If the problem occurred as a result of a security misconfiguration, then the deployment process needs to be reviewed to ensure that the mistake is not being duplicated, and similar devices on the network should be examined to ensure they are not susceptible to the same attack—or have already been subject to the same attack.

After the problem has been removed, extra vigilance should be paid to the rest of the network, to make sure the attacker was not able to gain access to another network device. Once an attacker is inside the network, it is easier to gain access to other network systems. Systems within the same VLAN should be thoroughly audited, and the log files should be closely examined looking for any anomalies that might point to the attacker gaining access to other systems.

This type of thorough audit will help to ensure that the attacker is not able to repeat the steps taken to enter the network in the first place. It also gives administrators confidence that the network was not further compromised.

18.5 Contact Appropriate Parties

While the problem is being removed from the network, forensics are being performed, and the system is being cleaned, appropriate parties should be contacted. The information about who is contacted should be logged, as well as whether that contact is made via e-mail or phone conversation.

The first organization contacted should be any organization adversely affected by the attack. If administrators are able to determine that the attacker used the compromised server to launch an attack against another server, that organization should be contacted to make them aware they may have a security breach.

Attacks are usually launched against one or more IP addresses. The IP addresses attacked can be used to track down the owners of the network block by querying the appropriate database (ARIN, RIPE, or APNIC). For example if the attacker used a server within the netblock to launch an attack against the IP address 12.25.233.110, a query of the ARIN database provides the following contact information:

```
[allan@ns1]$ whois -h whois.arin.net 12.25.233.110
[whois.arin.net]
AT&T ITS (NET-ATT) ATT12.0.0.0 - 12.255.255.255
Inflow (NETBLK-ATT137321616-232) ATT137321616-232 12.25.232.0 -
12.25.239.255
Rackmy.com (NETBLK-INFLOW-RACKMY-1) INFLOW-RACKMY-1
12.25.233.96 - 12.25.233.127
```

The search can be narrowed down to a query of the netblock that is of specific interest:

```
[allan@ns1]$ whois -h whois.arin.net NETBLK-INFLOW-RACKMY-1
[whois.arin.net]
Rackmy.com (NETBLK-INFLOW-RACKMY-1)
 710 N Tucker
 St. Louis, MO 63101
 US

 Netname: INFLOW-RACKMY-1
 Netblock: 12.25.233.96 - 12.25.233.127

 Coordinator:
    buller, patrick (ZZ1934-ARIN) pbuller@inflow.com
    314-754-0400

 Record last updated on 04-Apr-2001.
 Database last updated on 20-May-2002 20:01:13 EDT.
```

This information should be used to call the administrative contact for the netblock—in this case Patrick Buller—so the company can begin the investigation process. In addition to calling, it is a good idea to follow up with e-mail so the information is in writing.

In addition the administrators of the netblock from which the attack originated should be contacted. Most likely, the administrative contacts of this netblock are unaware that their servers have been compromised or used for an attack. It is best to approach them judiciously, rather than in an attacking manner, and explain what was discovered during the investigation process. The details of the attack do not need to be relayed, simply that the attack originated from their netblock; they should be provided with the source and destination IP addresses so they can start their own investigation.

If the source of an attack cannot be isolated, either the origin of an attack or the method used to gain access to the compromised device, then the information should be escalated to either CERT/CC or the Computer Incident Advisory Capability (CIAC).[2] Because these groups will require extensive server and network information in order to properly diagnose the attack, the decision to escalate this information to that level should be made by the CSO, or whoever serves in a similar capacity within an organization.

Finally, if a determination is made that the attacker used a security hole in an application or operating system that is not currently published, information about the attack should be communicated to the software vendor, CERT/CC, and CIAC. Again, this may involve providing third parties sensitive network information, the coordination should be handled by the CSO.

18.6 Prepare a Postmortem

The final step in the process of handling a security incident is preparing a postmortem. A postmortem should be a short report, no more than two or three pages, that details the attack and the steps taken to resolve the security hole that was exploited.

For serious security incidents, a postmortem should be presented to the senior officers of the company, as an explanation of what occurred, and what steps are being taken to prevent it from recurring. The senior company officials should sign off on the postmortem before it is distributed to other employees in the company.

A postmortem can be used as the basis for other documents, such as a press statement if the attack was particularly high profile, and it can be the basis of any reports filed with law enforcement agencies.

The postmortem should include the date and time of all correspondence regarding the incident, as well as a broad overview of the system, or systems, that was compromised. A general explanation of how the attack was accomplished, how it was spotted, and how it was stopped should also be part of the document. Finally, the steps being taken to secure the system and prevent the

---

2. You can even escalate it to both.

attack from recurring, as well as any follow-up steps that need to be taken, should be part of this document.

The postmortem should serve as a quick guide for less technical staff members who need to be made aware of the incident. It is also useful to pass it on to customers who may have been impacted by the security incident, as long as it does not contain any confidential information about the organization.

Good communication is important when dealing with security incidents. Letting people know about the problem, in a clear, easy-to-understand manner, will help smooth any questions about the effectiveness of the current security system. This is especially true if the postmortem demonstrates that the appropriate groups reacted in a swift and decisive manner to deal with a security incident.

18.7 Summary

Security incidents occur in even the best-run networks. The important thing to remember is that since network attacks are inevitable, how an organization reacts to those attacks is important.

The response to an attack should be swift, and it should follow a well-thought-out security escalation policy. The better the procedures in place to deal with different types of attacks, the easier it will be to stop the attackers before any real damage can be inflicted on the network.

Index

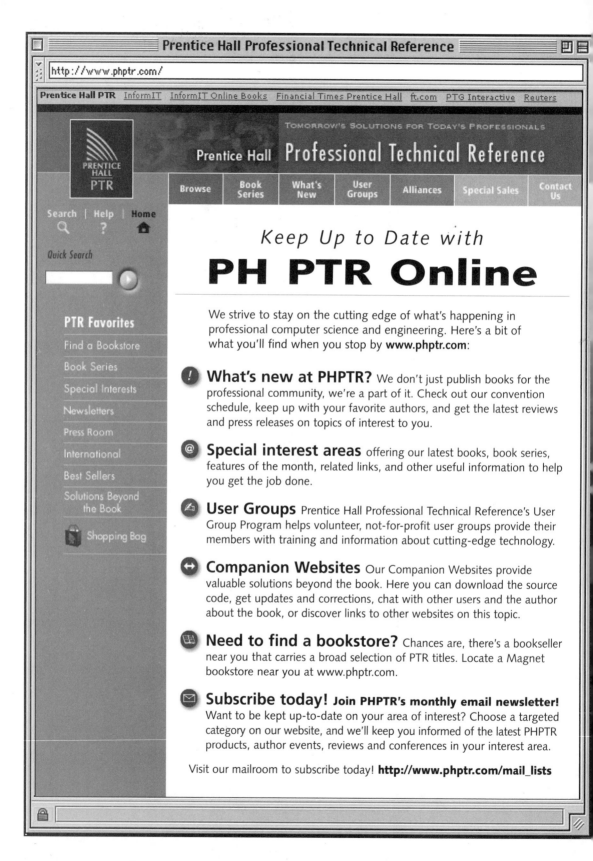